DATING GAME
SECRETS
FOR MARRYING A
GOOD MAN

DATING GAME
SECRETS
FOR MARRYING A
GOOD MAN

Alisa Goodwin Snell

Licensed Marriage and Family Therapist

Bonneville Books
Springville, Utah

ISBN 13: 978-1-59955-161-6

Published by Bonneville Books, an imprint of Cedar Fort, Inc., 2373 W. 700 S., Springville, UT, 84663
Distributed by Cedar Fort, Inc., www.cedarfort.com

Cover design by Nicole Williams
Cover design © 2008 by Lyle Mortimer
Edited and typeset by Kimiko M. Hammari

Printed in the United States of America

10 9 8 7 6 5 4 3 2 1

Printed on acid-free paper

acknowledgments

So many people have contributed to the development and progress of this book. First and foremost, my husband, Eric, and son, Todd, have made the greatest contributions and sacrifices throughout this process. Without their love, encouragement, and patience, I never would have finished it. Bob and Tiffiny Smalley provided stability and wisdom when I needed it most. Lindsey Beckwith helped me develop enthusiasm for the idea of doing the book. Louise Purdy, Eileen Sawyer, Janet Johnson, Sheila Murphy, Eva Oseguera, Chris Ann Woods, Lara Deppe, Kim Osborn, Megan Hyde, and Marilyn Parker helped me refine and develop the concepts, flow, and structure of the book from start to finish. Without their insights and suggestions, I might have quickly become too discouraged to finish the project. Aubrey Hemingway and the 110 women who participated in a pre-screening and seminar about the book gave me valuable feedback and measurable responses from which I made many revisions to the book prior to publication. Dennis and Joyce Ashton's support, guidance, and contacts helped me progress through the publishing process. Chad and Amy Swan, Ben and Colleen Hill, Darryl and Chris Snyder, and Becky and Don Child provided a variety of help from reading and responding to portions of the manuscript to assisting with my website, www.askalisa.org. Abel Keogh and Jon Madsen invited me on their radio call-in show, *The Abel Hour*, to advertise and discuss the concepts in the book and were great hosts who made the experience fun. Abel further advised and encouraged me in the arduous process of publishing the book, since he too was experiencing the trials of book publishing. Gina Pannettieri of Talcott Notch Literary Services provided seasoned experience and wisdom that helped me revise the book. Maurice and Nannette Harker shared their many insights about the writing process when working on an earlier book project.

My clients' experiences have provided the backdrop and insight into many of the case studies throughout this book. Their information has been altered to protect their privacy and anonymity, but hopefully it will help the reader either personally apply the information in the book or help her understand the significance behind some of the concepts.

There are many more people I cannot specifically mention, but my gratitude goes out to them as well. Thank you.

contents

preface

Necessity is the mother of invention

Had I, a licensed marriage and family therapist, not found myself to be a divorced mother of a one-year-old baby boy at the age of twenty-eight, I never would have spent the hours, days, months, and years that followed trying to discover the secrets to marrying a good man. I never would have searched through the wreckage of my unhealthy relationships, my mistaken beliefs, and my fears. I never would have relied on faith bringing light into darkness. I never would have learned the empowering secrets of successful dating. And I never would have understood how much I did not understand about men and their needs, feelings, and goodness.

When my marriage ended so disastrously, I felt I simply could not risk repeating the same mistakes again. The quality of my son's life depended upon my choices. The stakes were higher than ever before. The necessity for knowledge, wisdom, and clarity of mind had never been greater. I simply had to choose well the second time.

This necessity drove me to do what we woman do best—analyze everything. I read professional books, pondered, meditated, prayed, and talked with girlfriends, colleagues, and church leaders until I felt confident I had discovered a way to increase my odds for marrying a good man. Next came the challenge of trying, trusting, risking, and getting married again. The result this time was unmistakably good.

Since I worked with so many single women who wanted what I wanted—a loving relationship, a feeling of safety and security, a peaceful family life, and a good man who would love their children—I shared my theories with them. They tested these theories, gave me feedback, and experienced success.

Thus, this book is a result of my personal journey turned into a professional experience. I wrote it from a professional perspective. Perhaps you will find it useful in guiding you to marry a good man as well. Good luck and God bless your efforts.

—Alisa Goodwin Snell

The Dating Game

introduction

So, you want to marry a good man?

I t seems like it shouldn't be so hard to meet, date, and marry a good man, but many women feel it is almost impossible. However, there is a way.

The first thing you need to know is that finding a good man and dating effectively is like playing a contact sport. However, most women either don't have a clue how to get into the game, so they aren't dating at all, or they don't know the rules of the game so they end up getting battered. Thus, some women sit on the Bleachers, wondering what is wrong with them. Others walk around on the Field with a friendly smile, unaware of the hulking maniac (or Jerk*) about to tackle, smash, and throw them to the ground. A few lay waiting for serious medical intervention, crying, "Don't send me back out there!" And many more make quick retreats to the Bench, deciding there is no way they want to play any longer. If it weren't for the few who seem to be having a blast, dodging the Jerks, jumping past obstacles, giggling, and scoring big-time rewards, most women might just convince themselves to give up on the game altogether. If only those lucky few weren't so happy and in love, many women could resign themselves to lonely contentment far, far away from the Dating Game. But alas, most women just can't seem to give up on the hope of loving and being loved. After all, it doesn't seem like too much to ask for—fun, love, companionship, support, and a hopeful future with someone who adores them. If others have it, why can't they?

....

* Jerk = someone without empathy who acts without regard for the feelings, needs, and rights of others.

So, like many other women, you might ask the question, "How? How do I become safe, confident, and successful in dating and love? How do I marry a good man?"

There is a way, but first you need to know how to protect yourself from those who are more likely to abuse, exploit, manipulate, deceive, neglect, or betray you (also known as Jerks). Abusers and manipulators have specific behaviors in common, and this book can coach you on how to see them and their behaviors before you get attached and hurt (or in other words, tackled*)! For this purpose, the BE SAFE section of this book was created. Second, you need to have faith in your ability to succeed at marrying a good man, which the BE CONFIDENT section will address. And, third, you need to know the tips for successful dating so you can feel empowered and confident while dating, which the BE SUCCESSFUL section will help you understand.

For now, all you need to know is that you have a Coach who will guide you every step of the way—one who understands how hard it is to be in the game, one who has experienced the highs and lows of the game, one who knows your fears and disappointments and wants you to succeed, one who has helped countless women before they reached their goal of marriage with a good man. You are not alone. She has helped others succeed, and you, too, can succeed.

---

* Tackle = abuse and manipulation (which include all forms of abuse: neglect; exploitation; emotional, physical, or sexual abuse; and all forms of manipulation, such as blaming, shaming, lying, deception, and anger to get what the manipulator wants or to avoid taking responsibility for the manipulator's problems).

BE SAFE

*What is it about this man or me that
tells me I am going to be safe?*

chapter one

DANGER!

Many years ago, I worked with a teenager who had been a victim of child sexual abuse for over ten years. Unfortunately, the incarceration of her abuser did not end her victimization. Others seemed eager to exploit her vulnerability, and sadly, some did. During the short time she was in counseling with me, I observed this pattern continue as several older men approached her to give her a ride home just outside my office. (Fortunately, she found an excuse to refuse their requests.) On one occasion, I returned from lunch and observed her rifling through her purse to give a transient some money. She followed me into the building for her one o'clock appointment, sat down in a somewhat curled position, and sheepishly looked at me.

I began asking her a series of questions, which I am sure at the time seemed confusing and aggravating to her. "What was it about that man that told you 'I am going to be safe'?" She stared at me. I continued, "What was it about where you were that told you 'I am going to be safe'?" (The County Mental Health agency I worked for was in a bad part of town.)

She said sheepishly, "I can't be mean."

I continued, "What was it about who you were with, or were not with, that told you 'I am going to be safe'?" (She was alone in a parking lot with the transient.)

She said again, "I can't be mean."

I continued, "What was it about yourself that told you 'I am going to be safe'?"

At that point, she sat up, stared me in the eyes, raised her voice, and nearly screamed, "I don't know why these men follow me. I don't know why they like me. I try not to get their attention. I don't wear makeup. I don't do my hair. I wear baggy clothes. I don't know why men like me, but I can't be mean!"

This young woman left a lasting impression on me. Her pain was intense. Her confusion was great. Her efforts were desperate. And her fear was relentless. She was doing everything she knew to do, but with no success. Abusive men kept flocking to her as if she wore a sign that could be seen a mile away, and the very thing she was screaming at me in that moment—"I CAN'T BE MEAN!"—was what drew them to her. Of course, her lack of attention to her appearance presented a sheepishness that attracts many perpetrators, but her refusal to "be mean" was their ticket to exploiting her.

There was nothing about this transient, the situation, or the reality that she was alone that guaranteed her safety. She didn't have to be right about her judgment that this man might be abusive or manipulative. She just needed to be safe. Yet, as long as she feared that others would believe she was mean if she refused their requests, she would never assert her rights and ensure her safety. She had much to learn and do if she was going to learn to be safe, and it would all force her to defy her fears.

This story often invokes many feelings, from deep horror and sadness about this teenager's abuse to feelings of discomfort about such penetrating questions, to anger, despair, and a desire to protect someone who seems so vulnerable to further abuse. However, it relates more to you than you may know.

Most single women dream of being married to their best friend. They long for a relationship with someone who will care about their feelings. They hope for someone who will invest in their happiness. They envision their partner being loyal, loving, kind, forgiving, compassionate, sharing, and faithful. They look forward to intimacy, companionship, passion, support, and fun. And, they imagine loving relationships that last a lifetime.

Not surprisingly, singles don't daydream about abusive or manipulative relationships with the hope that they will be belittled, frightened, betrayed, deceived, neglected, or exploited. They don't long for the challenges and strug-gles imposed by those who are addicted to drugs, alcohol, prescription medica-tions, or pornography. They don't fantasize about being neglected or emotion-ally abandoned. They don't look forward to relationships with those who will financially devastate or exploit them. And they don't yearn to be replaced and rejected. Thus, singles want and don't want many things in relationships. Yet, what they want doesn't always match what they get. Many men and women are hopeful that their relationships will match their dreams, only to discover the result to be devastating.

Thus, this BE SAFE section will coach you on how to recognize the poten-tially abusive and manipulative by helping you answer the same questions I asked this teenage girl:

- What is it about this man that tells me I am going to be safe? (which chapters 3, 4, and 5 will address)
- What is it about who I am with, or not with, that tells me I am going to be safe? (which chapter 6 will address)
- What is it about where I am that tells me I am going to be safe? (which chapter 6 will address)
- What is it about myself that tells me I am going to be safe? (which chapters 2 and 7 will address)

Like sitting with the Coach in a Locker Room, you are encouraged to take a break from the Dating Game and spend some valuable time analyz-ing what you must do to ensure your emotional, physical, and sexual safety.*
Knowing how to answer these questions will be invaluable in helping you ensure your safety.

Getting back into the Dating Game requires you to take risks and be vulnerable, but this should not be at the cost of your emotional or physical safety. After carefully considering the things you learn in the next few chap-ters, you should feel more hopeful and courageous as you move forward with dating, because this time you will know those you need to avoid and feel confident in your ability to dodge danger.

---

* If you are freshly out of a bad relationship or have suffered a recent loss of a spouse, you may want this break to last at least six months to one year.

chapter two

Safety first!

Many women refuse to get back into the Dating Game because they want to protect themselves from the Jerks who might bash them. However, abuse and manipulation are not by-products of the Dating Game. Those who abuse and manipulate are opportunistic exploiters looking for vulnerability and weakness. The Dating Game may give them many opportunities to take advantage, but it is not the only place they will do this.

An abuser needs a victim. A manipulator needs someone who can be manipulated. All that is required is an easy target—someone who lacks assertiveness, lives by faulty beliefs, or has a history of being abused or manipulated. When the opportunity presents itself, those who are abusive and manipulative just can't seem to help but go in for the tackle. Thus, if you have these issues, you are vulnerable whether you are in the Dating Game, in the Bleachers, at work, in your neighborhood, or anywhere else. So, mere avoidance of the Dating Game is not enough.

Take this self-test to discover how vulnerable you are to abuse or manipulation. Your answers to the self-test may convince you that you need the information in this BE SAFE section more than you thought you did. The more you recognize your vulnerabilities to abuse or manipulation, the more you can prevent and avoid them. Thus, your first game play strategy requires that you assess your vulnerability to abuse. Later chapters will coach you on how to change and protect yourself from these vulnerabilities, but first you need to see and recognize them.

GAME PLAY STRATEGY #1
Recognize your vulnerability to abuse.

Mark the following statements based on whether you believe that they are true or false for you. If you feel that you only sometimes believe it is true for you, then mark false. If you want to believe it is not true for you but all of your behaviors say it is true for you, then mark true (if in doubt, you may want to ask a friend what they see in you).[1]

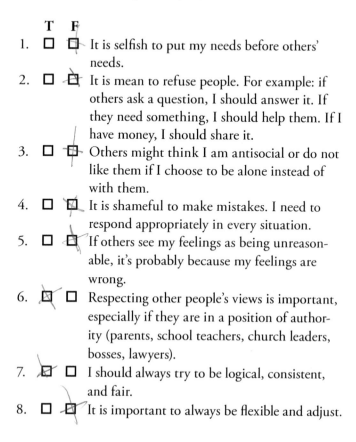

	T	F	
1.	☐	☑	It is selfish to put my needs before others' needs.
2.	☐	☑	It is mean to refuse people. For example: if others ask a question, I should answer it. If they need something, I should help them. If I have money, I should share it.
3.	☐	☑	Others might think I am antisocial or do not like them if I choose to be alone instead of with them.
4.	☐	☑	It is shameful to make mistakes. I need to respond appropriately in every situation.
5.	☐	☑	If others see my feelings as being unreasonable, it's probably because my feelings are wrong.
6.	☑	☐	Respecting other people's views is important, especially if they are in a position of authority (parents, school teachers, church leaders, bosses, lawyers).
7.	☑	☐	I should always try to be logical, consistent, and fair.
8.	☐	☑	It is important to always be flexible and adjust.

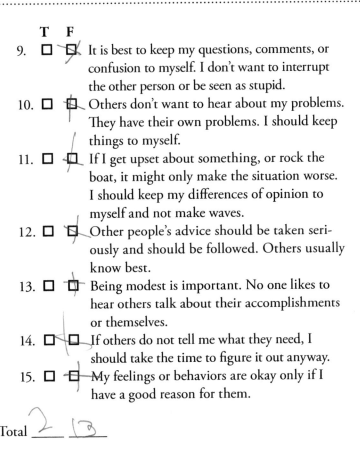

T F

9. ☐ ☒ It is best to keep my questions, comments, or confusion to myself. I don't want to interrupt the other person or be seen as stupid.

10. ☐ ☒ Others don't want to hear about my problems. They have their own problems. I should keep things to myself.

11. ☐ ☒ If I get upset about something, or rock the boat, it might only make the situation worse. I should keep my differences of opinion to myself and not make waves.

12. ☐ ☒ Other people's advice should be taken seriously and should be followed. Others usually know best.

13. ☐ ☒ Being modest is important. No one likes to hear others talk about their accomplishments or themselves.

14. ☐ ☒ If others do not tell me what they need, I should take the time to figure it out anyway.

15. ☐ ☒ My feelings or behaviors are okay only if I have a good reason for them.

Total __2__ __13__

Add up the number of true statements. If you answered true to six or more of the above statements, you probably have a problem with being assertive about your feelings, rights, opinions, and needs. The higher your score, the more likely you are to doubt yourself, assume too much responsibility for maintaining your relationships, or get manipulated or abused by others. If you answered true to nine or more statements, you may be experiencing depression or anxiety as well. You may also feel you have to walk on eggshells in order to avoid upsetting others.

Consider your relationships over the last year (include friends, family, boyfriends, and work relationships). Answer the following questions yes or no if they describe your behavior in these relationships.[2]

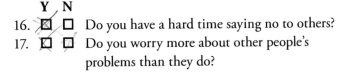

Y N

16. ☒ ☐ Do you have a hard time saying no to others?

17. ☒ ☐ Do you worry more about other people's problems than they do?

Y   N

18. ☐ ☑ Do you trust others even when there is evidence that they are not worthy of that trust?

19. ☐ ☑ Are you unable to share your feelings, problems, or needs or stand up for your rights because you fear the reactions, criticism, rejection, or anger of others?

20. ☐ ☑ Do you rarely feel or express anger?

21. ☑ ☐ When others say unkind things, break their promises, lie, or act aggressively, do you forgive them quickly, make excuses for their behavior, or ignore the problem?

22. ☐ ☑ Do you trust others you have just met to the point that you quickly share your deeply personal feelings or experiences, give them money, help them with their problems, become physically involved, or do other things that might put you in danger?

23. ☐ ☑ Do you do things you don't want to do, feel guilty about, or resent?

24. ☑ ☐ Do you work very hard at being fair, consistent, reliable, kind, caring, and logical?

25. ☐ ☑ Do other people tell you that you are too trusting or naïve, or that you're a doormat?

26. ☐ ☑ Do you get others involved in fixing your problems because you feel your life, finances, kids, ex-husband, or problems are beyond your ability to control?

27. ☐ ☑ Have you dated anyone in the last year who drinks to excess, lies, cheats, steals, manipulates, abuses drugs, threatens others, has legal problems, has an anger management problem, or acts aggressively?

28. ☐ ☑ Do you ignore your first impressions or gut feelings, believing you should give others a second date or more time?

29. ☐ ☑ Do you second guess your judgment and follow the advice of others because you feel they may know better than you?

30. ☑ ☐ Do you fix other people's problems and do

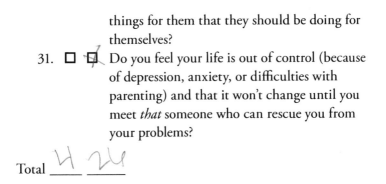

things for them that they should be doing for themselves?

31. ☐ ☑ Do you feel your life is out of control (because of depression, anxiety, or difficulties with parenting) and that it won't change until you meet *that* someone who can rescue you from your problems?

Total ___4___ ___24___

Add up the number of yes answers. If you answered yes to six or more questions, you probably have beliefs that make you vulnerable to being manipulated or abused. You may also feel stressed, overwhelmed, and anxious on a regular basis. The higher your score, the more you may be caught in a pattern of taking care of others at your own expense. This may result in attracting people who are irresponsible, controlling, or neglectful. A fear of loneliness, criticism, rejection, and the reactions of others may be keeping you from changing your behaviors and your relationships. If you answered yes to more than nine questions, you may be waiting for some external event or person to help you control your life or end your unhealthy relationships. You may also feel that other people have more control over your happiness than you do.

Review the following questions. Answer yes or no if the statement adequately reflects your experiences with family members or your current situations with important people in your life (long-term boyfriends, ex-spouse, family, friends, colleagues).

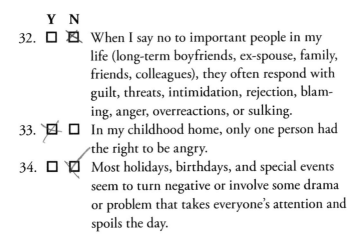

Y N

32. ☐ ☒ When I say no to important people in my life (long-term boyfriends, ex-spouse, family, friends, colleagues), they often respond with guilt, threats, intimidation, rejection, blaming, anger, overreactions, or sulking.

33. ☒ ☐ In my childhood home, only one person had the right to be angry.

34. ☐ ☒ Most holidays, birthdays, and special events seem to turn negative or involve some drama or problem that takes everyone's attention and spoils the day.

35. ☐ ☒ In my family and love relationships, I often
have to deal with my feelings and problems
alone. When I involve others, their reactions
often make the problem worse.
36. ☐ ☒ Others often don't give me a break or help me
unless I am desperately sick.
37. ☐ ☒ I have struggled with self-destructive behaviors
like cutting on myself, eating disorders, or suicidal behaviors at some time in the past.
38. ☐ ☒ The people I love the most cause me the most
stress, anxiety, self-doubt, anger, fear, and
worry. Sometimes I feel torn apart by conflicting feelings I feel I shouldn't have about these
people.
39. ☒ ☐ I often feel overwhelmed, worthless, and desperate for love and acceptance.
40. ☒ ☐ In my family, one or more of my family members
or myself was abused (physically, sexually, or
emotionally) by someone they knew.
41. ☐ ☒ I witnessed or experienced abuse from a
family member, boyfriend, or husband.
42. ☐ ☒ I have recently experienced a significant loss
(death, betrayal, being fired from a job) or
left a bad relationship.*

Total __3____

*If you answered yes to four or more of the above statements, you have most
likely lived in a dysfunctional or abusive relationship for an extended period of
time. This may have been in your family relationships or in a long-term relationship or marriage. Either way, you are significantly more vulnerable to getting
back into a manipulative or abusive relationship. This is partially caused by your
limited positive experiences and your tolerance for inappropriate behaviors. Thus,
do not skip the next few chapters. Your ability to recognize the warning signs of
the manipulative and abusive (or emotionally immature) will be essential to your
success.*

**If you answered yes to question 42 but no to questions 31–41, you are more
vulnerable to abuse and manipulation than you may realize because of your
recent loss. You need to exercise caution.*

List your responses here:

Questions 1–15: True answers ___2___ (six or more indicates a problem with assertiveness)

Questions 16–31: Yes answers ___4___ (six or more indicates you have a problem with beliefs that make you more vulnerable to manipulation and abuse)

Questions 32–42: Yes answers ___3___ (four or more indicates that you are vulnerable to manipulative or abusive relationships because of your family or past relationship histories or your recent loss)

The higher your scores in any one area or the presence of problems in all three areas puts you at a greater risk to get into an abusive or manipulative relationship. Thus, you would be wise to complete all of this BE SAFE section before you continue your efforts to join the Dating Game.

Review the following case study. (1) Analyze how Lori might have some of the faulty beliefs above (questions 1–15). (2) Identify those behaviors (questions 16–31) that make it easy for her to be abused or manipulated. (3) Consider how her parents' recent divorce, along with her isolation from her father (questions 32–42) might add to her vulnerability for abuse.

CASE STUDY

Lori did not get much attention from boys in high school, though she was fairly attractive. Thus, her first few experiences with men caused her to feel more desperate and insecure about keeping their affection and attention. This, paired with her parents' recent divorce and her father's limited interest in her, caused her to cling even more tightly to her first boyfriend.

He was attractive, confident, funny, and intense. She liked him immediately. Unfortunately, he also pushed the limits of what she felt comfortable with when kissing. He often tried to get too physical, and when she would move his hands, he just pushed them aside and tried again. When she would stop kissing him to tell him why she was uncomfortable with what he was doing, he would make light of her religious beliefs about pre-marital sex (even though he was a member of her church). When she tried to argue with him about it, he would get more intense and persist in explaining how wrong she was. When he successfully managed to hold her down so she couldn't resist, she finally gave up. She felt too exhausted to fight him over it anymore. "It doesn't make a difference anyway," she told herself. She really wanted to keep the relationship. Maybe what they were doing wasn't so wrong after all. No man wants to be with a prude.

The relationship eventually ended. Lori moved on and began dating others. With each new relationship, it seemed kissing quickly progressed to being too physical. She never resisted their advances, though it usually made her feel guilty later. Many of the men didn't call and ask her out again. Sometimes she felt hurt about it, but most of the time she ignored her feelings of being used and discarded. She prided herself on not actually having sex with any of these men, but she often felt powerless and ashamed after they left (and especially after they didn't call again). When she would consider not being physical with men, beyond kissing, she just couldn't imagine that a guy would go for that. It seemed they had to have some kind of sexual contact or they would lose interest. It was easier to just give them a little of what they wanted rather then risk their outright rejection or criticism. After all, she really wanted a relationship.

THERAPEUTIC ASSESSMENT

Lori had many issues, most of which may seem like low self-esteem; however, she was confident and capable in many other areas of her life. She just had little positive experience in her relationships with men, which caused her to have less confidence in men and her ability to be respected and appreciated by them.

Many of her faulty beliefs developed in her family of origin. Her father was too distant and often too critical. She didn't feel comfortable and confident in his interest in her. Her parents' marriage had never included much effective communication, and she often observed that her father ignored her mother's needs and requests (which Lori felt he did to his daughters as well).

Additionally, she had few good examples of male/female relationships among the other important people in her life.

When her first boyfriend acted much like her father, it was easy to assume that all relationships must be this way. Though she was not responsible for the sexual assaults of her first boyfriend, she was responsible for getting herself out of that relationship and asserting her appropriate needs and rights in her future relationships (many of these men did not abuse her, though her lack of assertiveness continued to make her feel victimized).

Until Lori believes that her rights, feelings, and needs are legitimate and begins asserting them, she will continue to be vulnerable to abuse and manipulation. Though no victim is responsible for the abuse inflicted on them by their abuser, the fact still remains: abuse is painful, and it is almost always up to the victims to get themselves out of the abusive relationships and any patterns they may have that attract them to these relationships.

Notes
1. These questions were adapted from an assertiveness training handout I acquired years ago. Unfortunately, its author is unknown, but the approach used here is consistent with Albert Ellis's theories of irrational thinking and A. T. Beck's approach in cognitive therapy.
2. Adapted from Davis, Martha, PhD; Elizabeth Robbins Eshelman, MSW; and Matthew McKay, PhD. *The Relaxation & Stress Reduction Workbook*, fifth edition. Oakland: New Harbinger Publications, Inc., 2000.

chapter three

Not all men can love— and loving them hurts

W hether you are on the Field of the Dating Game, at the office, in an alley, or chatting on the Internet, you will want to know how to answer the question, "What is it about this man that tells me I am going to be safe?" Most abuse occurs at the hands of someone the victim knows, not strangers—so how do you know who is safe and who is not? This chapter and the next few chapters are dedicated to coaching you on this question. And the first thing you need to know is that not all men (or women) can love—and loving them hurts!*

....

* According to the statistical information gathered by the Battered Women's National Crisis Center Organization, 7 percent of women were physically abused (3.9 million women) and 37 percent (20.7 million) were verbally or emotionally abused by their spouses or partners in a given year (Appleton, Catherine. *But I Have Such a Great Catch: Treating abusive controlling relationship,* homestudy.com).

The National Statistics—Community Violence Intervention Center at www.civiconline.org/stats.htm reports: Over 30 percent of all rapes/sexual assaults were perpetrated by a stranger, with 68 percent perpetrated by someone the victim knew (according to the Bureau of Justice's National Crime Victimization Survey, 1997). Fifty-five percent (55,383,350) of women surveyed had experienced rape or some form of physical assault during their lifetime

Now you may be asking, "How is that possible since all people will report feeling love at some point in their lives?" Of course that is true, but if love is separated from infatuation and other immature forms of love, it is easier to see that not all people truly love.

We all can feel passion for another person. We all can feel excitement about being in a relationship with someone who makes us feel great about ourselves. We all can feel a deep desire to be loved, admired, and accepted. But do we all feel a deep concern for the feelings and needs of another person? Do we all feel an interest in the other person's goals, dreams, and aspirations? Do we all recognize with concern the other person's feelings when we have unintentionally done or said something hurtful? Do we all forgo a selfish desire when our loved one's need is greater?

Unfortunately, many people desire to be loved deeply but do not envision themselves loving deeply. In this way, they want the *selfish* experience of love, not the *selfless* experience of love.

They view love and their responsibilities to those they love with emotional *immaturity* rather than emotional *maturity*. Thus, they do not see beyond themselves as they give and receive love. Their self-centered perceptions of love limit their ability to recognize and respect the feelings, needs, and rights of others, making it easy for them to justify doing whatever it takes to get what they desire. This often leaves those they love feeling manipulated, abused, deceived, neglected, exploited, betrayed, and asking the question, "Would someone who loves me treat me this way?"

Because those who are emotionally immature often have behaviors that are emotionally, financially, psychologically, or physically damaging to those who love them (most important, their spouses and children), it is in your best interest to know as much as you can about the emotionally immature before you fall in love with them. Understanding the many difficult and complex issues that those who love the emotionally immature often face can help you feel convinced to shun abusive and manipulative behavior while dating. Abuse and manipulation only become worse after marriage. Thus, your future success depends on your commitment to avoiding abuse and manipulation now.

(according to the National Institute of Justice, 1998). Nearly one in three adult women experience at least one physical assault by a partner during their adult years (according to the American Psychological Association, Violence and the Family, 1996). And, 38 percent of women had been sexually abused by an adult relative, acquaintance, or stranger before they were eighteen: 28 percent before they were fourteen (according to the MN Coalition for Battered Women, 1997).

The Coach knows that it is by far better to be happily single than miserably married. Verbal abuse can be as devastating to one's psychology as physical abuse. Years of suffering from manipulation, neglect, or exploitation can alter a person considerably. Therefore, your next game play strategy cannot be ignored if you are to remain safe and happy and maintain a hope that you can experience the rewards and pleasures of a happy marriage with a good man.

GAME PLAY STRATEGY #2
shun any and all forms of abuse and manipulation in your relationships.

CASE STUDY

Susan often talked with sadness about her relationship with her first husband. "He had such potential. We could have had a great life together. If only he had had enough support and help, perhaps he could have changed," she often said. These statements were usually made with a tone of regret in her voice. "He was always so kind and patient with me," she would state. "Perhaps if I had been more supportive or waited a little longer, he would have been able to overcome his drug and alcohol addictions. His affairs were just so painful that I moved forward with the divorce very quickly. If only I had taken more time and thought through the divorce, perhaps my daughter would not have been sexually abused by my second husband." Susan felt gripped with regret and self-blame.

As you read the information in this chapter, ask yourself, "What might happen to Susan if she does not better understand and change her part in her relationship patterns?" Throughout this chapter, you may find some insights to this question. The case study review at the end of this chapter will also bring additional clarity.

Those who act abusively and manipulatively (or in other words, those who are emotionally immature) need others desperately, though they may often say they don't need anyone. Without the enabling behavior of others (who take care of them, fix their problems, make excuses for their behavior, and make their lives comfortable), their life may quickly fall into collapse. Though they may initially act loving toward those they need, they often hate and resent their dependence on others. This hatred often spills out in episodes that swing from love and affection to hate and aggression, which may be manifest verbally, physically, and even by neglect. They often react to any perceptions of rejection, abandonment, or criticism from those they depend on with fear, anxiety, desperation, or rage in order to manipulate or frighten the person to stay or change the rejection or criticism they felt.

This dependence on others (combined with their intense fears of rejection) causes them to desperately seek control over their relationships, spouse, and children. Their attempts to maintain control over these relationships fall into three categories: the passive aggressive response, the aggressive response, and the combined response. The emotional effects of these responses on those who love them (spouses and children) can be very painful and confusing.

The passive aggressive response

The passive aggressive response in marriage is built on the principle of least interest—the person with the least amount of interest in the relationship has the greatest amount of control over it.[1] For example, the emotionally immature might behave in the following ways:

- Disengaging from the relationship.
- Becoming disinterested in physical contact.
- Being excessively busy.
- Staying at work late.
- Always helping the neighbors instead of the family.
- Being too sick or depressed to meet the family's needs.
- Maintaining secretive behaviors (such as shopping, credit card debt, addiction, flirting, or infidelity).

In this way, the emotionally immature person looks like the ultimate nice guy who "would do it if he could," but in reality he is neglectful, apathetic, distant, and secretive.* His pleasant and easygoing (or in some cases, fragile) nature makes it difficult for the spouse to feel justified in being angry, but the neglect causes the feelings anyway.

The spouse's efforts (complaining, pleading, nagging) to engage the emotionally immature person into becoming more involved often cause him to disengage further. To get his spouse off his back, the emotionally immature person may promise to come home on time, give up the secretive behavior, or meet his spouse's needs, but he always has a dozen excuses for not following through. Thus, his words and actions rarely match.

The emotionally immature person may also show great offense or overreactions to the other person's complaints. He may express all or nothing statements such as, "You can never be satisfied," "I am so horrible," or "Everyone would be better off without me." This victim or all-bad position serves to overcompensate for his problems, taking the issue to an extreme that causes others to feel guilty, back off, or apologize for the complaint rather than getting the complaint acknowledged.

Because the emotionally immature person fears that knowledge is power, sharing his daily frustrations (about the relationship or unfulfilled needs in the relationship) with his spouse would be equal to giving his spouse control. Thus, he may refuse to express emotion or legitimate complaints in front of his spouse, which would show weakness or bring about change that would fix the problem. Instead, he may openly complain about his spouse to friends, coworkers, or family members, while the spouse has no knowledge of the complaints or unfulfilled needs. The attention and validation the emotionally immature person receives from others serves as a secondary reward for not fixing the problem. This validation from others reinforces and rewards his victim position, decreasing his interest in sharing the problem with his spouse. If the problem were to be resolved, he would not have as much to share with others or a means for getting support from others.

The more the emotionally immature person withdraws from the spouse, the more power he has over the relationship. For these reasons he may deny feeling anger (in spite or his tendency to secretly brood over offenses for years) and may not tell his spouse the things he doesn't like

---

* For purposes of clarity and brevity, this chapter will refer to those whom act emotionally immature as "he" rather than as "he or she." In no way is this intended to single men out as being more emotionally immature (or potentially abusive and manipulative) than women, which is not the case. Please be sure to analyze the men and women you know (as well as yourself) as you attempt to personally apply the information in this chapter.

or has been hurt by (even if he is in counseling). Additionally, his ability to exercise emotional restraint may be used against his spouse to support his claims that his spouse is too emotional—thus, irrational, overreacting, crazy, or controlling.

Because the spouse is in the dark about the emotionally immature person's feelings and needs, she is consequently unable to address them and resolve them. Thus, the emotionally immature person's excuses for not engaging in the relationship remain. These excuses may drive him to feel justified in his alcohol or drug use, viewing of pornography, secretive behavior, avoidance of home, frequent threats of divorce, infidelities, and use of the ever powerful tool—the silent treatment. Sometimes the only hint to the passive aggressive person's true feelings is found in the sarcasm he uses or in the hidden message behind his behavior.

In parenting, the spouse is usually burdened with the responsibility for disciplining the children and is seen by the children as too strict, mean, and angry all the time. While the spouse is the disciplinarian, the emotionally immature person is often the friend to their children and seen by the children as fun, easygoing, loving, and a pushover. This often causes marital problems since the emotionally immature person may regularly undermine the spouse's parenting as a way of establishing the "nice parent" role. The children may also distance themselves from the spouse or feel justified in being angry, resentful, or disrespectful to her (especially if the emotionally immature person supports this disrespect).

It is common for the emotionally immature parent to burden his children with his emotional needs, problems, feelings, and relationship issues. In exchange for the child's emotional support, the emotionally immature parent may neglect parental discipline and structure. Thus, the child may have more freedom and independence than would be wise or appropriate. This can lead to increased opportunities for the child to become involved with drugs, alcohol, gangs, or sex (especially if one or both of the parents acts deceptive, uses drugs, misuses alcohol, or is involved with pornography or sexual acting out as well). In some cases, the emotionally immature parent may even encourage or accompany the child in his destructive behaviors (either through involving the child in the parent's drug use, accompanying the teen at a local party, using drugs along with the child's friends, flirting with other teens, or encouraging the teen's sexual behaviors), thus acting like a teen himself rather than like a parent.

When upset, the emotionally immature parent often reacts to the child more like a sibling than like an adult. For example, the emotionally immature parent may withhold affection, use guilt trips, or utilize the all-powerful silent treatment as tools for punishing the child (much like a sibling might). He may respond to a child's rejection or criticism with strong reactions of anger, rage, shaming, and even deep hurt, rather than expecting the child's rejection or criticism to be a sad but inevitable reality associated with the responsibilities of parenting and not something that should be taken personally.

The emotionally immature parent often prefers to bribe or excessively use rewards to get the child to perform everyday, necessary tasks such as getting up in the morning, getting dressed, going to school, or eating. If a child resists the bribery, the parent may quickly give up, saying, "I can't make them do it," rather than finding other ways to fulfill his parental responsibilities (thus, he gives up quickly, rather than enforcing the consequences, when his third grader refuses to go to school). He may then overindulge, coddle, or rescue the child from any pain or consequences of the child's poor behavior, thus contributing to the child's development of irresponsibility.

If the emotionally immature person becomes divorced or is left with the full-time responsibilities of the children, he will often continue the passive or disengaged behaviors he once used when ignoring his spouse's needs, this time with his children (being out late instead of coming home to be with the children, letting the children roam the streets, not disciplining the children, or focusing on dating instead of the children).

If the emotionally immature person does not have the children after the divorce, he is likely to show minimal effort in maintaining his relationships with his children, especially when he is dating (which usually occurs immediately since he desperately fears being alone). He may even put the responsibility for the relationship on the children or become quickly offended by the children's normal behaviors, feelings, or needs. This can result in the children feeling blamed, abandoned, or neglected.

He may also neglect his financial obligations to the children, justifying that the ex-wife shouldn't get the money, the children don't need the money, or his needs are too great to sacrifice the money. He often shows little recognition for the children's needs for the money and may make excuses that his ex-wife is capable of working or the grandparents are helping out anyway.

When the emotionally immature person sexually abuses children, he may use kindness, playfulness, gift giving, pleading, or guilt trips to manipulate the child into fulfilling his sexual desires. This is often not an isolated event since those who sexually abuse usually have a history of disregarding the boundaries, feelings, needs, or rights of others for self-serving purposes. Sexual abuse usually results in multiple offenses with multiple victims.

Manipulating others in funny, charming, needy, or desperate ways does not reduce the trauma of abuse and can even make it more confusing for the victim, who feels pressure to take care of the emotionally immature parent while not feeling free to feel or express anger about the incestuous behavior.

Consequently, the effects of the passive aggressive response on the spouse and children can be many. The spouse often feels dissatisfied, unhappy, confused, stressed, powerless, hopeless, blamed, anxious, or depressed. The spouse's relationships with the kids are often strained by the consequences the spouse alone must enforce and by the undermining influence of the emotionally immature parent. The spouse is often plagued with self-doubts (wondering if she is too emotional, high strung, or unappreciative) and fears becoming someone she does not want to be (always tired, angry, controlling, critical, or nagging). Furthermore, the spouse often feels isolated from the support of others because everybody else thinks the emotionally immature person is so friendly, always eager to help others, the nicest guy in the world, and so forth.

The children may suffer from anxiety, depression, stomach-related pain, headaches, difficulty concentrating at school, or social problems because of the emotional problems at home. Not only can the child feel the silent treatment and coldness between the parents, but the child also feels burdened by the marital problems the emotionally immature parent has inappropriately shared. Additionally, the child often feels pressure to be loyal to one parent over another—which causes great internal turmoil. In many cases, a child may become a surrogate spouse or parent to one of the parents. This role can cause multiple short- and long-term problems in the child's ability to relate to peers and others of the opposite sex, make transitions into important stages of development, and create appropriate romantic relationships.

The child may later feel great resentment about the emotional burden the parents created at such a young age. Additionally, the child is more likely to continue the behaviors the parents modeled, such as irresponsibility, passive aggressive responses, enabling behaviors, dishonesty, drug and alcohol addiction, sexual addiction, excessive dependence on others, secretive behavior, anger, resentment, attention, and avoidance of responsibility through sickness, depression, or weakness.

The aggressive response

The aggressive response in marriage is built upon the principle of control through fear. By using criticism, rejection, belittling, anger, threats, intimidation, and even force, the emotionally immature person is able to control their family relationships through exploiting their spouse's or child's fears of inadequacy (feeling not good enough, capable enough, or lovable enough), rejection, or physical harm.

Verbally berating a spouse or child, limiting contact with friends and extended family, becoming angry at seemingly small offenses, and blaming the spouse or child for the emotionally immature person's behavior creates an environment of fear and self-doubt within the spouse or child.

Because the spouse or child anxiously desires the love and approval of the emotionally immature person, feelings of desperation, a desire to please, and even an intense loyalty to the emotionally immature person may develop. Thus, the spouse or child may walk on eggshells in order to avoid setting off the emotionally immature person, only to find their efforts do not stop the shaming, blaming, name calling, excessive criticism, and other forms of verbal abuse. This process can have a powerfully controlling effect upon the spouse or child, who often assumes more and more blame and responsibility for making everything all right for the emotionally immature person, all in an attempt to avoid further verbal and emotional abuse.

Intimidation, threats, controlling the family finances, limiting access to the car, destroying the spouse's or child's possessions, throwing things at the spouse or child, shaking, slapping, kicking, hitting, restraining, or other forms of physical abuse cause intense fears and trauma for the spouse or child, which deepens the control the emotionally immature person has over their family. Although those who are verbally abusive may never become physically abusive, it is rare for those who are physically abusive to not also be verbally abusive. Thus, family members who experience physical abuse often live with verbal abuse as well. Together, the impact can be psychologically debilitating.

Sexually demeaning, exploitative, invasive, or cruel behaviors are devastatingly toxic to the spouse or child. At any age, sexual abuse has terrifying, destructive, and debilitating effects on the psychology of a person, but children suffer the most. A spouse who is sexually abused may at times feel responsible for the abuse, but a child who is sexually abused is often convinced he is to blame. Additionally, the child's fears of being dirty, unworthy of love, and so forth may cause a lifetime of self-esteem issues.

Consequently, the effects of the aggressive response on the spouse and children can be many. The psychological effect of the whirlwind romance, along with the spouse's dependence on the emotionally immature person, make it difficult for the spouse to leave the relationship, especially when the emotionally immature person acts loving, apologetic, and romantic following the verbal, physical, or sexual abuse. This honeymoon effect keeps the spouse desperately hopeful that the loving relationship she had at the beginning will return, making everything okay again.

In spite of these unlikely hopes, the aggressive behavior of the emotionally immature person usually just increases (while the loving, honeymoon stages become less frequent), causing the spouse to feel frightened, powerless, hopeless, more dependent, anxious, depressed, isolated, weak, incapable, incompetent, or blamed. The spouse's feelings of hopelessness are often deepened by the fact that the emotionally immature person is rarely willing to read self-help books or participate in counseling (often saying, "I'm not going to let anyone tell me what to do" or "I know more than those quacks do").

If the spouse refuses to accept the blame, demands that the abuse stop, or threatens divorce, the emotionally immature person may escalate his behavior through saying cruel things, throwing things, towering over the person, becoming violent, destroying the spouse's property, threatening to harm or kill himself (hoping the other person will panic or beg them to stay), refusing to let the spouse leave the room, sabotaging vehicles (or taking keys) so the spouse can't leave him, or threatening to kill the spouse. If physical abuse was already present prior to the spouse's demands, the emotionally immature person may become more dangerous.* Wise planning along with the support of others will be necessary in order to ensure the spouse's and children's safety. If the spouse takes these measures and ends the abusive relationship before the children begin to suffer from the effects of abuse in the home, the children may have significantly fewer issues than if the spouse and children stay in the abusive situation.

In contrast, if the spouse accepts blame and responsibility for the abuse, the spouse may in time consider suicide, gain excessive amounts of weight, develop an eating disorder, have an affair, turn to drugs or alcohol, become a workaholic, become a perfectionist, develop chronic illness, or have a mental breakdown. Additionally, the spouse may become blind to the abuse of the children, fail to protect the children, or even neglect the children (unfortunately, this outcome can be common when both parents are emotionally immature).

The effects of verbal, physical, or sexual abuse on the children can be just as great as those on the spouse, if not more so. The children may suffer

---

* Unfortunately, it is when a woman tries to leave a physically abusive relationship that she is more likely to be seriously harmed or killed.

from anxiety, depression, stomach-related pain, headaches, difficulty concentrating at school, or social problems caused by the multiple emotional burdens that abuse at home causes. They may act aggressively with others or be bullied by others. They may struggle in learning situations because of a fear of being criticized. And they may fear making decisions or mistakes.

But the children also fear for other members of the family as well, especially if they witness other family members (including a parent) being verbally, physically, or sexually abused. They often feel they must be loyal to one parent over another—which causes great internal turmoil. The children may be conflicted by their anger, hurt, and resentment about the abuse while still feeling a deep and desperate love for the abusive parent. They may appreciate the non-abusive spouse's calming words but resent her for not doing more to protect them.

Any verbal, physical, or sexual abuse the children experience from the emotionally immature parent cannot go unnoticed or unaddressed by the non-abusive spouse without causing the children to feel abandoned, betrayed, and blamed. Thus, unless the spouse diligently attempts to protect the child, the child will likely experience great anger, resentment, and distrust of the spouse.

Feeling alone, vulnerable, powerless, and distrusting of adults who fail to protect them, the children often become more susceptible to the influences of peers, gangs, drugs, and alcohol. They may seek immediate gratification or numbing of emotional pain through sex, drugs, stealing, self-harming behaviors (such as eating disorders, self-mutilation, or suicidal attempts). Additionally, the child's emotional vulnerability makes them more susceptible to other abusive individuals and less trusting of teachers, cops, social workers, bosses, and other authority figures. Without learning how to heal, break the destructive patterns, and develop trusting relationships with adults, the children are also more likely to fall into an abuser or victim role in their adult relationships.

The combined response

Although some of the emotionally immature keep more strictly to just a passive aggressive response or an aggressive response, many more fluctuate between the two types. For instance, those who are verbally abusive (but not physically or sexually abusive) often use passive aggressive behaviors (such as blaming, withholding affection, lying, neglecting, shaming, or denying the other person their legitimate needs) as a way of enforcing their verbal threats since using physical abuse is not something they like to do.

Many of the effects of this combined response on the spouse and children will be similar to those described above but with one significant difference: the spouse and children feel more permission to be angry about the passive aggressive behaviors they experience from the emotionally immature person because they also see the aggressive behaviors. Thus, it is easier to see how selfish and manipulative an emotionally immature person really is.

Now that you understand the emotionally immature person's need for control in relationships (which drives them to act abusively and manipulatively in the three styles above: passive aggressive, aggressive, and combined), reread the case study at the beginning of this chapter, and then consider the following therapeutic assessment.

THERAPEUTIC ASSESSMENT

If you, like Susan, struggled to see that her first husband's behavior was passive aggressive, you might understand why Susan clung to her unrealistic perception that her first marriage had such great potential and that she ruined her and her daughter's life by not being more patient. Unfortunately, Susan falsely blamed herself for her first husband's behavior more than she blamed him. He was not as supportive or available as she wanted to believe. In reality, he was rarely home and often did not fulfill her many appropriate needs and requests. Yes, he was kind, but only on the surface—his behaviors were very unkind, self-centered, and destructive to the relationship. Her refusal to see the relationship, himself, and his behaviors for what they were kept her in a fantasy.

In this fantasy life, love and happiness could have been hers if only she had not messed it up by giving up too soon and being imperfect—hence, her regret and blame. However, her perceptions and self-blame were not founded. In reality, she could not change or control her husbands' choices and behaviors (no matter how much she tried to be perfect, emotionally controlled, and "Christlike" in the marriage). In reality, there was no connection between her daughter's sexual abuse and her decision to divorce her first husband (her second husband was solely to blame for his abusive behavior). And, in reality, there were warning signs of both her husbands' manipulations, deceptions, and abuse even before marriage (though she didn't trust her gut feelings and judgment enough to draw attention to those issues then). Thus, she didn't make her husbands become what they became.

For Susan to move forward, she needed to accept both of her husbands' choices as being theirs, not hers. She also needed to rebuild her confidence in herself (she had lost as much faith and trust in herself and her decision-making as she had in men). And she needed to shun all abusive and manipulative behavior in her relationships while she was still single. It wasn't too late to change her life and alter her future, but it all depended on her maintaining logical beliefs and making good choices now, as a single woman.

Susan needed to start seeing things logically and expecting life to follow good reasoning and realistic consequences. A man who drinks to excess when dating will likely continue partying, drinking, or acting irresponsibly after marriage (which were the early warning signs Susan ignored before her first marriage). A man who dismisses a woman's feelings when dating will likely not recognize or respect her feelings and needs when married; a man who gets offended when she spends time with her daughter before marriage may control her relationship with her daughter or resent and punish her for the time and money she spends on her daughter after marriage (both of which her second husband did before and after marriage). The secret to her future success was in her thinking logically and realistically about the facts she observes during dating rather than emotionally and idealistically (while ignoring or minimizing the facts before her).

Notes
1.   Waller, W. W., and R. Hill. *The Family: A Dynamic Interpretation*. New York: Warner Books, 1951.

chapter four

It takes two emotionally mature people to make a relationship successful

Love relationships with the emotionally immature often start out by being extremely intense, romantic, exciting, and idealistic. The emotionally immature are often striking, intelligent, fun, and thrilling with an ability to make others feel special, needed, unique, and attractive. They often express immediate admiration or love and are willing to commit. They can also be extremely helpful and friendly. Thus, it may seem confusing why a relationship with someone who is emotionally immature would be discouraged. There is so much good there. However, being with someone who is emotionally immature can hurt in more ways than you realize, and the Coach knows it is better to be happily single than miserably married.

Thus, just when you're having fun with a good-looking, charming man, you may hear him say something, and everything changes. The Coach (in this book and now in your head) starts calling you to the Bench, and you know you have to decide if you are going to ignore the warning signs and stay in your fantasy of what you want this man to be, or drop the ball, go to the Bench, and choose reality.

If you want the kind of marriage that will make you feel safe and secure in your husband's love, commitment, and loyalty to you and your kids, you cannot marry a fantasy. Things are what they are. And those who are emotionally immature are significantly impaired in their ability to feel empathy, exercise self-control, and accept personal responsibility for their choices, consequences, and quality of life.

The effects of marrying someone who is emotionally immature on spouses and their children are many; and few, if any, anticipated (when they were dating) that such painful outcomes would happen to them. After marriage, the emotionally immature person's limitations leave the spouse with few options: (1) desperately spin in circles, trying to change someone who does not want to be changed and doesn't even see they have a problem; (2) feel angry, betrayed, and depressed about the emotionally immature person's limitations and behaviors; (3) accept the limitations of the emotionally immature person, grieve the many needs that will never be met by the emotionally immature person, and discover effective tools for *managing* the relationship; or (4) get divorced. None of these options seem desirable, nor will they make the relationship evolve into the type of relationship the spouse truly desires.

Thus, if you can recognize the person you are dating as emotionally immature and choose to stop seeing him before you get emotionally attached, you may save yourself years of frustration, neglect, shattered self-esteem, fear, depression, or abuse. This chapter will coach you on how to identify those who are emotionally immature through recognizing their problems with empathy, self-control, and personal responsibility. However, this knowledge alone will not save you from a tragic relationship.

If you are to successfully avoid relationships with those who are emotionally immature, you need to both identify the emotionally immature and accept the fact that you cannot change them. Without this acceptance, you will likely become enamored by their good qualities while holding on for the perfect solution that will make their bad qualities go away. The longer you interact with them, the more the psychological impact of these relationships will ensnare you. You cannot change another person. You cannot make those who never emotionally matured (due to abuse, neglect, brain injury, poor parenting, early drug use, or any other cause) mature just because you love them.

Now is a time to think about what is best for you and what the person you are dating has to offer you. Now is not the time to accept a new charity project or feel obligated to stay in a relationship just because you are good for them. You need to ask yourself, "What is it about this person that makes them good for me?" just as much as you ask yourself, *"What is it about this man that tells me I am going to be safe?"* This is not selfish. This is "self-worthish." And your present or future children depend upon the quality of your choice.

You will not be able to feel justified in asking either of these questions if you falsely believe you can create any kind of relationship you want independent of the person you are in a relationship with. Good relationships require two emotionally mature people. The skills of empathy, self-control, and personal responsibility in both partners are a must if a relationship is to endure the many challenges of life and marriage while still meeting the needs of each individual and the relationship.

This brings us to our next game play strategy.

> ## GAME PLAY STRATEGY #3
> Accept that not all men can love, that loving them will hurt you, and that you cannot make someone emotionally mature.

As you read the following information about the problems of the emotionally immature, ask yourself, "Was Peter a supportive boyfriend, or was he actually emotionally immature and, as such, acting controlling?"

CASE STUDY

Olivia was a twenty-two-year-old college student. She had many friends, earned good grades, and had a supportive family. Her parents had been happily married for twenty-six years. She had close relationships with several of her siblings and enjoyed her family time. Peter was her first significant boyfriend. He was attractive, articulate, intelligent, and motivated. He had just completed his bachelor's degree and was applying for medical school. His father was a doctor, and his mother had been a stay-at-home mom who seemed active and involved in the community. Olivia and Peter had just become engaged, and their lives together seemed promising and idealistic.

Sadly, Olivia's parents seemed less than enthusiastic about Peter and their upcoming marriage. They often encouraged her to take more time and get to know him better, stating they had a few concerns about him. She believed their concerns were minor in that her parents felt he kept her out too late, made her drive to meet him in town or at his home too often, and rarely wanted to spend time with her around her family. Peter often stated that her parents were just being too protective, smothering, and enmeshed. When she would talk about how close the family was, he often rolled his eyes and stated something from his psychology class about how dysfunctional her family was.

Most of their time was spent alone. He rarely wanted to go on double dates with her friends or be around her family. When he would agree to spend some time with her friends or family, he and Olivia often ended up arriving late and leaving early. Peter often stated he felt their relationship was most important and other relationships didn't really matter.

After she would spend some time with her family or friends, he would often point out what a negative impact they had on her. He would spend hours trying to help Olivia see that her parents and friends controlled her, told her what to do, and made her dependent on them. She often felt grateful to be with someone who was so concerned about how others treated her. She believed his protectiveness and defensiveness of her would help her become stronger, since he consistently encouraged her to stand up to her parents and not take their "crap."

However, she wasn't truly sure if he had the best ideas on relationships and knew the right way to act in them. She often felt uncomfortable with how he and his family treated his mother. On one occasion, she tried to point out how hurtful she felt his dad's comments to his mom must be, but Peter just snapped at her and said, "Like a future school teacher knows how relationships should be." When she pulled back and said that his comment hurt her feelings, he gave her a hug and said, "Don't worry your little head about it."

When making arrangements for the wedding, she often felt he was overly concerned about how the wedding should be planned, who should be invited, and what she should wear. He seemed concerned about whether or not the wedding would seem too "hickish," like her family. He didn't want to embarrass his family or make them look bad to their friends. She knew she had a great catch and didn't want to embarrass him either. She had always looked forward to her wedding day and had many ideas of her own, but she began to doubt herself. So, she started running all of the wedding plans by him "out of concern for his feelings."

The development of emotional maturity

As children mature, they experience multiple changes in their thinking, emotions, and connections to others. Preschool children (one to four years old) seek immediate gratification and are inherently narcissist. Their behavior is often self-serving and shortsighted. They want what they want and will do what it takes to get it. They often only control their behavior because they fear a punishment or want to gain a reward. They do best in well-structured environments with firm limits and consistent consequences.

Elementary school children (five to ten years old) seek validation and approval from others. Their behavior is often motivated by acknowledgment, praise, and recognition. They draw comfort from established rules and beliefs regarding right and wrong and good and bad. In well-structured environments, they often control selfish behaviors because of a desire for acceptance through obedience.

Junior high students (eleven to fourteen years old) seek acceptance and avoid rejection. Their behavior is often motivated by social norms, rules, and structure. Their fears of rejection or embarrassment are great, especially in social situations or with peers. They show little insight into their actions and often assume a victim position when caught doing something wrong. (They say things like, "If Paul had not hurt my feelings, I would not have punched him.")

High schoolers and young adults (fifteen to twenty-plus years old) seek personal insight and meaningful connections with others. Their transition to adulthood occurs in many important and significant ways. They begin taking responsibility for how their behaviors are linked to their consequences. They become motivated to change their behaviors and self-serving impulses based on the needs, feelings, and rights of others. They see themselves as linked to important people and the world. They begin to develop an internal value system that guides their choices independent of punishments or rewards. They accept community standards, rules, and laws as being important to social order but often question the rules and structure of society as measured against their own value system (which frequently changes). This does not suggest that they are defiant to authority. On the contrary, they often have many trusting relationships with authority figures but enjoy analyzing social, political, and religious beliefs to form their own opinions.

Therefore, somewhere between fifteen and twenty, teens or young adults mature to the point that they choose not to steal because they are concerned about what hardships it might cause someone else or because it makes them feel personally bad. They don't call someone names or hit them because they know what it feels like and they don't want to cause anyone else to feel this way. They don't lie because their personal value system says it's wrong and they wouldn't be able to respect themselves if they acted contrary to their beliefs. Thus, they have learned to control self-serving desires because of their concern for others and for themselves. They have internalized the golden rule, "do unto others as you would have done unto you," the Christian belief of "love thy neighbor as thyself," the philosophy of "if it is to be, it's up to me," and the belief that "it is not what a person says that defines them but what they do."

This development in emotional maturity is essential to long-term happiness and success in the adult world. It prepares teens for the responsibilities of adulthood as well as the needs of others in relationships. This transition does not only occur in high school alone but can be spanned over many years, perhaps between fifteen and twenty-four years of age. However, the more time passes, the more likely the person may not develop the traits at all. By the mid-twenties, those who have not developed these emotionally mature insights and self-restraints may never make the essential connections they need for successful relationships and adult life-skills.

This important emotional stage of development cannot be missed or skipped, for all additional developments in emotional maturity seem to hinge upon it. This is the time when the teen learns empathy for others, personal responsibility and accountability, and self-control. If a teen or young adult does not develop this emotional maturity, his capacity to love will reflect the level of maturity he did acquire.

The longer a person continues into adulthood without these skills of empathy, personal responsibility, and self-control, the less likely it is they will emotionally mature and the more likely it is they will have relationship problems, work-related problems, or legal conflicts.

Adults with these issues are often classified by mental health professionals as having personality disorders.* However, for your purposes you need only recognize them as emotionally immature with a probability of never acquiring the necessary and important skills needed for long-term, successful relationships—no matter how much you love them.

Unfortunately, about 15 to 25 percent of the adult human population never emotionally matures beyond fourteen years of age. Their behaviors remain motivated by selfish desire, reward or punishment, acknowledgment and recognition, or social acceptance or rejection—but not love. They feel a desperate longing for love, approval, and acceptance, but they make little to no connection to their responsibility *to love.*

These people are much like children in adult bodies. Sadly, they don't know any other way to be. It is as if a light of understanding never turned on in their minds. They simply do not know the emotional darkness they live in. And it is all related to the emotional maturity that did not develop in their teens, **specifically the skills of empathy, self-control, and personal responsibility.**

Empathy

Empathy for the feelings, needs, and rights of others assists a person in looking beyond him or herself to consider another person's perspective. Most people may appear to have empathy when they cry at a sad movie or state concern when they see someone hurt another person's feelings; how-

....

* Personality disorders, as defined in the *Diagnostic and Statistical Manual of Mental Disorder*, include Antisocial Personality Disorder, Avoidant Personality Disorder, Borderline Personality Disorder, Dependent Personality Disorder, Histrionic Personality Disorder, Narcissistic Personality Disorder, Obsessive Compulsive Personality Disorder, Paranoid Personality Disorder, Schizoid Personality Disorder, and Schizotypal Personality Disorder (American Psychiatric Association. *Diagnostic and Statistical Manual of Mental Disorders*, fourth edition. Washington, DC: American Psychiatric Association, 2000).

ever, this is not an indicator that the person has developed the skill of empathy for others. There are many important differences between empathy and a superficial interest in others (which often meets a self-serving purpose).

Empathy is truly present when a person controls his behavior because of his concern about how his behavior may affect others, and especially someone he loves. Thus, a husband with empathy who becomes angry about the bills may change his tone of voice when he sees his wife appear fearful or sad. He may still feel upset, but he changes how he expresses his anger in order to meet her needs or out of respect for her feelings.

On the contrary, a husband who is emotionally immature (and, as such, lacking empathy) may yell and scream at his wife, even call her stupid, all the while feeling justified that she deserved to be yelled at. This behavior may continue even though she is crying or telling him he is hurting her feelings. Her behaviors and feelings do not elicit concern; if anything, they are seen as further evidence of her weakness, inferiority, and illogical nature. If the husband later says he is sorry about what he said but does not change his behavior next time, it is likely his statement of apology is not a reflection of empathy. It may be an attempt to avoid consequences for his behavior (her leaving him or requiring him go to anger management counseling) or to meet a self-serving purpose (calming his wife down so she will be more interested in having sex or in going to his company party), but it is not a reflection of his care and concern for her feelings, rights, and needs.

Since the demand and need for empathy largely exists among family relationships, the emotionally immature person's lack of empathy may not be as apparent in other settings. Helping out a coworker or neighbor often elicits many personal rewards, such as praise, recognition, and social acceptance; thus, the emotionally immature person may be apt to be helpful and friendly to others because the social rewards or recognition are self-serving. However, at home he may respond to similar requests for help with anger, intimidation, belittling, or a refusal to help.

Because the emotionally immature are limited in their ability to feel empathy, the feelings, demands, or expectations of others (especially those close to them or in a position of authority over them) often elicit anger. The self-centered world they live in makes it difficult for them to legitimize others' needs, especially if those needs seem to threaten their own wants, needs, or desires. Furthermore, they are quick to assume that others have a hidden agenda or are thinking negatively about them; thus, they perceive the demand or expectation as a manipulation or an insult.

Much like teenagers, they do not like being told what to do. They often feel their ideas are superior to others' ideas. They have a better way and are therefore entitled to do things their own way and on their own terms. Thus, they take great offense at the demands or expectations of others. They are quick to argue that the other person's thinking or feelings are flawed. They are often critical of authority and may openly oppose supervisors, bosses, cops, or other authority figures. If they do respect their authority figures, they are often likely to treat others in lesser positions than themselves with condescension and disrespect.

In some cases (and more commonly in women) they may respond to others' feelings, demands, and expectations with self-destructive behaviors such as stating they are worthless, unworthy of love, and undeserving of forgiveness or self-love, or reacting by overeating (binging and purging), cutting on themselves, spending money they don't have, or threatening to commit suicide. Some of these behaviors are attention-seeking in nature and are meant to solicit the support and sympathy of others.

In most cases, if their anger, manipulations, or victim-playing do not change the demands or expectations that were placed on them, they tend to calm down in time and comply with the demands. However, they will often hold a grudge and ruminate over the offense they feel they received from those who placed the demand or expectation.

Self-control

Just like children and teenagers, the emotionally immature show little to no impulse control and are prone to act irresponsibly and recklessly. They may struggle with irresponsible money management, excessive spending, substance abuse, pornography addiction, flirting, attention-seeking behaviors, infidelity, eating disorders, angry or violent reactions, stealing, dishonest behaviors, sexual promiscuity, or suicidal threats or behaviors.

The motivations for their poor impulse control may vary from a need for approval to recognition, attention, order, control, or status. For some, an internal feeling of emptiness or worthlessness may drive their drug and alcohol use, unfaithful behavior, or excessive spending. In these cases, they turn to substances, others, or the possession of material items as a distraction from their pain and emptiness. Others may be driven by a desire for power and control. These individuals may become verbally or physically abusive or even break the law if necessary to get what they want or to force others into doing what they demand. Others may be driven by a desire to look good in the public eye. These people may throw things, scream, or become violent with their spouse or children if their excessive expectations of public performance have not been met or when personal or family problems have become exposed to others.

Regardless of the emotional issue, which they are usually unaware of, they hope that through obtaining immediate emotional gratification, in any form, they will feel better, maintain control, or get others to do what they want.

The emotionally immature may appear to have strong values. They may openly condemn those who abuse substances, mistreat family members, have affairs, and so forth. However, there are often great inconsistencies between their words and their actions. It isn't that they don't believe these values are right or best; it's just that when the opportunity for immediate gratification presents itself, their commitment to their value system quickly becomes discarded. They may then hide, deny, or rationalize their behaviors.

If pressed to confront their behaviors, they will often employ a variety of manipulation tactics to avoid taking responsibility for their actions. Eventually they may concede that they alone are responsible for their choices, but this insight does not seem to run very deep or last very long. In the end, consequences or the fear of consequences are the only things that cause them to exercise more self-control.

If, in an act of desperation, they promise to make changes, these changes are often difficult for them to maintain on their own. In many cases their commitment to the changes will not last more than four months before it is abandoned. Changes are often deserted within the first few weeks if others become critical of their efforts. Thus, their behaviors and reactions seem to be driven more by the external events around them than by an internal value system.

Personal responsibility

The emotionally immature employ many manipulative tools in an effort to evade accountability for their own choices and consequences of diverting their responsibility for rationalization, justification, minimization, distraction, blaming, playing the victim, playing innocent, lying, deceiving, denying, anger, threats, and intimidation.

There are several reasons the emotionally immature will employ these manipulative tools: (1) they fear the ugly and selfish reality behind their behaviors; (2) they worry about the reactions and rejections of others; (3) they don't want to give up their self-serving behaviors; (4) they fear they are unable to face their consequences or are incapable of living with their conse-quences; and (5) they don't want to take the responsibility for changing their problems. Additionally, when the manipulations succeed in getting others to back down on their accusations, the manipulations become reinforced and rewarded. Thus, the emotionally immature conceal their behaviors, some-times for years, to escape facing the truth and its consequences.

Because the emotionally immature resist acknowledging that their poor behaviors were their choice (since other appropriate options were available to them), they often refuse to acknowledge their consequences as being just and fair. If you confront them long enough, they will eventually concede that it was their drinking that caused the DUI and not a faulty breathalyzer, that their affair was their choice and not a result of their spouse's nagging, or that their violence toward their spouse was not the only option they had for getting their spouse's attention. However, even if he acknowledges that he did something wrong and should therefore experience consequences, he will often debate what those consequences should be and will feel persecuted if the consequences are not changed to match his expectations. Regardless of the efforts of others to help the immature person see the connection between his behaviors and con-sequences, it seems that he shows very little insight into his behaviors for long. Therefore, he usually does not commit himself to a course for lasting change, especially if he doubts others will impose consequences.

Furthermore, the emotionally immature often have irrational expectations with beliefs that project responsibility for change onto others rather than them-selves. Thus, they may expect immediate rewards for minimal behavior (spon-taneous trust after very little change, instant forgiveness after saying they are sorry, management positions with very little experience). They may believe that if others loved them, they would make good things happen for them. They may insist that it is someone else's responsibility (including spouses, parents, the gov-ernment, God, and church leaders) to improve their quality of life or make life fair for them. They may believe their wants are needs that others should respect and support. And they may insist that since someone failed them along the way, they are powerless to change their life (or other versions of the victim, martyr, underdog philosophy).

Additionally, they may illogically believe that others are an attachment of themselves or even a possession. The threat of losing something they believe they are entitled to have can cause rage. They may then react by becoming angry, verbally abusive, intimidating, threatening, belittling, or self-destruc-tive as a way of manipulating others not to leave them.

The emotionally immature can be high and low functioning

As you have read about the behaviors of the emotionally immature, you may feel tempted to believe that only the extreme examples (such as those who self-harm; threaten suicide; indulge in drug, alcohol, or sexual addictions; engage in affairs; perform illegal activities; or abuse others physically or sexually, which are behaviors common among the lower functioning) would determine the person to be emotionally immature. That is not the case. Those people who do not engage in activities that might threaten legal, social, or religious consequences (thus acting high functioning) may still lack empathy, self-control, and personal responsibility at home.

The higher functioning person's ability to control socially unacceptable behaviors (so they can gain respect in their professional, religious, and social circles) does not change the fact that they are emotionally immature in their relationships at home, where empathy, self-control, and personal responsibility matter most.

There are several reasons you need the skills for identifying those who are emotionally immature while you are single, regardless of whether they are higher or lower functioning:

1. The men you date who are lower functioning will be on their best behavior, thus acting higher functioning when you first start dating them. If you wait to recognize someone as emotionally immature until the first time they hit you or until you discover the first infidelity, you will be too emotionally connected to make a clean break.

2. Even those who are higher functioning can be difficult to be in relationships with, and the verbal abuse or neglect in these relationships will likely only get worse if the emotionally immature person feels any threat of criticism, expectations, rejection, or demands (which are unavoidable realities of life and relationships). Verbal abuse can be painful and even destroy self-esteem. Why take the risks of living with intermittent periods of severe verbal abuse while enduring low levels of consistent verbal slights, criticisms, and jabs? Furthermore, there is no guarantee that the emotionally immature person will remain higher functioning. If they begin drinking excessively, abusing substances, embracing sexually addictive behaviors, or

initiating an affair, the behavior that was better controlled when higher functioning will regress to lower functioning, and the relationship will be greatly threatened, if not impossible to maintain.

3. The psychological impact of these relationships makes it difficult to end the relationship.
4. You will have lost precious time and emotional energy that would have been better spent on someone who would have returned your love.
5. Your children will have been affected by the behaviors of the emotionally immature person and the instability of your relationship.

Now that you have learned about emotional immaturity and how to recognize it in others through their problems with self-control, personal responsibility, and empathy, reread the case study from the beginning of the chapter to see if you can identify Peter's issues with empathy, self-control, and personal responsibility. Then read the following therapeutic assessment.

THERAPEUTIC ASSESSMENT

Olivia did not see the many changes in herself that her parents saw since she began dating Peter. In the few short months of their relationship, Olivia had become more moody, irritable, snappy, and tearful. She seemed preoccupied with her weight and appearance. Her grades in college were dropping, and she seemed content to drop out of school, with only a few semesters left before she would receive her teaching degree. Olivia did not seem like herself. She had always talked with excitement about being a teacher. Now it seemed as if all of her goals were disappearing. Her parents expressed to Olivia their concerns that Peter did not seem more interested in and supportive of Olivia's goals. They stated their concern that the late nights she was spending with Peter and the things she was doing to help Peter were affecting her sleep and contributing to her irritability and failure at school. Olivia initially agreed with them that she needed to refocus her attention on her goals and find more balance in her relationship, but after talking to Peter about it, she seemed even more resolved that dropping out of college and starting a family right away was what she wanted to do. She would no longer discuss it with her parents.

Most of Olivia's friends and roommates did not like Peter. He seemed arrogant and often condescending to them. He rarely talked with them when he came to pick Olivia up, and he often interfered with any plans Olivia made with them. She would be on the phone with him for hours and then cry herself to sleep, yet she always talked about him as if she was lucky to have him. On occasion she would tell her friends about her and Peter's fights, but later she would explain how wrong she had been and that she was glad to be learning so much about relationships and how to make them work. She didn't seem happy or confident. She seemed to doubt herself more and more and was even running her decisions past Peter. She often waited by the phone and refused to go with her friends to movies or dinner, stating she needed to be home when Peter called. Her friends and family wanted to be happy for Olivia's engagement, but they often spent hours talking about how worried they were about her. Something just didn't seem right.

Olivia's parents and friends were right to be concerned about Peter. They knew very little about him and what was going on in the relationship, but they felt uncomfortable when they were with him and saw the relationship was having a negative effect on Olivia. They knew there were many things Olivia was not telling them about the relationship and how he was treating her. They didn't want to interfere in Olivia's life, but they wished she would slow down her wedding plans and talk to them more.

Olivia could have had enough evidence to see Peter's emotional immaturity if she had wanted to. Peter's emotionally immaturity was obvious in that he didn't feel empathy for Olivia's feelings, opinions, goals, or needs; he used his arrogance and better-than-you attitude to successfully intimidate, blame, and manipulate others so they would not hold him personally responsible for his behaviors (though he did much of this unconsciously). And he occasionally reacted with outbursts of anger that showed his problems with self-control (though he was currently managing his anger and self-control issues well enough to be higher functioning—at least for the time being).

• • •

To improve your skills for identifying the emotionally immature and to assess your own emotional immaturity, you may want to review appendix a (at the end of this book). Recognizing others' and your emotional immaturity can be one of the most important things you do for your safety and success in dating a good man because birds of a feather flock together—you cannot hope to attract someone who has skills you do not. Furthermore, when dating, you will want to review the list in appendix a to solidify your assessment of your date's tendency to act emotionally immature.

chapter five

Ohhhhh!
That's a warning sign!

When will the first defining moment be, when you say, "Ohhhhh! That's a warning sign!"? Will it be when someone is trying to set you up on a blind date? Will it be the first email? Will it be the first phone call, the first date, the first criticism? When will you know that this man is potentially abusive or manipulative?

One strike, two, and then three—when do you say you know enough and call it quits? You may be in the Dating Game, but your happiness and safety is no game. When do you say, "This man scares me, and I am not going to be emotionally, physically, sexually, or financially safe if I stay"?

Those who have ever been in an emotionally or physically abusive relationship know how hard it is to end the relationship. Additionally, healing from the relationship often takes months or years. Then there is the daunting task of dating again, but this time their confidence may be shot because they don't know if they are getting back into another abusive relationship. Furthermore, it probably took them at least four or six months to recognize that their relationship was becoming abusive. They simply cannot afford to take four months or more again before seeing if their next relationship is going to be abusive.

The good news is, you can answer the question, *"What is it about this man that tells me I am going to be safe?"* Anyone can learn to identify a majority of those who are abusive and manipulative within the first three dates. Since those who are abusive and manipulative lack empathy, self-control, and personal responsibility, they can't help but give themselves away, in spite of their efforts to be on their best behavior.

Thus, if you know what to look for, you can identify the potentially abusive and manipulative before you get attached. But you must do this within the first three dates to prevent yourself from denying your gut feelings, delaying your decision about the person (just one more date, week, or month), or waiting until a more convenient moment. The reality is, the longer you know them, the more confused you will get, the more you will feel attached, the more you will want their approval and validation, and the more you may become dependent upon them.

Additionally, if you use the three-date rule and discover the guy you are dating passes the test, you can have confidence and assurance that you are safe (then you just have to decide if you are compatible—which will be addressed in chapters 8 and 15). So, your next game play strategy is to know, use, and keep using the three-date rule.

GAME PLAY STRATEGY #4
keep to the three-Date RuLe

Before learning about the three-date rule, read the following case study and ask yourself, "Are there any warning signs in Mike's behavior?"

As you review the four steps to the three-date rule, compare what you are learning to you own experiences and to the case study on the next page.

CASE STUDY

Janis met Mike over the Internet. He called on Monday and asked her out for Saturday. He did not call to confirm their date, so when he didn't show up, she began to wonder if she got the time wrong. She tried to call him but only got a busy signal. Forty-five minutes later she called some friends and was on her way out the door when he called saying he was ten minutes away. She cancelled her plans with her friends and waited another thirty minutes for him to show up.

She decided at dinner an hour into the date to mention her confusion and the inconvenience he caused her by being late. She thought carefully about how to bring it up without being too critical or seeming rude. Since she felt she had stated her feelings respectfully, she was greatly shocked by his reaction. He immediately became angry and distant. He told her, "You aren't one of those girls are you? I don't put up with high maintenance girls. Don't you appreciate the fact that I asked you out days in advance, am paying for your meal, and haven't criticized you for being cold and rude when I picked you up?" He then became silent and brooding. She felt uncertain and uncomfortable. She resisted apologizing but felt an immediate need to soothe the situation. She tried to bring up casual conversations and ask him about his family and work, but he seemed cool and uninterested. He paid the bill and then started driving her home.

When they got to her house, he began telling her about how hard his life had been and how lonely he felt. He talked, mostly about himself, for about an hour. In time he reached for her hand and told her how wrong he had been about her, stating she was obviously a warm and kind woman and he would like to see her again. She was attracted to him and found their conversation enjoyable. Her earlier discomfort had faded when he warmed up to her, and she knew she would like to see him again.

He kissed her and then asked to use the restroom before he left. Once in the house, he kissed her again. She felt a bit anxious about the time and was concerned about how she was going to tell him she needed him to go, fearing he may become upset and rejecting like before. Though she enjoyed kissing him, she was unsure how far he might try to go. Eventually, and after being more intimate than she would have liked on a first date, she told him she needed to get to bed and he would need to go. He left.

She wanted to feel okay about the evening, but she also felt a little anxious and uncomfortable—she wasn't sure why.

To do the three-date rule

1. Familiarize yourself with the early warning signs of the' potentially abusive and manipulative.

The following warning signs reflect the emotionally immature person's lack of empathy, self-control, and personal responsibility and can often be observed early in the dating process. To ensure your safety, you may want to review these warning signs often or memorize them. Additionally, discussing them with a friend after a date may build your confidence in what you are seeing. *If you date a person who appears to have these warning signs (especially those in italics), take the warning signs seriously—remember what you are seeing is the person's best behavior; thus, their behavior will get worse.*

Problems with self-control

- They drink to excess on the first few dates.
- They openly use drugs.
- Each night they are with you, they miss work the next day.
- They spend all their time with you immediately— discarding family, friends, work, or school responsibilities to be with you.
- They don't call when they say they will. They arrive more than half an hour late for the first date. They get angry when you don't immediately accept their apology and drop it.
- They brag about their past or present drug, alcohol, or sexual behaviors.
- *They talk very early on about sex or make sexual comments about you, your body, or things they would like to do to you or*

have you do to them.

- As they talk about their past, it becomes apparent that they have had frequent job losses for mysterious, illogical, or concerning reasons.
- *When they talk about their past, they have multiple criminal charges or appear to minimize their illegal behaviors and consequences. (For instance, they might say something like, "An ex-wife received a protective order against me, but even the judge knew it wasn't warranted." Yet the judge granted it?)*
- As they talk about past relationships, they appear to have a history of jumping from one relationship to the next or have a history of infidelity.
- They may ask on a first date, "How do you feel about me or us?" They may justify this premature attempt to define the relationship by stating, "I hate to waste time on girls I am not sure are interested in me or are not willing to pursue commitment." They give the impression that if you don't tell them what they want to hear, they will not call you again.
- Their past marriages or significant relationships all ended up being with someone who was abusive, neglectful, unfaithful, addicted, or psychotic. They don't appear to be taking any responsibility, and their stories seem too extreme to believe. They seem too innocent or too good. It just doesn't add up.
- *As they talk about their experiences, they appear to have a history of reacting with anger (for example: they may talk about experiences in which they quickly got into fist fights over small offenses, lost jobs because of anger management issues, punched holes in walls, yelled, or called names).*
- *As they talk about times they have felt rejected, criticized, or stressed with demands, they appear to have reacted with destructive behaviors (for example: acting violent, doing drugs, procrastinating, cutting on themselves, spending excessively, having a one-night stand, binging and purging, threatening or attempting suicide).*
- As they talk about their moral beliefs or values, they seem to act impulsively and immorally. They either show little

recognition of the inconsistency, rationalize their behavior, or say they need to change but keep doing the behavior anyway.

- *As they talk about their childhood behaviors, it appears they had little discipline from parents. Their behaviors seemed out of control (early drug use, sexual behaviors, truancies, aggression to others, destruction of property, disrespect to authority).*
- They say things like, "You are going to be so good for me," "With you I will become the person I have wanted to be for years," or "You are so strong and honest. I need someone who calls me on my stuff. It will be so good for me to have someone I know won't let me manipulate them."
- As they talk about their history, they appear to have secretive behaviors and stories that don't match up or make sense.
- *When you express concern about some irresponsible or dangerous behaviors they want to spontaneously do with you (call in sick to work and go to Hawaii for the week, go skydiving, go skinny dipping), they become rejecting (or threaten to take another woman instead), critical, angry, pouting, and punishing, or they immediately take you home.*

Problems with empathy

- *They encourage you to get drunk or to participate in drug use.*
- *They pressure you on the first phone call or date to share your personal feelings, problems, issues, and past. And, they don't back off when you appear uncomfortable with their probing questions.*
- *They immediately want to know your phone number and where you live or work, and they want to go on a date away. When you express concern about giving them this information, they may say, "You can trust me," or they may act sweet, charming, pressuring, downplaying, or criticizing until you give in.*
- Within the first few phone calls or dates, they ask for money, a loan, or help paying off a bill or making an

expensive purchase. They give long explanations for why their luck has been so bad and their need for the money is great, without recognizing that you may be a college student, single mom, or a woman who is merely working a minimum-wage job. They seem praising, adoring, or sweet while asking for your help, but critical, distant, or angry if you do not immediately give them what they want.

- *They minimize or criticize your family, work, or educational responsibilities or personal goals, saying they are not that important or that you take them too seriously. They may even do this while setting up the first date and as a way of trying to get you to see them sooner.*
- They very quickly say things to you like, "I have never loved anyone like this before" or "I've never felt this way before." (If they have been married before and in a few days they love you more than they ever loved their spouse, what does that say about their ability to love?)
- They seem critical of others' appearance, weight, clothing, social skills, or personal weaknesses. (A little bit of this may be normal for younger adults, but too much criticism of others' appearance shows emotional immaturity.)
- They seem overly concerned with their appearance and how others perceive them. They may make an issue out of your appearance, either stating that you make them look good or immediately trying to make you over so you will better match their standards.
- As they talk incessantly about themselves, they ask few comfortable questions about you. Then they may praise you for your looks and talk about how the two of you are so much alike, but they still know very little about you.
- They talk as if they know more than others and act as if they are better than others. They may even act condescending, critical, or demeaning to the waitress at dinner, right in front of you.
- When talking about those they work with or those they are in authority over, they may brag about things they have done and said to coworkers, as if they have no concern for the feelings of these people.
- As they talk about their failed past relationships, they seem

to have little to no awareness of the feelings, frustrations, issues, or needs the other person may have had with them or the relationship. They do not provide solid examples of things they did to try to repair their relationship or meet their spouse's emotional needs. If you asked them, "What would your ex-wife say was the reason for your divorce?" they either change the subject, get uncomfortable, give all the blame to the ex-wife, or say they don't know.

- When talking about their relationships, they have no long-term friendships, or they have many family members who they have no contact with. They may talk as if they have suffered great rejection or betrayal from everyone they have loved.

- They appear to have love/hate relationships. They express idealistic feelings about you and your personality, calling you an angel, a saint, the perfect woman, the nicest girl they have ever met, someone they know they can trust and won't ever hurt them (though they just met you), while talking about how everyone else they have loved has betrayed or abandoned them. They appear to ruminate over their injuries, resentments, or anger toward others, feeling these people are evil, crazy, bad, or cruel. Yet they seem to still want contact with these people. Thus, their tendency to love quickly seems to switch to hate quickly and even back to love quickly.

- When they talk about their past relationships, they express hatred, resentment, and anger toward the women in their lives (mothers, sisters, girlfriends, wives, doctors, bosses, coworkers), even years after the offense.

- *They seem proud of jokes or behaviors that could cause problems for others. For example, they may throw gum into a crowd, hoping it will fall in someone's hair, or turn on an outside faucet, hoping the water will freeze and cause someone to fall. This could also include littering, small acts of vandalism, stealing, and so forth. They don't seem to see the difference between a harmless joke and a cruel prank.*

- *They get too close too quickly and seem to get in "your space" even though you may appear to be uncomfortable with their affection. They may do this when you are around others because you may be less likely to say no in front of others.*

- *They take your things, damage your property, or get in your space without permission. They may do this jokingly, playfully, or aggressively even on the first date (for instance, they might take your purse and teasingly riffle through it even though you've asked them to give it back).*

- *They joke, criticize, tease, or make sarcastic comments about you or your behavior within the first few dates. When you ask them to stop, they downplay your requests, tease you more, tell you that you are taking it too seriously, or get mad.*

- *They appear to intentionally show up at your work or home during a time they know you need to focus your attention elsewhere. Then they distract you from these responsibilities with humor, fun, affection, guilt trips, sadness, anger, or brooding. They may become offended, blaming, angry, or rejecting if you don't give them the attention they want.*

- *Within the first few dates, they seem offended when you go on a date with someone else, act rejected when you don't rearrange your plans to be with them, or take it personally if you don't answer the phone or return their calls right away.*

- *They pressure you to fulfill their physical requests—any resistance you give does not stop them. They continue to pursue their desires through humor, playfulness, pleading, anger, appealing to sympathy, outright ignoring your efforts to say no, or doing what they want anyway.*

- *They may quickly pull you from activities with friends or family or become easily threatened by your friends or family. They may do this in a variety of ways, acting sick just when you are about to leave, picking a fight that makes you stay and work it out, making excuses that keep you from leaving, or complaining that your friends or family members don't like them.*

- *They put down or minimize the importance of your interests, hobbies, athletic pursuits, and so forth. They may quickly interfere with you continuing these interests, especially if these hobbies or sports involve other men.*

- *When talking about their childhood, you get the impression that they may have been cruel to animals, acted sexually aggressive, or acted violently toward younger children. While*

*on the date, you notice that they have acted or are acting cruel
to animals, children, or others (their pets are poorly taken
care of, appear injured, or seem to have been tormented; their
younger siblings seem frightened by them or want nothing to do
with them; their comments to others seem cruel or demeaning).*

- *If you express your feelings about their behaviors toward you,
they react personally and dramatically to your feelings without
any acknowledgment or concern for your feelings (for example,
they may say, "How could you say that to me? That is so
mean!" instead of saying, "I'm sorry. I didn't think about it at
the time, but now I can see why you would feel that way.")*

Problems with taking personal responsibility

- They seem too good to be true and everything any woman
  would want them to be. They seem to have it all together
  (money, possessions, status, good looks, confidence, the
  respect and admiration of others) and they never express
  human weakness, fear, insecurity, or doubt.
- When you are with them, you feel desperate to look
  good, make them approve of you, or act perfect. You
  fear showing them your weaknesses, when this is not a
  usual pattern for you. You begin to feel more insecure,
  self-doubting, prone to eating disorders you did not have
  before, and even depressed and anxious.
- They burden you with their problems immediately. This
  may include emotional, financial, family, or parental
  problems (for example, "I forgot my wallet. Can you pay
  for dinner?" on the first date. "My babysitter flaked on me.
  Could you take my kids?" within the first week of meeting
  you—how can that be good for his kids?).
- *They jump in to fix your problems, save you from others, pay
  your debts, discipline your kids, and tell you what you are doing
  wrong. They continue to pressure you to let them take care of
  you even when you resist their efforts. They may say to you,
  "You shouldn't be so independent. Men don't like that. You will
  never have a relationship if you don't let men take care of you."
  Then, they threaten to reject you if you don't let them take care*

of you (or in other words, if you don't let them take over).

- *They treat you as if your judgment is flawed and they know how to take care of you better than you do. They may say things like, "You don't really want that" or "I know what would be perfect for you."*
- *They become immediately romantic, gift-giving, or over-indulging. At first it doesn't seem like strings are attached, but later you see that there are strings attached because they keep you in their debt, remind you of their sacrifices, or expect you to pay them back for their gifts if you don't do what they want.*
- They immediately want commitment, are willing to marry you right away, or want to move in with you.
- *They always seem confused or baffled about the things you have said you need or the things you have told them no about. They may act like it is the first time you have ever said it, or they may apologize and promise to not do whatever it is again, but within a few minutes, an hour, or a few days, they do it anyway. Then, they act surprised, as if you never told them. They promise again, do it again, act surprised again, and the process repeats itself. Somehow it is always your fault that they aren't getting the message.*
- *They use psychology, sales techniques, self-help information, or religious/spiritual principles to convince you to share personal information with them, trust them right away, or do things for them. They may also use these tools as a way of convincing you that you are the problem, that you have issues, or that you caused any conflict between the two of you. They don't apply these principles to themselves, except when it makes them look good, superior, or more sophisticated. You may recognize this misuse of psychology or spiritual principles by the mixed feelings it creates within you (anxiety, depression, uncertainty, self-doubt, shame, a greater desire to gain their approval, acceptance, validation, or concern about what they think of you).*
- When they talk about themselves and their experiences, they blame others for their problems or issues. They seem like the perpetual underdog who just needs a break or is always rejected, persecuted, and misunderstood by others.
- When they talk about their life, they express a distrust

of or anger toward authority figures (cops, supervisors, bosses, or religious leaders). They talk as if they know more and are better than the experts.

- When they talk about their behaviors, they talk as if they are above the rules, laws, regulations, or tax requirements that others must live by. They talk as if they are unique and therefore do not have to follow the same rules as others. They believe they should not be required to live with natural or imposed consequences for their behaviors (which were someone else's fault anyway).

- When talking about how others feel about them, they talk as if others immediately love, approve of, understand, or see them as exceptional.

- *They talk as if their disrespectful, critical, or abusive behavior toward others (or animals) is justified, not a big deal, or someone else's fault.*

- *When talking about past anger management problems, they talk as if they would never be aggressive again, but they can't explain how they overcame the issue (such as going to counseling, reading books, taking an anger management course, using tools for controlling their behavior, mapping out those emotions or circumstances that trigger their behaviors, or creating an appropriate plan to control their reactions).*

- *When confronted about their behaviors (like being late, not calling when they said they would, or having conflicting stories), they blame others or you, act confused, tell you that you remembered it wrong, make excuses, lie, get angry, become withdrawn, criticize or attack you, or take you home immediately.*

- *When you say no, express a desire to slow the relationship down, or limit how much time you can spend with them, they use the silent treatment, withhold affection, threaten to end the relationship, become angry, criticize your priorities, ask for their gifts back, compare you to an ex, or call you names.*

- *When you express your feelings or needs, show human weakness, or act in any way they consider unfaithful or unattractive, they react immediately and dramatically and do not let up on their criticisms until you apologize. If they do accept that they did something wrong, it is still only because they were reacting to you.*

As you assess those you date and the things they say and do when interacting with you, you should:

- Be concerned if the person fits three or more of the descriptions in each of these three categories.
- Be very concerned if the person fits several descriptions in italics (since the italics indicate a significant risk to your emotional, physical, or sexual safety).
- Be very concerned if the person fits many of the descriptions in all three categories.

Everyone will have a few of these issues, so you need not be concerned if the person fits five or less of the descriptions not in italics from all three categories, especially if you and your friends believe their explanations sound legitimate. They may have issues, but that doesn't mean they are emotionally immature.

The warning signs of the potentially abusive and manipulative are usually pretty clear during the first few interactions; however, you should not become blind to the warning signs just because the guy you like passed the three-date rule. Those who are therapy-wise, have a psychology or sales background, or live far away (so that you have few in-person interactions with them) are more likely to get past the three-date rule; however, most people cannot maintain their best behavior, deceptions, or fraud longer than four to six months unless those they are interacting with put blinders on or refuse to see the inconsistencies that would expose the deceptions. The truth is usually visible to those who want to see it. Thus, never ignore warning signs of abuse or manipulation in the first four to six months.

2. Assert your feelings, needs, wants, likes, and dislikes at least once on each date to observe the person's reactions.

Many of the warning signs above cannot be discovered if you do not assert yourself. You can begin this process with even the first email or phone call so you can test whether or not you feel safe enough to accept a date. Of course, you don't have to ruin the date by being controlling and difficult (which would turn a good man off). You just want to test your date a few times to learn,

"What is it about this man that tells me I am going to be safe?" Testing your date is an important part of the process. *If you act perfect or too accommodating on the first few dates, you just learn what he is like when you are being what he wants, instead of seeing who he really is.*

There are a variety of ways you can assert yourself with a date. Here are some examples:

- During the first phone call, tell him you would like to meet him in town for the first date until you get to know him better. Then watch how he responds. Does he tell you, "You can trust me. I would never hurt anyone" (which is a way of trying to talk you out of your boundary)? Does he sarcastically comment, "Oh, you're one of those paranoid types of girls. Ha ha. That's cool. Okay," and then keeps teasing you about it (which is a way of criticizing the boundary and using passive aggression to show his anger about it)? Or does he say, "Oh, I totally understand. Where would you like to meet" (which is a good man's way of supporting your boundary)?

- When you are on the date, he may ask you where you would like to go to eat. Express an opinion or give him two options you would enjoy (so he feels you aren't unreasonable). Then see how he responds. Does he tell you none of your options are good: "Yuck, how can you like that place? You don't want to go there. I'll take you somewhere better" (which is a way of criticizing your decision-making and saying he knows better than you)? Does he take you to the restaurant you requested but complains constantly about the food or service (thus punishing you for your request by ruining your ability to enjoy the meal)? Does he support your choice or negotiate with you for some more mutually agreeable options, without putting you down for your preferences (which is a good man's way of acknowledging your feelings while being assertive about his own needs)?

- When he doesn't call on the day he said he would, simply comment on it by saying, "I'm glad to hear from you." Then wait a few moments and ask in a friendly tone, "Did something happen yesterday? I thought you were going to call." (The purpose of this is not to make him feel bad but to see how he reacts. Just bring it up and observe). Does he ignore your comment, act confused, deny that he said he would call, get annoyed, make a lame excuse, or tell you that you must have misunderstood him (which are all ways to avoid taking responsibility)? Or, does he say, "You know what? I did say I would call. I apologize if my flakiness caused a problem for you" (which is a good man's way of accepting responsibility and showing empathy for your feelings. His emotional maturity is further demonstrated if he exercises more control in the future by not saying things he is not sure he can follow through with or by trying harder to be consistent)?

3. Talk with at least one friend (who you trust is good at speaking the truth, even when you don't want to hear it) after every date, and include details about the person and the date that relate to these warning signs.

There is something about speaking the truth aloud that shifts fantasy into reality, which is part of the reason we are so tempted to avoid being completely honest. If, when talking about a date, you find yourself skipping important details, protecting your date so he won't be seen in a bad light, or minimizing the significant warning signs in your date's history, you know you are in trouble. Obviously, your gut feeling is telling you there is something wrong. If you refuse to discuss it with others, you deny yourself the comfort that can only come from the truth. If you live in a fantasy of what you want your date to be, you will eventually become hurt by the reality you refused to see earlier.

Speaking the truth with others (who you know are not afraid to speak the truth as well) is important to your safety because it will help you feel more confident and give you the support you need to act quickly. As others recognize the warning signs you saw, the disrespect you felt, or the criticism you experienced, their confirmation of the truth will help you feel more confident in your ability to see things accurately so you can act quickly. Furthermore, the more you speak the truth openly, the less you will fear the truth.

Your friends and family will also not be swayed by emotion. They will not feel attached to this person like you, so they will not be as likely to minimize his behaviors. Usually a parent can see the warning signs more clearly than their teenager who is infatuated with the rebel at school. Do not dismiss the gut feelings of those who love you. They may see things you do not. Take the time to hear their concerns, and give it sufficient consideration.

There is one more important reason you will want to speak the truth about every date. When you are on a date with a good man, exploring every detail of that date will only increase your confidence in the emotional maturity you saw in him. You and your friend will likely recognize that he has problems or issues, but the way he handles those issues will engender respect. Thus, he will not appear to be too good to be true. The truth about his issues will feel real. He will seem real. And the skills you see him use relative to his issues will reflect his ability to take responsibility, show empathy, and exercise increasing levels of self-control.

For example, a man who is emotionally mature but has some issues with excessive drinking will show empathy for how his problem affects others while also taking personal responsibility for fixing the problems he has created. He will be willing, if necessary, to seek help in his efforts to gain self-control as well (which you will see he has done in the past or is doing now). Thus, a good man may have issues, but his emotional maturity will be obvious in his behaviors, words, and attitudes.

Thus, talking about the truth with a friend will help you feel more confident and secure about your ability to live in reality and make solid choices about those realities you see.

4. Trust your gut feelings and act on them quickly. Do not go on all three dates if you feel unnerved, uncomfortable, manipulated, put down, pressured, or for any reason disturbed by the first phone call, interaction, or date.

Our gut feelings are rarely wrong. Thus, recognizing your feelings, understanding them, and then acting on them when they seem to be telling you something is wrong can probably do more to help you ensure your safety than anything else you can learn.

These gut feelings usually express themselves in two ways: they produce negative emotions in response to abuse and manipulation, and they produce positive emotions to stimulate courage, action, and confidence in the truth. For example: when your personal space has been invaded or when you have been falsely blamed, punished, belittled, demeaned, pressured, or exploited, you may experience confusion, a stupor of thought, anger, powerlessness, depression, anxiety, self-doubt, or fear. Once you recognize these negative emotions as reactions to abuse and manipulation, you may experience righteous anger, building courage, clarity of mind, renewed energy, commitment to action, and then feelings of confidence, peace, and self-respect.

Unfortunately, if you do not listen to the messages your gut feelings are sending and you continue to choose a destructive course, you are likely to lose your connection to your gut feelings. In time you may see only what you want to see instead of what you needed to see. You may also discover increased levels of anxiety, low self-esteem, depression, anger, or fear, while not understanding why.

Thus, it is important to act on your gut feelings within the first three dates or sooner. This rule is not so much to protect you from him as it is to protect you from any tendency you may have to dismiss, ignore, or invalidate your gut feelings. You can't afford to loose such a powerful ally.

Now that you have learned how to recognize the potentially abusive or manipulative (the emotionally immature) in the first three dates, reread the case study from the beginning of the chapter. Identify warning signs in Mike's behavior? Then read the following therapeutic assessment.

THERAPEUTIC ASSESSMENT

Janis was right to be upset about Mike being late. She had been appropriate and wise to make a comment about it (step 2 of the three-date rule). A good man would never have responded the way Mike did. Mike's reaction was highly manipulative. He quickly diverted his responsibility for her legitimate feelings about him being late back on her. He criticized her (saying she was high maintenance), threatened her with the possibility of rejection, and shamed her with descriptions of his "good" behavior (of asking her out in advance and not criticizing her, both of which he should do anyway) and her "bad" behavior (of being cold and rude, which she had not been). Then he punished her with the silent treatment. Her first warning sign that she was allowing herself to be manipulated came when she attempted to soothe and calm the situation (though he created the problem, not her; she just appropriately commented on the problem).

Mike's descriptions of his hard life showed that he was assuming a victim position and wanted her to rescue him, which she did the minute he praised her (by forgetting and immediately forgiving his bad behavior over dinner, another warning sign of her vulnerability to manipulation).

Mike's attempt to praise and kiss Janis was simply his way of manipulating the situation so they could go in the house and make out (he did not even use the restroom when he first went in the house). Once in the house, Janis became immediately anxious and afraid that he might not react well if she asked him to leave. His aggressive reaction over dinner was enough to intimidate her now. This caused her to be less assertive about her feelings and needs and even give him more intimate contact than she would have liked to give. Once he left, she wanted to make the evening feel okay, but she couldn't—her gut feelings reminded her that something just wasn't right.

It was fortunate that Janis had this experience. Though Mike manipulated her, it did not happen again. She talked with her friends and immediately began to see the warning signs. She never went out with him again. Her righteous anger about Mike's manipulations made her more confident in her own discernment, rights, and gut feelings when she was on dates with other men. This experience also made her more appreciative when good men recognized and respected her legitimate needs and requests.

• • •

No one responds perfectly to the warning signs of abuse and manipulation. Nor will you, especially when you don't anticipate the abusive or manipulative behavior. However, the sooner you recognize the warning signs in a date's behavior, your vulnerabilities to being abused and manipulated (which chapter 2 identified for you and which chapters 6 and 7 will help you change) and stop contact with the abuser or manipulator, the better. You can take confidence and hope in the fact that you are getting better with each experience.

Learning the first four game play strategies should have helped you answer the question, *"What is it about this person that tells me I am going to be safe?"* You still need to know the answers to the other questions, so read on.

chapter six

Always avoid
unnecessary risks

Taking risks in the Dating Game is essential to becoming successful; however, these risks should only be taken when you can feel
confident about your overall safety. Whether the risk is flirting,
giving a guy your phone number, going on a date, or deciding to kiss the
guy you like, each step you take implies emotional and physical vulnerability. However, do not take more risks than you can control or recover
from. Until you know enough about the man you like to discern that he
is not a threat to your physical safety, it is best to limit the situations and
circumstances you place yourself in.

Predators are skilled at looking for weakness and vulnerability in others.
They test others' boundaries to identify those who are easily manipulated
and then set the situation up to their advantage to exploit the vulnerability
they see. For these reasons, it is always best to keep control over the situation
you first meet someone in, regardless of how you meet him, until you know
enough about him to believe taking a few risks may be wise.

If you can answer the question, ***What is it about where I am (or am
going) and who I am with that tells me I am going to be safe?*** before
you go on a first date, you will likely maintain control over your safety and

prevent many unnecessary risks. Your next game play strategy will coach you on how to answer this question so you can ensure your safety.

GAME PLAY STRATEGY #5
Don't take unnecessary risks. Stay in safe places and around others until you know you are safe.

Before reviewing some safety rules, consider the following case study.

CASE STUDY

Megan hesitated before answering the phone at 11:30 at night, but she worried about missing Jason's call. Though she had just met Jason on a singles website the night before, there seemed to be something special about him, and she didn't want to discourage him from pursuing her, so she woke up and answered the call. He apologized for calling so late but explained that he just needed someone to talk to and he had felt such an immediate connection to her that he hoped she didn't mind.

The night before he had seemed charming and sweet. His picture on the Internet had seemed attractive, so she was a bit disappointed to realize that he just wanted to talk about his ex-girlfriend. He talked for over an hour about the hard time he was having getting over her, about his bad childhood, and about his desperate need to talk to someone face to face.

At first Megan had thought she could be of some help and support, since she too had come from a divorced family and had difficulty getting over an ex-boyfriend, but she felt nervous about letting Jason come to her house that late at night. Jason just seemed so persistent that if he could come, for even one hour, it would help him feel so much better. He promised her that he just needed a friend and would not do anything to make her feel uncomfortable. "Believe me. You can trust me. I wouldn't hurt a fly," he said.

Finally, she agreed and gave him her address and directions. He came over forty-five minutes later. However, he didn't seem so interested in talking about his ex-girlfriend anymore. He kept commenting on how sweet Megan was and how pleasantly surprised he was to see that she was more beautiful than her picture on the Internet. He then moved to sit next to her on the couch. She couldn't deny she was glad he didn't want to talk about his ex anymore and was actually showing interest in her, but she felt a little nervous that he was moving so close. Then he came in for a kiss and seemed to overpower her on the couch. Before she knew it, they had had sex and he was leaving.

Megan was sure she had not wanted to have sex with him. But it all happened so fast. She definitely recalled saying no to him several times and trying to move him away from her. He hadn't physically abused her or been violent, so she wondered what had just happened. She immediately called a friend, and as soon as her friend answered the phone, Megan broke down into sobs. As she related the story, her friend convinced her that she didn't ever have sex with her dates, she had never told Jason she had an interest in having sex with him, and she had in fact said no several times and tried to get him off of her. Her friend picked her up and immediately took her to the police station.

The police performed a rape assessment and determined that Jason's manipulations of the situation were characteristic of sexual assault. Jason was later booked and charged. During his prosecution, two other victims came forward with similar accounts of how he had manipulated and overpowered them into having sex.

Few people foreshadow what might create a potentially vulnerable situation—but perpetrators do. Here are some safety rules you may want to follow to help you avoid most unnecessary risks.

Basic safety rules

1. If you or someone you know has never met the man with whom you are chatting on the Internet,* setting up a first date, or giving your phone number to at the grocery store, do not give out your home or work address during your first few contacts. Do not give any information that may help the person identify your work or home address. We all consider our home to be a safe place, but it is not safe if you are alone and with a man who is not safe. Thus, it becomes imperative that you safeguard your address until you have enough contact with someone (or references from others) to determine if the man is safe.

2. Do not share any telephone numbers that can be used to get your address from the Internet. This includes calling from your home phone because your number will show up on caller ID. If you type your telephone number into Google.com's search engine and your address comes up, someone else can get it also. Make sure your address is unlisted, or only give out your cell phone number (which usually cannot be tracked to a home address).

3. Look for the warning signs that he may be potentially abusive or manipulative (from chapter 5) during your first few interactions (Internet chats, phone calls, conversations at the grocery store). You do not need to wait until the first date to discern if someone is exhibiting warning signs.

4. Very early on, set boundaries that support your feelings, needs, and rights, and limit what you are willing to do or not do during your Internet chats, phone calls, or dates. *This is the second step in the three-date rule (from chapter 5)—watching his reactions will indicate if he is potentially abusive or manipulative.* Thus, it is recommended that you do the following:

---

* The Internet often gets a bad rap. Unfortunately, predators find the Internet a good place to prey upon the vulnerabilities of others, but if you know what warning signs to look for (from chapter 5) and you keep to these safety rules, you should be able to navigate the Internet, ensure your safety, and meet a lot of good people. For many people thirty and over, the Internet's dating sites can offer good opportunities to meet others with similar values and goals. Thus, the Internet should not be discounted for its benefits. It just needs to be used with caution and wisdom.

a) Set limits about sexual conversations, especially in the first interactions (emails, telephone conversations, dates) because (1) sexual conversations may make you more vulnerable to sexual predators (who may be abusive or just players looking for one night stands); (2) you do not know how safe you will feel with this person when you meet them, and you do not want to feel committed to doing something you may not feel comfortable doing; (3) talking sexually may increase the pressure the person puts on you to be alone with him, which is not safe; (4) there is no good reason to take such risks just to satisfy a temporary sexual desire; and (5) you want a man who is interested in you—not your body. Remember, no good man would bring up such topics. If he does, you can take that as a sign that he is potentially abusive or manipulative.

b) Set limits about how much personal information you feel comfortable sharing with him, especially information that exposes your vulnerability to abuse or manipulation (this should include details of past abuse) until you have known him for a while. Again, the potentially abusive and manipulative often try to pry into your personal experiences for the psychological leverage it may give them over you. Good men do not use these tactics. Good men won't usually ask detailed, probing questions about your past or personal experiences. If you offer this information, they may listen and ask questions, but they will quickly back off when you appear uncomfortable. Good men are often content with light and casual conversation and are willing to let you share things on your terms.

c) Set limits about how much information and access they can have to your children until you know them well. This may include where your children go to school, what they look like, or what their names are. Do not post pictures of your children on the Internet for everyone to see. Share these pictures with only those you choose. Until you know the person is safe, protect your children from any unnecessary risks or emotional attachments by not getting others involved in your children's lives too quickly.

5. Expect him to meet you in a crowded place for the first date or interaction. Restaurants, ice cream shops, cafés, crowded parks, museums, and public buildings are great places to meet someone for the first time. Doing a quick breakfast or lunch at a restaurant can be an effective and easy way to learn what you need to about the person (like whether you are attracted or how comfortable you feel with them) without condemning yourself to a potentially lengthy, torturous date, in the event you do not like him. Stay in public places throughout the date. Do not return to his or your home to watch a movie, make out, or talk. You will have plenty of time for this later. Keep your first few dates simple until you feel confident about him being a safe person who will respect your feelings, rights, and needs.

6. If in doubt, ask him to go on a double date. Ask a friend and her date or spouse to join you on the first date. Not only will this ensure your safety, but it can also take some of the pressure off you and your date for keeping the conversation going. Additionally, your friend may see your date and his behavior more clearly than you do. If you both see warning signs, your friend may give you additional confidence to stop seeing him.

7. Expect him to call you and see you during reasonable times of the day. You should be concerned any time a near stranger calls you late at night. Usually these calls turn sexual very quickly. They may also turn to requests that you get together that night. Making decisions after 11 PM is a bad idea. Not only are you tired (which makes you emotionally drunk), but you are also unable to get help from others if you need it. Most men who selfishly begin an evening with you this late at night are not concerned about what is best for you or your life (especially if you have to go to work the next day). Eliminate the problem by setting boundaries about how late you will get together, and keep your dates to reasonable hours when you feel confident about the choices you make and the help you can get from others.

8. Tell a friend everything you know about the man you are going on a date with. Tell her where you are going, what time you are leaving, when you should be home, what your date's name is, and his phone number, email address, or Internet dating profile so she knows how to send help or identify him if there are any problems. You may also want to have a secret message for a friend so if needed you could call or text her and in code let her know you need help.

9. Take your cell phone and extra money. Cell phones provide immediate access to help and should be carried by any woman going on a date. However, it is also a good idea to carry cash. If you decide to ride in his car, you may need the money to help you get home if you feel uncomfortable while on the date. Just knowing you can call a cab rather than being stranded with someone who makes you uncomfortable can empower you to protect yourself.

10. Do not use drugs or drink. It is never a good idea to impair your judgment when on a date; additionally, those who are potentially abusive and manipulative will abuse this vulnerability to their advantage. Also, always keep an eye on your glass to prevent the possibility that your date might slip something into it. Take good care of yourself—stay sober.

11. Act and dress in a manner that engenders respect. If you dress and act in a feminine, attractive, yet modest manner, you are more likely to feel self-respect and get respect from your date. You will also be more likely to get help from others if you need it. It is always a good idea to be somewhat fashionable when you are single, but avoid dressing provocatively. Though many women feel she should be able to wear anything she wants in public and not be sexually assaulted, we do not live in a world where what should happen does happen. Those who are abusive and manipulative look for vulnerability, and unfortunately, provocative attire makes women look needy, desperate, easy, and vulnerable.

CASE STUDY
REVIEW

THERAPEUTIC ASSESSMENT

Once Jason was in Megan's home, her options were greatly limited. He was a skilled manipulator and ignored all her feelings and requests. He quickly overpowered her, and she was not confident enough in her feelings and needs to boldly and authoritatively raise her voice and intensely say, "Get out of my house NOW!" His predatory style was that of manipulation, not force. He likely would have left had she been more threatening.

However, teaching Megan how to recognize danger and respond immediately and powerfully was unrealistic and would take her months, if not years, to confidently develop. She often doubted her own judgment and felt too overwhelmed in conflictual situations to recognize her feelings, needs, or fears in the moment. Thus, the best way to help Megan be safe was to help her plan and anticipate problems before they happened. Once on her guard, committed to safety rules she would not break, and empowered with options she could use when on a date (which she regularly processed with girlfriends before going on a date), she no longer had to worry about getting into a situation she could not respond to effectively because it was beyond her power to control. Until the fourth date, she refused to take any risks, with good men or manipulators, that gave them more control over the situation than she had. She went on double dates, met men for lunch in a public place, took her cell phone, drove her own car, and did whatever the situation required. Some of the men she dated seemed put off by her rules, so she immediately stopped talking to them. Others seemed more than willing to do whatever she felt she needed. Her commitment to this process not only made her safer, but it also made her feel more confident in herself and in the good men who respected her needs.

• • •

Because good men are in the majority, not the minority, and because few men are sexual predators, at the end of a date you may feel these measures required too much work, were unnecessary, and were somewhat embarrassing. However, these measures don't just ensure your safety; they also provide an opportunity for the men you date to meet your needs. If you are too accommodating and willing to please, all you will learn about your date is what he is like when everything is easy and non-taxing (which won't help you to identify him as potentially abusive or manipulative). Furthermore, it is by far better to know how a man will respond to your feelings, needs, and rights from the beginning because real relationships are not all about him.

These measures may seem excessive and unnecessary, but good men will support them without hesitation. So why take any unnecessary risks? An ounce of prevention is worth a pound of cure.

Additionally, setting a challenge before a man and seeing him rise to it just to be with you is an opportunity that most women will want to have. These experiences are not only beneficial to women, but they also meet the deep needs of men.

Most men want to be heroes. They want to please women. They want to make a difference. They want to help. Don't deny men the privilege of sacrificing for you. Most men do small things for others every day. They don't expect fanfare or do things with strings attached. They do good things because they know it is the right thing to do, because they like the way it makes them feel, and because they want to know they made a difference.

By putting your needs and challenges before a date so you can do what is best for you and ensure your safety, you give your date the opportunity to work, sacrifice, and appreciate the thing he desired—you and your time. A good man will never complain about the sacrifice. An abuser and manipulator will. What a powerful way to tell the two apart.

chapter seven

Create a new pattern for yourself and your relationships

If you are like many single women, you probably feel like:

- You are in the Bleachers, unable to break into the Dating Game, condemned to observing others living your dreams.
- You are one of many woman on the Field, holding a ball while calling out to the guys around you, "Do you want to play," but all they do is shrug their shoulders and say, "Maybe."
- You are ready to announce your new lower standards, just to get some attention coming your way.
- You are standing in shock watching the great guy you were playing ball with drop it and walk away without a word— or worse yet, to play with someone else.
- You are sitting comfortably on the Bench, taking a much-needed break, but the Coach just keeps yelling, "Get back out there!"
- You are wandering the Field, checking out the Sidelines, exploring the Bleachers, even venturing into a place Far,

Far, Away, looking for proof that good men exist, but all you see is evidence of Jerks.
• Or maybe you are recovering from a tackle, questioning why the Referee does nothing, and wondering if you are the only one who is going to help you get up and away from the other Jerks that are zooming in on you.

Regardless of where you are in the Dating Game, you are likely not where you want to be—the Final Stretch heading for the Final Goal. The good news is, the next four game play strategies will do more than just help you ensure your safety through answering the question "What is it about myself that tells me I am going to be safe?" These game play strategies will also help you be successful in attracting good men. In this way, you are preparing for the BE CONFIDENT and BE SUCCESSFUL sections that follow this chapter.

> # GAME PLAY STRATEGY #6
> ## Recognize and change your pattern in relationships.

CASE STUDY

"I hate men," Jennifer said emphatically. "They want only one thing, and they don't care who they hurt to get it. They think only about themselves." Her anger quickly collapsed into sadness as she hung her shoulders, buried her face in her hands, and cried. "I just feel so angry, torn, hurt, and helpless. I want love so badly, but every guy I care about hurts me. Do I have to date nerds or weirdos to be treated well?"

Analyze your relationship pattern

Consider your most important relationships. Choose at least three relationships to answer the following questions. Write your answers on a separate piece of paper so you can have more room to complete these questions. *If you don't date much, analyze your behaviors related to those you have had a significant attraction to (even though you may have never dated them). A pattern may emerge in your behavior that will give you insight into what you may be doing wrong. If you have very little experience with relationships, or have recently come out of a long-term marriage, thus making it difficult to analyze more than one love relationship, you will need to analyze three or more of your closest family relationships or friendships. Your behavior in these relationships may coincide with your behavior in your love relationships, thus exposing a pattern.*

On a piece (or several pieces) of paper, draw four columns:

1. In the first column,

    a. Write the name of each person you will be reviewing these questions about. (If you did not actually date, but he was a significant crush, then you still experienced a relationship with him—whether he knew it or not. If you are writing about other important relationships, then assume every question stating him also means him or her.)

    b. Describe what first attracted you to him (physically, emotionally, intellectually, financially, spiritually).

    c. Explain what you think attracted him to you.

2. In the second column, write about *his* behaviors and characteristics during the relationship.

3. In the third column, write about *your* behaviors and characteristics during the relationship.

As you do steps 2 and 3, write about how the relationship began, developed, and ended. Describe your role, what you did or didn't do, and said or didn't say. Describe those things he did or did not do and said or did not say. Remember what attracted you to him and him to you. Describe if either of you were guilty of abusive, manipulative, exploitive, unfaithful, dishonest, neglectful, substance abusing, secretive, or irresponsible behaviors. If the relationship didn't last long or never really began, describe what you were doing while you were waiting to see what might happen (sat by the phone, analyzed what he was thinking, excused his behaviors). Recall how quickly the relationship progressed (became committed, became physical). Describe who was more into whom. Analyze how the relationship affected both of you (improved both people, contributed to old habits resurfacing, began an addiction, affected personal standards, changed beliefs).

4. Review and analyze the information you have written in each column. Circle those things that seem to be in common. Write the circled words in the fourth column. Also write notes about those patterns you saw emerge in each section. Take careful note of your behaviors, choices, and responses because the secrets you need for changing your future lie in you and your behavior more than in the choices of others.

GAME PLAY STRATEGY #7
Be true to the truth.

Have you ever had a friend who was in love with a Jerk? Sure, he was handsome, but he was also irresponsible, self-absorbed, unfaithful, and rude. You couldn't understand what she saw in him. What made him so desirable? He had "bad boy" written all over him, but it only seemed to make her more attracted to him.

For some mysterious reason, many women find the cocky, arrogant, irreverent, disrespectful, spontaneous boy attractive. What makes these men seem alluring, exciting, and romantic when their love and commitment is always beyond reach, while the love and commitment of good men (who are steady, even-tempered, constant, respectful, faithful, and responsible) goes unappreciated, devalued, and easily discarded? Why do so many women think "bad boys" look good and "good men" look bad?

Why is so much of what is good discredited, mocked, or ignored in our society? Why do men (and women) who act irresponsible, angry, lustful, indulgent, selfish, violent, and neglectful get so much attention?

Answers to these questions may be hard to find. Perhaps the news, violent movies, irreverent comedies, depressing music about infidelity, attractive actors playing jerks on television, and the negative personal experiences of many women have contributed to "good" men being lost in the shuffle of attention that is given to "bad" men.

Nonetheless, you cannot call "bad" (or emotionally immature) men good, give them your love and devotion, and then get a "good" outcome. You need more than just a wish and a prayer to help you dodge the Jerks and partner up with a good man. You need the power and energy that can only be found when you are being true to the truth in reality and your relationships.

In spite of the opinions of the world, each person has a conscience.

We all know what is right and wrong and good and bad. In our heart of hearts, we know that lying, cheating, stealing, pornography, sex outside of marriage, infidelity, abuse, drunkenness, and drug use are wrong. And we know we don't want these behaviors in our relationships. We know that when we, or the men we date, do these things, a painful consequence will follow. But we deceive ourselves into believing this time will be different. Our circumstances somehow will exempt us from the rules and consequences we see others suffering under. We then doggedly pursue our foolish choices to the bitter end, hoping against all odds that we will be the exception to the rule. We sometimes go a long way down our destructive path, feeling we truly can have it all without the price and hard work of self-control.

However, our destructive choices always catch up with us, exposing our lies both to others and ourselves. And then we discover our self-respect was lost, our relationships were damaged, we did get addicted, our word did lose its meaning, and on and on. In the end, the reality that we must learn self-control remains, but now with the heavy burden of being alone again while we heal our shame.

So, how does a woman marry a good man? By choosing to be realistic about everything she sees in the men she dates and in her relationships. By choosing to be committed to her emotional maturity and its demands for ever-increasing self-control. By risking rejection, criticism, and even loneliness for a time rather than deceiving herself into believing that this time the "bad boy" will really become the responsible, loving, and faithful "good man" she needs him to be.

Good men exist. They are everywhere, and if you want to marry one, you need to take a definitive position within yourself and your relationships to embrace goodness. Make it tangible and real in your life. Define what is right and wrong and how you know you need to act. Take a stand now. No matter what you have done in the past, you can change. Define your beliefs. Be brave. Do not rationalize or justify. Do not convince yourself to settle for less in the men you date because you are somehow too flawed, weak, or sinful to ever obtain anything that is lasting or good. Think of your children (whether you have any now or not—because someday you may have children). Love them enough to want the best for you and them.

Once you have committed yourself to your values, then you will be ready for your next game play strategy.

GAME PLAY STRATEGY #8
Recognize, appreciate, respect, and enjoy good men.

CASE STUDY
REVIEW

THERAPEUTIC ASSESSMENT

Jennifer did have many bad experiences, but it didn't have to be that way. There were many good men all around Jennifer; she just didn't recognize or appreciate them. She was giving her energy and attention to selfish, manipulative, and exploitive men through watching the news, reading magazines that showed celebrities in and out of relationships and affairs, and talking with girlfriends who were having similar bad experiences. She then concluded all men were Jerks.

What Jennifer did not realize is that a person is more likely to attract what she gives her attention to. Her choice to focus her attention and energy on the Jerks in the world kept her perpetually ensnared in a pattern of bad relationships. Giving her attention to Jerks only increased her tolerance for their behaviors while she remained largely unaware of the good men all around her who would have treated her with respect and love.

When Jennifer dated a good man, he and his ways were so foreign and unusual to her that she did not appreciate and respect the goodness he offered her. For example, when a good man respected her space and didn't try to kiss her right away, she felt he wasn't interested in her (because the other men she dated always seemed interested in scoring right away). When he didn't immediately spend all of his time with her (because he was focused on maintaining his full-time job, family, friendships, and other important interests), she quickly lost interest in him (falsely assuming that he was boring because the relationship lacked the immediate drama and intensity she was used to from the Jerks she dated before). Furthermore, when he didn't pursue her the way the Jerks did, she gave up on flirting and encouraging him to date her. Thus, she eliminated him as an option.

• • •

Without a personal commitment and loyalty to goodness, how can you expect to appreciate good traits in good men? Their consistent dedication and hard work might seem only boring, menial, and too predictable, causing you to lose the thrill and excitement that so many women seek in relationships.* However, if you come to appreciate these same responsible qualities as ones that will make him more devoted, loyal, and invested in you, how much more might you appreciate and respect all that makes a good man good? Only through seeing things as they truly are (good or bad, when appropriate) can you effectively increase your odds for attracting and loving a good man.

As you date men who seem committed to goodness, you will have multiple opportunities to observe how they exercise self-control, assume personal responsibility, and show empathy for the feelings, rights, and needs of others. These three skills are the ultimate test of someone's commitment to living a "good" life. Many people can preach their values and beliefs—but do they live them? The ultimate test of someone's values is in their actions. A man who is committed to family will treat his mother with respect and maintain contact with her. A man who is committed to work will not stay out all night on weekdays, because he knows he must go to work in the morning. A man who believes in being faithful to one woman or wife will say no to others in order to make sure he can meet his girlfriend or wife's needs. A man who believes in honesty will share things with his girlfriend or wife even though it might upset her, just because he thought she would want to know. Thus, good men can be known by the ordinary, kind, loving, and unnoticed things they do every day in addition to all the bad things they don't do.** It may seem too simple, but it is true.

This is not to say that men who appear to be good through their many good actions are always good. There are those who put on a good face but only do it for show. They seem to have a public face and a private face (as hypocrites do). However, you can know these men through the many warning signs in their behavior (since maintaining a false pretense is hard to do

....

* Certainly many women want a little variety and unpredictability—a spontaneous weekend vacation, a mysterious surprise, a flirtatious love note, all of which a good, predictable man may provide if his wife lets him know she would like such things. After all, good men want to please their wives, and they also enjoy having fun and breaking the monotony.

** Good men do not lie, cheat, steal, commit adultery, use drugs, abuse, or call names. If they ever had acted these ways for a short time, their goodness would have driven them to admit their wrongs, change their behaviors, and heal their relationships.

for more than six months). These men will not show empathy, self-control, and personal responsibility in their everyday actions to those they should be closest to, and their actions will not be predictably consistent and good (like good men). This is why taking someone's religious status, professed goodness, or psychological superiority at face value is such a bad idea. Hopefully those with devout religious convictions or a dedicated study of psychology are made all the better through their regular and consistent religious worships or psychological evaluations, but it is no guarantee. One of the more painful forms of abuse can include spiritual or psychological abuse (the misuse of spiritual or psychological principles for the exploitation and control of others).

Thus, focusing on a person's behaviors so you can realistically look for and see the truth that reveals their emotional maturity is your best bet for assessing their goodness. Good men go to work, pay their bills, make time for those they care about, accept responsibility, fix their problems, listen and communicate, share their feelings, talk about their needs, read to their children, say they are sorry, and myriad other things every day and without fanfare. Good men do not expect attention for doing "good" things. However, they are often drawn to those who recognize and appreciate their efforts.

Thus, as you become more aware (and appreciative) of the good men around you, you may find that more good men are drawn to you. Good men abound. They are in the majority, not the minority. Focus your energy and attention on good men, and you will likely attract them and become more attracted to them as well.

GAME PLAY STRATEGY #9
Be true to yourself.

The most important reason for the two game play strategies of being true to the truth and recognizing and appreciating good men is to develop the skills and confidence you need. Too many women refuse to date because they doubt their judgment. They fear they might trust a man to be a good man, only to discover he is not. As you begin this process, know that you will most likely trust someone to be a good man, to discover later that he did not in fact have the skills of empathy, self-control, and personal responsibility that you thought he had. As unfortunate as this is, it is an unavoidable part of the process.

You cannot make a muscle strong if you do not exercise it. No one's judgment is infallible. Just believe in yourself that you will remain true to the truth. Believe that you are learning from your experiences, getting stronger every day, and getting better at seeing things as they really are. And choose to believe in (and appreciate) the good men you know. Move on and keep practicing your skills while trusting your judgment. This will be essential if you are to embrace the process of being true to yourself. (Note: To further build your confidence in identifying men with empathy, self-control, and personal responsibility, appendix b has been provided as an additional resource.)

To further assist you in learning to be true to yourself, you will also want to confront and change your problematic thoughts and beliefs.

Many beliefs can cause problems. Most of them seem to have their foundation in ideas such as "I must have love and approval to be okay; I must be perfect; everything is either black or white, right or wrong; life must be fair and the way I believe it should be; others should protect, save, and take care of me; anything that is unknown or uncertain should be feared; other people and events have more control over my life than I do; it is best to avoid conflict; the past controls the present; happiness can be found in leisure and inactivity; others are fragile and should not be hurt or experience pain; anger is bad; sacrificing for others is the key to being loved; emotions and feelings are beyond my control; I must be wrong if others don't agree with me; I cannot be happy if I am not with others; a perfect love relationship will fulfill me; life is supposed to be good and free from pain; my worth is based on my successes."[1]

Many of us accept these beliefs as true without question. Unfortunately, these beliefs often cause multiple emotional and relationship problems while also undermining a person's confidence in themselves and their judgment. These beliefs are rigid and extreme, and they put the quality of one's life in the hands of others. This victim position usually leaves the person waiting for "the one" who will save them from their problems. Those who are manipulative and abusive often seize these opportunities to "save the day" because of the control and influence over others it allows. On the contrary, this victim position also repels healthy individuals. Thus, those who embrace these beliefs are often more vulnerable to those who are manipulative, and are less likely to attract those who are healthy.

That is why this game play strategy of being true to yourself is so important to your safety and success in marrying a good man. You may not know or understand what it means to be true to yourself, but you alone can and must define this for yourself. You may find, like many others, that being true to yourself feels like a gut feeling you can't shake, a logical belief that creates peace and confidence, a voice from within yourself that seems to compel you to take action in spite of your fears, or a simple faith in your own feelings, needs, wants, likes, and dislikes that drives you to express yourself and be heard.

Whatever you decide, to be true to yourself you will need to know and exercise your legitimate rights if you are to stay committed to the path you know you need to take. Thus, you may find the following descriptions of your legitimate rights helpful. The more you accept and believe these legitimate rights, the freer you will feel to follow the path you know is best for you.

Place a check mark next to those you believe are true for you. *Do not place a check mark next to those rights you believe others can enjoy but you cannot.*

"I agree"—My legitimate rights[3]

___ I have a right to sometimes put myself first.
___ I have a right to make decisions and mistakes.
___ I have a right to judge my feelings as legitimate, independent of other's opinions.
___ I have a right to develop opinions and convictions.
___ I have a right to change my mind, behaviors, commitments, and opinions.
___ I have a right to object to unfair criticism, expectation, or treatment.
___ I have a right to ask for help or support.
___ I have a right to assert my desire for something to change.
___ I have a right to feel anger, sadness, and pain.
___ I have a right to not follow the advice of others.
___ I have a right to receive recognition for my accomplishments, successes, and work.
___ I have a right to say no.
___ I have a right to say yes.
___ I have a right to decide when I want to be alone.
___ I have a right to not justify or explain my decisions, feelings, wants, and needs.
___ I have a right to allow others to fix their problems.
___ I have a right to wait for others to express their needs, rather than feeling responsible to anticipate their needs or wants.
___ I have a right to not always feel responsible for the welfare of others.
___ I have a right to not respond to a situation or problem.

As you read about your rights, you may have agreed with many, if not most of them. However, do you act accordingly? You may agree that you have the right to say no, but do you say no? (You may want to review your "yes" responses to questions 1–15 in chapter 2 to help you see what your behaviors really say about whether you exercise your legitimate rights.) If you have not exercised your rights at least on a few occasions, you most likely fear doing so. (Read your responses again and erase those you have not acted on in the past.)

Asserting some of these legitimate rights may cause you fear initially. However, if you do what is best for you, in spite of your fears, you may discover like many others have that your fears quickly disappear or weaken; you receive unexpected support from others; you feel more confident than you previously thought possible; you feel stronger and freer; and you see more options for solving other problems as well. Certainly some people will oppose you, but if you continue on the path you know you must follow, you will be surprised at how many people may be drawn to you.

Therefore, repeat these legitimate rights in your mind. Talk about them with others. Do whatever it takes until you can assert them in your life and relationships. Do this for weeks or months, if necessary.

If you find asserting these rights to be uncomfortable at first, start with your safest relationship (this can include a friend you know won't reject you or a person you don't have a relationship with such as a salesman, clerk, or stranger on the street). As you practice these skills, in time your ability to assert your rights with those you fear will grow. Remind yourself often that being true to yourself through asserting your rights is your single most effective tool for repelling the abusive and manipulative and attracting good men.

Notes
1. Adapted from Davis, Martha, PhD; Elizabeth Robbins Eshelman, MSW; and Matthew McKay, PhD. *The Relaxation and Stress Reduction Workbook*, fifth edition. Oakland: New Harbinger Publications, Inc., 2000. This approach is consistent with Albert Ellis's theories of irrational thinking and A. T. Beck's approach in cognitive therapy.
2. Some of these questions were adapted from *The Relaxation and Stress Reduction Workbook*, fifth edition.
3. These legitimate rights were adapted from an assertiveness training handout I acquired years ago. Unfortunately, its author is unknown, but its approach is consistent with Albert Ellis's theories of irrational thinking and A. T. Beck's approach in cognitive therapy.

BE CONFIDENT

Before you go back on the Field, you will want to spend some time with the Coach, building your confidence in the good men you seek and in yourself.

chapter eight

What you don't know about dating can hurt you

W hat you don't know about dating good men can hurt you. It won't kill you. It won't leave you broken or bleeding, but it will leave you bruised for a while, spinning in place and asking the question, *Why?*

Dating has many unknown dangers, hazards, and risks. If you don't know the rules and secrets to avoiding and navigating them, you may feel the Dating Game keeps injuring you. These injuries are not Tackles. They are just the result of stumbling blocks, potholes, curve balls, game-play collisions, and other hazards resulting from risk-taking. Some of these injuries occur from ignorance of the rules, flawed strategies, overanxious enthusiasm, and inaccurate information about the other players. But a skilled Coach can help you learn how to navigate the game with fewer injuries and better success.

A good Coach's past experiences, observations, and successes can help you create a game plan that ensures your safety from Tackles and Jerks (which section 1 addresses) but also helps you navigate the other injuries that are a common part of the Dating Game.

Thus, before you go back on the Field, you will want to spend some time with the Coach in the locker room, building your confidence in the good men you seek and in yourself. In this way, SECTION 2: BE CONFIDENT, will coach you over the next three chapters before sending you back onto the Field.

Good luck.

CASE STUDY

Kris was in a bad relationship for over three years. She tried everything she knew to improve it. In the end she finally realized that the problem wasn't her, her commitment, or her willingness to work at the relationship. It was her boyfriend and her pattern of attracting men like him. Getting out of the relationship was a difficult and long process. She couldn't bring herself to date again for more than a year. But once she was ready to date, her sense of confidence had been greatly improved. She knew what she had to offer a relationship, and she had a conviction that no relationship, like the ones she had had in the past, was worth the price she paid. She had come to sense her worth, both personally and in a relationship, and she was only interested in giving these great gifts to a good man, one who would understand, respect, and appreciate all she brought to him and the relationship. Until then, she was content to be alone.

Dating the second time around was entirely different for her. She dated less but felt much more confident. When others offered to set her up on a blind date, she never hesitated to respond by asking, "What is it about this man that tells you he would be good for me?"

CASE STUDY

Review

Kris's statement embodied the confidence she needed for success. It was not how much she dated that mattered. It was knowing what she wanted and being confident in her ability to have it.

She was not focused on the need to date to feel good about herself. She knew her worth. She wanted love, but only if it improved her situation. She had much to offer a relationship and was willing to work hard and give but was only interested in investing in a relationship with someone who could and would give as much back as she gave to him. She was ready to love and be loved and would accept nothing less.

Thus, when others said (as so many did), "You would be so good for this guy I know," she wanted to be convinced he would be as good for her before she thought about accepting a blind date.

chapter nine

Not just any
relationship will do!

Now that you have learned how to ensure your safety, you may want to learn a few things about the other players and the game before you step onto the Field. You probably already know that the object of the Dating Game is to find a partner so you can progress to the Final Goal (marriage) and leave the Dating Game once and for all. There are many game play strategies the Coach can offer you that may help you reach your goal (which the BE SUCCESSFUL section will provide), but first you need to know what kind of partner you are looking for.

Not all players are the same, and partnering up with one may have a vastly different outcome than partnering up with another. Knowing how to avoid the Jerks is not enough. You need to know what kind of person you are looking to attract. In this way the old saying, "Most people don't plan to fail; they fail to plan," applies perfectly. If you wander about the Field looking to partner up with the first good man you find, you may feel disappointed with the lack of compatibility you discover later.

Most emotionally mature people are not too picky or too shallow in the things they are looking for in relationships. Sadly, so many single women report that friends and family keep telling them, "Your standards are too high" or "You will never get married if you don't stop being so picky." What a misguided belief.

Having high standards is not the problem. The problem is that many women have not clearly defined what they are looking for, how they will recognize it when they find it, and what qualities and skills they need to attract it. Thus, their standards may be high, but their efforts are largely ineffectual.

Knowing what you seek is essential to appreciating it when you find it. Furthermore, focusing your search helps you harness your energy, faith, and vision so you can be more confident and successful. To help you do this, your next game play strategy will encourage you to exercise faith in the belief that *you will have the opportunity to marry the kind of person you say you want to marry*—you just need to *be specific*.

GAME PLAY STRATEGY #10
Exercise faith that you will have the opportunity to marry the kind of person you are looking for.

CASE STUDY

Katelyn dated a lot, but her relationships never seemed to progress beyond two months. She couldn't understand why it seemed most of the men she dated were either lukewarm about their feelings toward her or she was lukewarm in her feelings toward them.

She longed to feel passionate and excited about someone and to feel they were the same about her, yet all her relationships seemed to just flicker and die before they ever got started.

She tried dating different kinds of men: some were intellectuals, others athletic, some mechanics, others outdoorsy. But the result was usually the same—nothing. She just couldn't understand what she was doing wrong, and she feared her luck in love would never change.

To begin the process of defining what you are looking for in a relationship, you will first need to understand a few things about the safety and security needs of women and the faith and trust needs of men. Reflecting upon these needs may help you prioritize those issues that are of greatest importance to you and your future relationship's success.

Women need safety and security, men need trust and respect

I titled this book *Dating Game Secrets for Marrying a Good Man*, knowing all too well what women mean when they think of a good man. A good man is someone who treats his wife as a priority, someone whose behaviors match his words, someone who is honest and faithful. A good man works hard to provide for his wife and family members' physical, emotional, and financial needs. A good man takes time to communicate and work out problems. A good man keeps trying even when things are hard. A good man thinks through his choices, considering the needs of those he loves. A good man makes his wife feel safe and secure in his commitment, loyalty, and love for her. A good man earns and maintains his wife's trust and respect in him and his choices.

Unfortunately, when a woman is with a man whom she feels does not provide her all of the above, she often loses trust and respect for him and feels insecure in the relationship and his commitment to her. When this occurs, she usually withdraws emotionally, pushes him back, puts up walls of defense to protect herself from further injury, and convinces herself that she doesn't need him or may be better off without him. She will then ruminate over the things he does (or doesn't do) and says (or doesn't say) to further convince herself that her walls and defenses need to remain. The more time she spends analyzing her relationship and feeling hopeless or helpless about his behaviors, especially those that impact her feelings of safety and security, the more likely she will emotionally divorce herself from him and fall out of love with him.

However, just as a woman needs to feel safe and secure to thrive in a relationship, a man needs the faith and trust of a woman in a relationship if he is to thrive. When a woman treats a man as if he is incapable, untrustworthy, or incompetent, he often experiences powerful emotions that compel him to fight or escape the situation (especially if he is worthy of her trust and she doesn't see it). In the beginning of a relationship, a man will respond to these emotions by fighting for the relationship and trying harder to please her, but if her disrespect and distrust persist over time, he will give up trying and either start fighting back or withdraw into other activities where he can feel like a success. He will then become less involved in trying to pursue and please her and become apathetic to her needs, because trying to please her only results in her dissatisfaction (making him feel worse).

In this way a good man tends to rise or fall according to a woman's expectations. If he believes she expects him to fail in the relationship, he will. If he believes she expects (or trusts) him to succeed in the relationship, he will. It is the woman who makes a man feel like a success. And when he feels like a success, he will do almost anything for her and will give his heart and loyalty to her.

Though many women fear men are unworthy of a woman's faith and trust (due to the selfish, indulgent, dishonest, manipulative, addictive, or unfaithful behaviors of some men), many men can and should be trusted and respected. They exercise the self-control, feel the care and concern for others, and take the responsibility necessary to ensure a woman's safety and security in a relationship.

You have learned how to recognize good men from the potentially abusive and manipulative, you have developed a greater appreciation for good men, and you have learned how to assert your needs, feelings, and rights in relationships. Now is the time to trust your judgment and the goodness of men and commit yourself to having a male-friendly psychology in your relationships. To help you accomplish this, each chapter that follows will have a section called "Have a Male-Friendly Psychology" along with additional information, hints, tips, and suggestions for lovingly asserting your needs in relationships (so he can develop a female-friendly psychology as well).

To prepare you to understand the male psychology, you will need to accept that women do not in most cases really understand men. Women think about their relationships, problems, feelings, and needs about 80 percent of the time, so they believe they understand men (what men should be, how men should act, and what potential their relationships could have if only the men they need did their part), but their perceptions of men are usually so limited that these women often end up undermining a man's role in their relationships and driving him away.

Therefore, as you define the kind of men you are looking for, try to focus on those qualities that you need to ensure your safety and security and to maintain your trust and respect in the goodness of the men you date. Also try to keep an open mind to the fact that there may be many unique and different ways for a man to manage his own problems while still showing you the empathy, self-control, and personal responsibility you need him to have. Future chapters will help you better understand the psychology of a man, but for now just keep an open mind to the idea that a man can be trusted to manage his problems in his own way.

While defining what you are looking for, you will also need to define the trials, problems, or issues you would be willing to choose in marriage. Everyone will experience trials in life and marriage. You will not escape the reality of problems in married life, but if you choose a spouse who has the skills of empathy, self-control, and personal responsibility (and if you have these skills as well), you and your spouse will likely feel more bonded through your trials as you unite with love and respect to address them.

That being said, you need to accept that there is no guarantee that marrying an emotionally mature person will ensure that you will never be betrayed, deceived, hurt, neglected, abused, or manipulated *for a short period* in your marriage. Many good people can fall into a bad pattern. They can become too familiar with someone at work; mistakenly believe they can control drug, alcohol, or prescription medications without becoming addicted; make poor decisions about finances and then do something dishonest in an attempt to quickly repair the damage; or become too emotionally overwhelmed and react in an unusual moment of violence (to which they immediately take steps to ensure it will not happen again). However, the difference is that their internal value system (or conscience) pains them deeply for it and compels them to confess and correct what they have done and *never* do it again.

These relationships, in time, can fully heal with both spouses feeling that much good, understanding, and growth resulted from the experience. Additionally, the efforts of the emotionally mature person to repair the damage done nearly always ensure that he will not quickly or easily return to his *brief,* yet destructive, behaviors. Thus, it is quite likely that he will not repeat the indiscretion.

Familiarizing yourself with the traits and behaviors of the emotionally mature or even assessing someone you are dating according to a detailed list of these qualities may help build your confidence in their goodness. Appendix b will assist you in assessing someone's skills (or even your own) of empathy, self-control, and personal responsibility.

Analyze what you need, want, and are willing to accept as problems in a marriage

Now that you understand men's and women's core needs in relationships, you should be better prepared to prioritize which qualities you are looking for in the good men you seek.

It will not be enough to know that you are with a good man if you have nothing in common. Compatibility is important. Thus, you need to clearly define what you are looking for. It is recommended that you make emotional maturity a must, but it's your decision. Describe what you want—be specific.

Provided on the next page is a chart for you to define what you are looking for in those you would want to marry. Place in each column those behaviors, attitudes, values, or problems you believe you need, want, can accept, or cannot live with in the person you would like to marry. For your assistance, a series of questions have been provided to help stimulate your thoughts. Please know, opposites attract but they don't last. Marital incompatibility over sexual, financial, parental, family, and religious differences add to the divorce rate. Thus, you would be wise to carefully consider your compatibility in these areas.

In many cases, differences can be good when both parties have the same goal or value system. People who have different ideas about how to achieve the same goal can bring their differences together and find synergistic success through creativity and sharing. Thus, you do not need to find someone who thinks like you to be happily married. You just need to find someone who is heading for the same destination and is open to merging both of your strengths to achieve your mutual goals.

Also remember that no one is free of issues. You will need to choose to deal with some problems (the signs of most problems are often evident before marriage), but which problems can you live with? Can you be with someone who is honest and responsible but doesn't make a lot of money? Can you feel fulfilled with someone who is a great provider but doesn't like the outdoors or is gone on business trips for several weeks in a month? You decide.

For your assistance

The following questions have been provided to help stimulate your thoughts. Read through each question, but answer only those that apply to you. Place your thoughts in the box on the following page or on a separate piece of paper to allow for more room.

A. Physical
- What do you feel you need and want in a man's appearance to be attracted to him?
- How important is the person's age, appearance, physical health, and fitness to you?

I Need or Must Have	I Want (but can live without)	Problems I Can Accept	Problems I Cannot Live With

- How important is chemistry to you?
- What physical health issues or problems could you choose? Which health issues could you not choose?

B. Recreational, sporting, entertainment, activities

- What sporting or recreational activities are important to you? Do you feel you need someone to share these activities with you? How would it affect you if it weren't important to a spouse?
- What problems may be caused by your or your spouse's interest in certain recreational activities? Which of these problems could you not choose to live with?

C. Financial

- What are your needs relative to debt, paying bills, investments, savings, college funds, living month to month, spending money for fun, buying clothing, buying toys, and going on trips?
- How much money do you feel you need to have annually in order to feel that your needs have been sufficiently met?
- What financial problems would you not be willing to live with? What problems could you accept?

D. Value-based needs

- Do you have specific religious, moral, spiritual, family, or philosophical values that you need the person you marry to share with you? (For example: do you need someone who goes to church each week, someone who is highly honest, someone who has high values and integrity, someone who has strong spiritual or personal beliefs but is religiously uncommitted, someone who has strong family values, someone who values education?)
- How do you feel about drinking, smoking, white lies, drug use, pornography, gambling, and R-rated movies? Which of these values do you need a spouse to share with you? If a spouse had a problem with one of these, could you choose to accept that problem, or would it be something you could not live with?
- Do you need to be with someone who shares your educational, political, or philosophical beliefs or goals?

E. Family

- Do you need someone who likes your family and will be open to you spending a lot of time with them?
- What family issues and problems could you choose or not choose?
- Do you need to be with someone who wants children?
- Do you need to be with someone who shares your parenting philosophy?
- Do you need to be with someone who will put you first before other family members or their dependent children?
- What role do you need your spouse to assume in the family and with the children?
- Do you need to be with someone who will stand up for you when other family members or children treat you badly?
- What ex-spouse or step-parenting issues or problems are you willing to choose? Are you willing to raise stepchildren in your home, and if so, how many?

F. Sexual

- Do you need to be with someone who shares your sexual interests, beliefs, or desires and respects them?
- Do you need to be with someone who can talk openly about

sexual matters?

- How do you feel about a spouse masturbating or looking at pornography? How might these activities cause marital or personal problems for you?
- Would you have a problem if you did not have sex as often as you desire? How often would that be?
- What sexual problems or performance issues would you be willing to choose? Which problems would you not be willing to choose?

G. Emotional

- What emotional qualities do you need in a spouse (for example: an ability to forgive, control anger, be able to cry when needed, be kind)?
- What emotional reactions could you not accept in a spouse?
- What emotional issues could you live with or not live with (depression, anxiety, mood swings, irritability, low self-esteem, obsessing over cleanliness, excessive eating, excessive exercising, anorexia, anger management issues)?
- What communication skills do you feel your spouse must have if you are to be happy in a marriage?
- How important is it to you that your spouse acts with empathy, self-control, or personal responsibility?
- If your spouse acted emotionally mature in his effort to resolve his emotional issues, would that make a difference in your desire to accept his emotional issues (such as depression, anxiety, obsessing over his health)?

H. Employment

- What kind of employment do you need a spouse to have to respect him?
- Is it important for your spouse to be educated or in employment that requires education?
- Do you need your spouse home a lot? Would business trips and long hours at the office negatively affect you?

I. Other

- Write down anything else you would need in order to feel happily married.

Carefully consider the list you have created. Your choices will define the strengths and weaknesses you choose in the spouse you marry and in the issues (good and bad) he brings to the relationship. (For example: a man who is loyal to you may have developed that trait of loyalty from his relationship with his mother—he will not easily abandon her, just like he will not easily abandon you. Can you respect and appreciate his connection to her, especially when he is willing to consistently make you first over her requests?)

Consider your list again. Is it true to the truth and the reality of life and relationships? Does it fit your values and definition of what is good, bad, right, and wrong? Will this list realistically lead you to a good man and a good relationship over time? Will the things you've listed fade in their importance within a few years?

Based on the information above, if you found a man with these traits, could you choose your love and love your choice? If not, change what you are looking for. Be sure you are clear about what you want before you move on with dating. Prioritize the top ten traits you need for your happiness. The first five should be considered a must-have in your next relationship. Do not settle for less. The next five need to be seriously considered for their potential to be realized over a period of time. In other words, if you need someone to share your religious values (or make a six-figure income or have a commitment to savings) as a top-five need, then be sure you are both compatible in this area before marriage. But if it is only a six or seven on the list, then explore the person's willingness to support your religious beliefs (or gain an education or begin a savings plan) without an expectation that he has already achieved this goal. If he is willing to provide this need or is already in progress toward this goal, then you may feel he is a compatible fit for you. The point is, you cannot have everything on your list all at once. Some traits in a spouse may require time and patience from you if they are to be realized, but be assured you can have the top-five things you desire, and don't settle for less.

Choose your love—love your choice

Contrary to popular belief, love is a choice. You are not a victim who just falls in love. You can act in such a way that you are more likely to feel love (and chemistry) for the kind of people you want to love. You can protect yourself from falling in love with the kind of people that would be bad for you or would not be what you are looking for by refusing to spend time with these kinds of people (thus, eliminating your chance of falling in love with them). And you can choose to love your choice through embracing on an ongoing basis the choice you made. Love, in all its forms, is a compilation of the many choices you make before and after you fall in love. Thus, if you want your love to last, you must choose your love and love your choice.

When you choose a man's problems just like you choose his strengths, you can focus your time and emotional energy on how to positively affect and cope with the problem rather than feeling consumed with anger or resentment about the struggles he brings to married life. Remember, you have strengths and weakness he will have to cope with too. Will you want him to be focused on your problems, or on his options for effectively managing and supporting those problems? Furthermore, it was your choice to choose his problems, so you are not a victim. If you can keep this in perspective, you will be more effective and happier.

Have faith you will marry the kind of person you described

In an uncertain single's world, it is easy to experience fear and doubt (about yourself, your future, men, and a man's interest in you). However, choosing to give your emotional energy and attention to your fears will likely only create a negative outcome (both now and later, because your fearful beliefs make you miserable now while also contributing to poor decision-making that will likely make you miserable later).

On the contrary, believing *you will have the opportunity to marry the kind of person you say you want to marry* will focus your energy while inspiring and motivating your faith. The resulting hope you feel will not only increase your present coping skills but will also inspire your decisions, increasing the likelihood that you will have a happier and more successful future. Thus, focusing your energy and attention on your faith will likely create the positive outcome you desire and believe in.

Now that you have defined what you are looking for, you need to choose to believe in your game play strategy—*that you will have the opportunity to marry the kind of man you have said you want to marry.*

Choosing to exercise faith in this belief can dramatically influence your ability to obtain a better outcome. Faith is not just a principle supported by religious philosophy; it has also received much attention from the scientific and medical communities because of the observed effects of faith on physical healing. Researchers have noted over the last several decades that those whose spiritual and personal beliefs or values give them the ability to view their medical circumstances with a hope or faith in a better outcome often experience unexplained improvements in their health. Scientific experiments have also noted the effect of faith when those receiving a sugar pill experience spontaneous improvement in their health due to their belief that they had received an experimental medication (this process is known as the placebo effect). Thus, when people believe something will help them, it often does.

Likewise, the role of faith in developing confidence cannot be underscored for its importance in helping you succeed in the Dating Game. Acting with faith in yourself and the kind of men and relationships you are looking for will likely create and attract an energy that draws those you seek to you. Just as birds of a feather flock together, those of a similar nature seem to be drawn to each other, and all you need to do to start this process is believe. Later chapters will help you learn how to act with faith, but if you can merely trust in this principle enough to believe for now, you will likely begin to act with more confidence than you did before.

CASE STUDY
REVIEW

THERAPEUTIC ASSESSMENT

Katelyn dated a lot, but her relationships never seemed to progress beyond two months because she only got out of her relationships what she put into them. She was passive and inactive. She knew how to flirt and get the attention of a variety of men, but she always doubted whether she was really interested in them from the moment she gave them her number. She didn't really know what she wanted, what it would look like if she found it, or whether she could really commit to it if it fell in her lap. She was looking for an emotionally elusive experience—a feeling, without understanding that many feelings are a by-product of our choices and actions. So, she remained passive and distant, making the passionate feelings she desired nearly impossible to feel. Once Karen learned that this was her problem, she defined what she was looking for and how she would recognize it. She then embraced and participated more in her relationships. In time she felt more passionate about the men she dated.

If she was going to experience more success, she was going to have to define what she wanted, seek after it (without becoming the pursuer in the relationship), and actively embrace and participate in the processes once she found it. Once she did that, she would likely find the men she dated were more passionate about her as well.

chapter ten

You must act with faith to be confident and successful

Too many single women fear what they aren't able to control. Since dating and relationships require the investment of another person, women often fear the uncertainty and vulnerability they experience in relationships. A woman's inability to control how her relationships begin, develop, or end often causes her to spend innumerable hours analyzing her relationships, becoming overanxiously involved in her relationships, or avoiding relationships in a desperate attempt to prevent pain and failure. However, where fear and doubt are present, faith is not. A woman will be less likely to succeed at the Dating Game if she does not act with faith—faith in herself, faith in men, and faith in her ability to have a successful relationship.

Just like any good Coach would spend numerous hours in the Locker Room prepping her players on how to confront self-defeating thoughts so they can be more focused and confident in the game, this chapter will help you act with faith in yourself, men, and relationships through believing *the kind of man you are looking for is looking for someone like you—and he will pursue you* (which is your next game play strategy).

GAME PLAY STRATEGY #11
BeLieve that the kinD of man you are LooKing for is someone LiKe you—anD he wiLL Pursue you.

CASE STUDY

Anna felt she could not hope to date if she did not put herself around other singles, so she often went to singles events, conferences, and dances. While there, she would approach men, initiate conversations, ask men about themselves, and try to be friendly, but few men ever asked for her number or followed up with a phone call to ask her out. So she increased her efforts and hosted parties at her house, invited men she met to have a homemade dinner with her and her friends, and made cookies for guys from her church group. Yet still nothing came of her efforts.

She was an attractive girl, educated, confident, and easygoing, so she didn't understand what she was doing wrong that she wasn't getting any significant attention from men. Were they just intimidated? Many of her friends, who were similarly well educated, had concluded that their lack of dating was because they were too intimidating to men. But was that right? She didn't feel she had an intimidating personality at all. Where was her mistake?

Unfortunately, many women mistakenly believe that if they don't pursue men, they will never have a relationship with a man. However, the following secrets to the male psychology simply show that this is not true. As a woman learns to understand and appreciate the male psychology, she may find that she actually has tremendous power to influence her relationships in ways she had never considered before.[1]

♂ Have a male-friendly psychology

The secrets below as well as those contained in the following chapters may be helpful to you as you learn to value and appreciate how men approach dating and relationships differently than women.

SECRET #1: Men seek out relationships that make them feel trusted and respected.

Men need to feel competent and will do almost anything for those who trust and respect their competence (as was discussed in chapter 7). Nothing feels more sobering and exhilarating for men (and women) than to be with someone who sees their value and has faith and trust in them and their choices. When a good man is with a woman who values his competence, he becomes even more skilled in his ability to empathize with others, take responsibility for his mistakes, assume responsibility for action when needed, and exercise self-control for the benefit of himself and others.

SECRET #2: Men love through sacrifice.

It has long been understood that men work hard for the things they love, and they love the things they work hard for. This includes sports, games, tools, toys, property, cars, careers, and women. Good men are not shy about pursuing the things they want and need—they expect it to be a reality of life. However, they see no point in sacrificing for things they can get for free. When toys, cars, money, or women come easily, a man is quick to enjoy them in the moment and then forget about them. Good men mean no harm to women in this way. Men just think about women (especially those they have only known a short time) much less than women think about them. That won't change until men have pursued and sacrificed for the relationship over a period of time. Thus, what good men get easily, they forget easily, but what they work hard for and achieve, they will cherish and adore for a lifetime.

SECRET #3: Good men are largely logical about their relationships and commitment. Thus, they do not commit easily to things they have not invested in over a period of time.

Men enjoy being with women and want companionship, but a man's decision to commit has nothing to do with the things he says when he is on a date. Men can express many emotions in the moment that they later discard when they realize the things they said were largely illogical, impractical, or too complex in their consequences to continue pursuing.

Unfortunately, many women take literally the positive things men say. They do not understand that men try on their emotions and decisions like we try on clothes at the mall. Good men like playing with ideas, feelings, purchases, and commitments in theory. They abandon quickly those things that get too complicated too fast when they are not sufficiently invested and committed to the idea they were exploring. Thus, until a man has invested his time, energy, money, and emotion into you or a relationship over a period of time, he simply does not have enough invested to stay when things get complicated or boring.

SECRET #4: Men are driven to succeed, face challenges, compete, and conquer.

Men seem to thrive in the face of reasonable challenges. The feelings of self-respect they experience when mastering a difficult task are often exhilarating and elicit a great passion and love for the thing they pursued and obtained (especially if they invested themselves in it over an extended period of time).

Yet, men love it when women pursue them. They love the attention, affection, and flattery that occur when an attractive woman expresses her interest. This is partially caused by the fact that the scales in a man's mind are always tilted toward the fear of rejection. However, no matter how much a good man may deeply enjoy a woman taking the lead, where there is no challenge, there is no conquest, and he is likely to become bored and start looking for something better within three weeks (because things that seem more challenging seem more rewarding). Therefore, if a woman initiates the first few steps in the dating process and the man does not then quickly match or exceed her efforts, she is at risk of becoming the good-for-now-until-something-better-comes-along girl or the nuisance that he must now gently dump or ignore.[2]

CASE STUDY
REVIEW

THERAPEUTIC ASSESSMENT

Despite all of Anna's efforts, she was unwittingly sabotaging the interest of the men she was pursuing. She was too immediately available. There was no challenge, no conquest. Before a man had a chance to recognize her, develop a feeling of anxious anticipation about approaching her, or summon the courage to ask her out, she was there. It spelled out boredom and took away the challenge.

Interestingly, the same day Anna realized her mistake, while attending a singles conference, she decided not to approach any men at the dance that evening (just to make herself more of a challenge). Instead, she stayed at a distance, made eye contact, and smiled warmly to several men, repeating in her mind, "If he is interested, he will pursue me, or someone else will." Sure enough, several men walked the distance of the dance floor to ask her for a dance. Before the end of the evening, two men asked her for her number, and they both called later.

●   ●   ●

Oftentimes women respond to their feelings of powerlessness over relationships by taking an assertive role in getting the dating process going. This is not recommended, because the way a relationship starts can often define the course the relationship maintains even after marriage. A woman who has to pursue a man all the way to the altar will likely find he is passive still, even in marriage.

As much as women want to believe that pursuing a man is just being assertive and moving things along, the fact still remains—women feel more confident and secure in relationships when men actively pursue them, and men feel more passionate, committed, and loving when they invest in the relationships they pursue. Thus, a woman would be wise to encourage a dating process that ensures the best possibility for the men she likes to take and maintain an active role in pursuing her.

This can often be a difficult task for a woman. Waiting patiently for others to take action (or fix problems) is not a strength many women intuitively possess. Women are often so overanxious to see things change or progress that they frequently push, prod, and pull others along (or outright do it for others) without recognizing the lack of faith this shows in others and themselves. It is as if underlying these behaviors, the woman:

- Fears the other person could not or would not do it if given a chance.
- Believes the other person could not or would not do it the right way.
- Fears the other person does not see her as important or valuable enough to do their part in the relationship.
- Fears she will be abandoned if she is not needed or taking

care of others (because she doubts her importance and
value either in her own eyes or in the eyes of others).

Therefore, she jumps in and takes over rather than risk the pain and rejection she might face if the person did not do their part. Not only does this unconscious process insult both the woman who believes it and those she codependently enables, but it further prevents those she enables from growing through sacrifice.

It is human nature to remain apathetic and passive if others allow it, but it always impacts one's feelings of self-respect as well as one's feelings of respect for those who jump in and do for others what they should be doing for themselves. Evidence of this loss of respect for self and others is often rampant in the person's ongoing destructive behaviors and in their frequent demonstrations of contempt and anger toward those family members who seem to be doing everything possible to fix the person's problems.

Thus, if you act on faulty beliefs like "If I don't do it, no one else will," you will accidentally encourage and support destructive behaviors in others while simultaneously communicating that you distrust and doubt the person's willingness or ability to handle problems on his own. Such actions and attitudes will only prove to weaken you, your relationship, and the person you are serving.

However, if you act on beliefs like "If I do it, no one else will" and "It is better for everyone if I just support others in fixing their own problems rather than fixing their problems for them," while lovingly standing back, you may find you communicate in both your words and actions, "I have faith you can work it out." Your commitment to standing back so others can have the time and space to resolve their problems, accept their consequences, and fix their mistakes allows them the opportunity to manage their own lives; but you may also find it builds your faith in yourself that others choose to be with you because they value you, not because they inappropriately need you. Thus, the faith you demonstrate in others can synergistically help both of you.

To help you know how to lovingly do this, the following tips may be helpful.

TIPS that can help you show faith in others as they solve their own problems

- When someone is talking about a problem, listen. Express
  sadness, concern, or other emotions that show you are
  trying to understand how hard the situation is. In other
  words, show empathy.

- There are many ways to express care and concern while not jumping in and fixing others' problems. Say things like, "That is so hard" or "That must feel frustrating." Then ask them:
  - What are you going to do?
  - What are the options you are considering?
  - I trust you will know what is best for you. Do you want to hear some options that might help you resolve the problem, or do you just need someone to listen?

  All of these questions send the message that you trust the person can manage and fix his problem. Plus, these questions can give you the opportunity to pause before rushing in and taking over.[3]

- After listening to someone and feeling they would like you to help them (rather than jumping in and taking over), get them to spend more time thinking about the problem by asking them:
  - What options have you tried for fixing the problem?
  - What other options could you try?
  - If you are not able to help, what other options do you have?
  - If this problem doesn't get fixed, how could you live with the situation?

  Many times this process may help the person come up with ideas that help you or him see that he doesn't really need your help. But if not, say, "I want to help you. Let me think about what I might be able to do to help, and I'll get back with you." After stating this, be sure to take enough time to consider how you can help and support him without doing it for him.

- If someone wants you to do for him what he should be doing for himself and his efforts to involve you feel manipulative, tell him:
  - I trust you can fix the problem. You will be in my thoughts and prayers. Good luck.
  - I want to help you, but I can't.
  - No!
  - I love you too much to do that for you. I hope in

time you will see that I am saying no because I
care. Feel free to be mad, but I must do what feels
best to me. I hope you will understand. I trust you
will be able to work it out. Good luck.
- When you struggle with feelings of guilt, duty, or
obligation, remind yourself that others can resolve their
problems better than you can, and the solution will mean
more to them if they find it themselves. *If you have faith in
God, turn your concern for his problems over to God, trusting
that He can help him better than you can.*

Defining and then sticking to the role you feel you should play in relationships and dating may test your faith in others, men, and yourself. When
the results of your faith do not come as quickly as you desire, your ability to
believe in the actions you are taking may feel challenged.

However, you need to understand one important principle of relationships—*it takes two to tango.* For instance, in order for there to be a manipulator, there has to be someone who is easily manipulated. Someone who is
abusive can't act abusive unless there is a victim who allows it. Someone who
is irresponsible can't function and maintain his irresponsibility unless there
is someone who is over-responsible and enables his lifestyle and behaviors.
Thus, for every relationship pattern, it takes two to maintain it.

If you refuse to play a role that you would only resent, that you would feel
burden by, or that you know would impair your relationship, the person you
are interacting with will have to decide to adapt to the needs of the relationship or let the relationship die. Some people may refuse to adapt to the new
demands of a relationship, but those who desire the relationship (because it is a
compatible fit for them) will care about maintaining it. They will play their role
as you play yours, and the relationship will survive (or better yet, thrive).

Even if you discover that several dating relationships with great potential
only ended when you did not do more than you felt comfortable with, trust
that this principle will still apply. As long as you commit yourself to staying
in the Dating Game, in time the kind of person you are looking for will find
you. And he will play his role as you play yours.

Certainly believing in these principles requires taking a leap of faith. You
may have to be willing to let some relationships end while clinging to a hope
that someone else will come along who will want the kind of relationship you
have to offer and invest in it. As scary as that may be, do you have any better
options? Faith in yourself and others may be difficult, but oftentimes it is the
best (and many times only) path to a better life.

Not only will having faith in the kind of person you are looking for and the idea that he will do his part to be with you help you unlock the confidence you need, it will also help you maintain hope (which is a precious commodity for single women). The following tips may further assist you in maintaining that hope.

TIPS for acting with faith in yourself and others that they will see your value and pursue you

- Tell yourself that others (especially single men) will choose to be with you because they value you, not because they need you. You do not need to feel confidence in this idea at first; just keep repeating it in your mind. In time, you will start to accept and believe it.
- When nurturing potentially good relationships with others (and single men), let them serve and help you when they offer, and expect that they will allow you to serve them as well. Sacrifice is essential to developing deep bonds of love. Furthermore, refusing others' sacrifices often sends the message that you believe you do not deserve their love or you do not trust them enough to let them get close to you.
- Trust your judgment, and protect yourself from people who have shown a pattern of acting emotionally immature in a way that hurts you. This will leave more room for you to participate in and enjoy good relationships. Believe and trust good relationships will come.
- Show warm and sincere faith that others (including single men) care about your feelings and needs and will respond respectfully when you assert them. For example, you might say, "I know you have my best interest in mind," or "I know you would care if you accidentally hurt my feelings," "I know you want to meet my needs when you can, so I thought I would let you know I could really use some help on Wednesday." Express gratitude for any of their words or actions that show they care about you.
- Encourage others (including single men) to say no to you so you can have confidence that they mean yes when they say yes. One way to encourage others to say no is by saying, "I am confident this need will be met, whether

by you or someone else, so if you need to say no, I will be fine." Furthermore, your ability to respond well to being told no shows your trust that they care about you even when they can't help you. Remember, when one door closes, another door opens. *If you have faith in God, rely on His ability to show you other options for resolving your needs rather than reacting to the "no" you just received.*

- When you choose to say no, show faith in yourself and those who attempt to manipulate you by not backing down, giving in, calling later, apologizing, or doing anything else just to avoid their anger, rejection, or criticism. Trust that when they calm down, they will still see and appreciate your value and do their part in the relationship. If you showed them respect, emotional control, and love while still being firm, you can feel confident you played your role. Give them space and trust that they will continue to play their role.

- Enjoy moments when you are alone. Trust that others (and single men) will be there later. Those who can be alone with themselves are more likely to make wise choices in their relationships; thus, try to find ways to increase you ability to be content and fulfilled when you want or need to be alone.

- Frequently remind yourself that **the kind of man you are looking for is looking for someone like you—and he will pursue you.**

Since the concept of having faith in yourself and the kind of man you are looking for is so pivotal to your success, each chapter of the upcoming BE SUCCESSFUL section will give you ideas on how to apply this concept in a subsection called "If you play your role—he'll play his." For now, you just need to begin having faith in the concept.

Notes
1. Schlessinger, Laura, PhD. *Woman Power: Transform your man, your marriage, your life. New York:* Harper Collins, 2004.
2. Gerstman, Bradley, ESQ; Pizzo, Christopher, CPA; and Seldes, Rich MD. *What Men Want: Three professional single men reveal to women what it takes to make a man yours.* New York: HarperPaperbacks, 1998.
3. For additional ideas on how to help others own their problems, you may find the theories of Foster Cline, MD and Jim Hay helpful. Read their book, *Parenting with Love and Logic* (Colorado Springs: Pinon Press, 1990).

chapter eleven

Fake it until you make it

A good Coach understands the value of teaching players to practice strategies and moves before getting into the game so they can act without hesitation when in the game. Those who lack confidence when in a game may hesitate, appear uncertain, or become easily intimidated by other players, resulting in someone else getting the ball. Likewise, this chapter will encourage you to practice new behaviors so you can act with more confidence when you are on the Field of the Dating Game.

Though you, like many women, may not feel confident, you need to know that you do not need to feel an emotion before you act in a way that supports an emotion. To have confidence, you must learn to act confident. If you choose your actions, independent of your emotions, your actions can have a great effect on your emotions. Sometimes faith begins when people desire enough to believe that they are willing to act in spite of their doubts.

Many women talk about their issues with low self-esteem, but these women don't have any different fears or problems than those women who act with self-confidence. Women who act with confidence and self-respect only feel it in spurts. They have mood swings, PMS, and emotional doubts like everyone else, but if their behaviors in relationships remain consistent, they appear confident to others and experience the benefits of the self-respect their behaviors engender.

Thus, to feel confident, a woman must take action in her life, even when she doesn't feel like doing so. In this way she may need to fake it until she makes it (which is your next game play strategy).

> # GAME PLAY STRATEGY #12
> ## fake it until you make it
> ## (to feel confidence).

In order to help you act with more confidence in yourself, men, and relationships, you will first need to learn a few more secrets of the male.

♂ Have a male-friendly psychology

SECRET #5: Men like women who like themselves.

Most men like a woman who is fun, friendly, outgoing, happy, nice, and active. They interpret these behaviors to indicate that the woman likes herself and others and that she has confidence others will like her as well. Not only is this confidence attractive, but it also fits well with the male need to compete, pursue challenges, and succeed. A woman who is well-liked is a woman who can have any man she wants; thus, if she chooses him, he has succeeded where other men have failed.

SECRET #6: Men love to be heroes.

Men love to make a difference. They like helping others (when they don't feel manipulated into it). And they enjoy the feeling of self-sacrifice for a greater good. This is not to say that they easily see or recognize the needs around them. Men are good at being focused on one thing at a time and are therefore prone to not observing the many needs of others; however, when a need becomes obvious and they feel they can make a difference, helping others (especially women) can be a rewarding experience and one that makes men feel a greater bond to those they serve.

SECRET #7: Men like being appreciated.

Because men like being heroes, they will go to great lengths to help, especially when their sacrifices seem to be appreciated and well received. Feeling appreciated is often enough reinforcement for a man that he may feel completely satisfied after giving hours of service or money once he has received a sincere expression of gratitude.

Along these lines, men feel invalidated and unappreciated when they compliment a woman, only to have her demean herself and their compliment. Not only does a woman's response of "No, I am not!" to his statement that she is attractive make her appear to lack confidence, it also denies him the opportunity to feel appreciated and heroic.

CASE STUDY

Aubrey would've loved to date but felt she didn't have the time or the emotional freedom to do so. There were always so many things to be done and people to take care of. She was a single mom with two kids who had to keep up with her full-time job, her house, her yard, her friends who needed her support, and her mother and sister, who had many problems they couldn't deal with on their own.

Helping her friends, mother, and sister took hours out of her day. It seemed her mother was always calling in some kind of a crisis. Her sister was consistently asking her to watch her kids, and her friends (one in particular) would regularly drop by unannounced and stay for hours, even though Aubrey needed to do homework with the kids, prepare meals, and get the kids to bed. Thus, Aubrey always felt she was running behind and trying to catch up on the essentials (like balancing the checkbook, mowing the lawn, cleaning the house, doing the laundry) until late in the night.

Aubrey loved helping her mother, sister, and friends, but the stress and demands of their needs were sapping all of her strength and causing her to feel she had no room in her life to pursue other options. When would she ever be able to make dating a priority without everything she cared about falling apart?

Not only did she feel that she carried the weight of all these problems on her shoulders, she also felt she simply did not have the confidence to approach men. She didn't have time to eat right, let alone exercise, buy new clothes, and go to a singles event. Meeting men and dating would just have to wait. But, then again, she was worried about her young children receiving the benefits of being raised in a family with two actively involved, loving parents, and she really believed her boys needed a positive male role model. How was she ever going to make time for dating? If she didn't make changes then, when would she? Every time she thought about it, she saw nothing but guilt, powerlessness, and impossibility. It was hopeless.

Take action to feel self-respect and confidence

Your ability to succeed in the Dating Game depends upon you taking an active role in improving yourself and your relationship skills now. When a woman passively waits for others to change her life, she is more likely to experience depression, anxiety, fear, doubt, anger, and feelings of victimization. Good men (although they love to be heroes) are not usually attracted to neediness. Women whose lives are out of control, who wait for a savior to rescue them from their problems, will not attract good men as often as they will attract the abusive and manipulative (who see neediness as vulnerability they can exploit).

If you want to ensure that you are on a path that will lead you to a good man, you will need to live your life with purpose and choose to refine and improve yourself. If a woman mistakenly waits for her life to begin when she is married, she will only discover misery and disappointment (both before and after marriage). When every date ends with the realization that he is not "the one," dating can seem pointless and depressing.

On the contrary, when a woman views her dating experiences as an opportunity for personal progress, options for discovering meaning and purpose in life and dating are found. The experience of having power over one's progress, independent of the dating process, can help a woman remain patient so the process she needs can unfold in its own way. Once married, she can use these same skills to further enhance her life and relationship.

To help you act confidently in ways that will assist you in progressing both personally and in your relationship skills, the following tips have been provided. As with any efforts you may take to progress, it is always wiser to consider your current strengths and then set realistic goals that can help you get one step closer to your larger goal.

Select one or two reasonable goals from each category. Once you have acted on those goals for a few weeks, come back to the list and set a few more or create some of your own, depending on your needs. As long as you are continually evaluating yourself and trying to progress, you will be better able to attract the positive attention of others; thus, you may want to review these ideas regularly.

When considering the ideas below, it is important to remember that all new behaviors feel awkward and unnatural when you first do them—so fake it until you make it. You do not need to feel like a behavior fits you for it to help you. Try the behavior out for three weeks. You may find in time it fits you well. If you don't, you can always alter or abandon it, but don't judge the new behavior until you have committed yourself to it for a period of time.

TIPS for improving feelings of self-love, self-respect, and self-confidence

- When thinking about your body, talk lovingly. Admire what is beautiful, soft, and feminine about your body. If you want to lose weight, either commit to action or be lovingly patient with the fact that it can't be your first goal right now. (For example: look for and find something beautiful about your body just the way it is and then say, "When I am ready to make weight loss my first priority, I know I will lose the weight. For now I love _____ about me.") Many men will overlook a woman's size (up to about forty pounds overweight) if the woman has confidence in herself; thus, emotionally mature men don't make a woman's weight an issue as much as women do. If you love yourself, he is likely to also. Always talk and think about your body in a positive manner.
- Invest in yourself. Buy clothes that make you feel great (because they flatter your physical strengths and hide your weaknesses). Get a stylish haircut. Buy good makeup. Pay for a massage. Make your needs part of your budget. Occasionally splurge on yourself like you would for someone you love.

- When thinking about yourself, your problems, your feelings, or your fears, give yourself the benefit of the doubt. Be as kind and generous about your strengths and weaknesses as you would be with someone you love. Replace self-depreciating thoughts with loving, kind, and patient thoughts. (For example: if you catch yourself saying, "I am so stupid," stop yourself and say, "You can't talk to my friend that way. She's awesome.") Remind yourself of difficult things you have done or accomplished in the past. Write a list of your successes and those qualities you like about yourself. And, most important, tell yourself, "Confident women have PMS, mood swings, and self-doubts too. My fears and insecurities are no different than any other woman's. Those who act confident just nurture their strengths rather than listening to their fears and doubts." In other words, choose to nurture self-loving and respectful thoughts.

- When talking with others about your issues or problems, laugh at your insecurities and fears (laughing at one's fears can be greatly liberating); talk about your weaknesses as if they do not define you or your potential; look for solutions and ideas that help you feel hope, faith, and confidence; accept advice and ideas that feel helpful, and take a timeout from any conversation you feel is going downhill fast. Sometimes sharing problems and issues with others can make a woman feel more inadequate rather than building her confidence, especially if she is experiencing PMS. If this is the case for you, you may do better only talking with friends who know you well or taking some time to be alone until you feel you have found emotional balance. Sometimes the best solutions to a problem are those found from within through pondering, meditation, or prayer. Getting a good night's sleep is always a good idea.

- Speak just as often about your strengths, the good intentions of your heart, your desires to improve, and your successes as you speak of your struggles, weaknesses, or issues. There is just as much truth in what you are doing right as there is truth in what you are doing that's ineffective or problematic. You are more likely to experience lasting change when you focus on and build upon your strengths as opposed to feeding and nurturing your weaknesses. Many people act as if self-loathing will increase their motivation for change, but it rarely creates lasting change. (For example: when a woman looks at her body and berates herself for being overweight, she may exercise that night out of pure anger and disgust, but her self-loathing will likely only sabotage her progress or cause her to give up when results don't come quickly.) Get in the habit of looking for your strengths and talking about them, even if it is just in the mirror to yourself.

- Act as if your life is going well. Tell others you are doing well, and then share one specific thing you are grateful is going well in your life (even if all you can say is you are having a good hair day). This will help you look for evidence of good things in your life. Furthermore, if you felt depressed prior to showing gratitude for your life, you may feel the experience made you less depressed. If you have a hard time finding something good in your life, take more responsibility for your happiness, and start talking about the efforts you are taking to improve your life.

- Say no to others so you can invest in the things you value. Setting boundaries with others tells them and you that you are a priority and worth the investment you are making. Not all boundaries need to be big. Avoid the temptation to give an excuse that justifies your boundary. Sometimes the most effective way to set a boundary is to say, "That is not going to work for me, but I trust you will be inspired about what other options you can pursue" or "That is not going to work for me tonight, but I would love to help you on Thursday (or any day and time you could feel good about helping them)."

- Act happy and busy (even when you don't feel it) at least a few times a week. You might find you feel happier when you act the part. Happy and busy people are more likely to draw positive attention from others.

- Walk with your shoulders erect. Use good posture. Look others in the eyes and smile. Do this at least three times a week, whether you feel like it or not.

- Face the things you fear. The more you face your fears or act in opposition to your fears, the less your fears will be able to define you and your life. For example: if you fear you are not smart, start challenging yourself to learn while telling yourself that you are capable, hardworking, and good at learning things you commit yourself to learn. Whatever the challenge, look at your strengths and use them to fight in the direction of your fears. Seek help from others as you do this, whether it is a friend, family member, or counselor. You are more likely to succeed if you have support.
- Set goals to go back to school, save money, get a home, or learn a new occupational skill. The more action you take to improve your situation, the more self-respect you will feel. Set realistic goals. Respect the limits of your time, money, and energy so you don't set yourself up for failure.

T⬆PS for increasing your feelings of confidence in your future

- When thinking about or talking about your future, don't say "if"—say "*when*" ("When I am in my next relationship," "When I go on my next date," "When I get married," or "When I fall in love").
- Repeat in your mind, "I will have the opportunity to marry the kind of person I want to marry—I am doing my part—I am pursuing a path that will lead to it—I not only can have a relationship, but I will have a good relationship."
- Repeat in your mind, "The kind of man I am looking for is looking for someone like me—I will know him by the fact that he will value and pursue me."
- Show your fears, doubts, insecurities, and emotional breakdowns about your future to those two or three friends or family members you feel support you best, but to everyone else, minimize how much you share your doubts. The more people you share your insecurities with, the more life you give to those insecurities. You need people to talk to, but you need to feed your faith in yourself, men, and your future more than

you feed your fears and doubts.

- When talking with others, say things like, "I am confident I will find the kind of person I am looking for," "I know I will get married," and "I believe the things I am doing are making a difference in that I am dating better men than I used to." The point is, the more you talk with faith in your future, even when you have moments of doubt, the more you will feel it.

- Practice patience and be realistic. When tempted to say, "I can't live one more year without a relationship," stop yourself and moderate your words. Try to avoid dramatic statements that exploit all-or-nothing thinking (such as "Nothing in my life is going right," "I never have any dating success," or "Everyone has someone but me"). Statements like, "Sometimes I feel discouraged," "I wish I could move things along faster," or "I feel like giving up on dating, but when I look at my experiences rationally, I can see evidence of positive changes," can help you stay emotionally balanced and can encourage you to remain patient. After all, marriage won't be the end of all your trials. You will need patience then too.

- Talk about your personal or religious beliefs that give you hope. When struggling, surround yourself with books, music, uplifting ideas, spiritual philosophies, and other sources that support your faith in men, the world, God, and yourself.

- Talk about your future as if you will not get married for two years. Plan your life, activities, and goals with this in mind. Do not live as if your life will only begin when you are in a relationship. And while you live your life, choose behaviors that help you progress in ways that encourage the dating process (which are described in part below and in detail throughout the chapters that follow).

TIPS that will help you attract good men

- Tell yourself daily, "Good men are in the majority, not the minority. If I look for and believe in the goodness of men, I will see it." Review chapters 7 and 9 as often as needed.

- Start looking for signs of single men around you. Single men are everywhere. Yet, so many single women act like married women. They avoid eye contact with men; they don't look around when at the grocery store or a restaurant; they don't dress up when they go to the movies; they don't say hello or ask attractive strangers questions. If you start looking for single men in your everyday activities, you may find your body language will change, your awareness of men will increase, and others will start to notice you.

- Repeat in your mind and to others, "Good men are and will be interested in me, and they will pursue me when I am ready to put more work into dating."

- Start imagining how it would feel to act with confidence. Imagine how you would interact with someone who you really enjoyed being with. What would you talk about, do, or say? Role-play your reactions, and have confidence that you can translate your mental practice into live action. Have faith that you will be able to act comfortable, excited, playful, and fun with someone you feel safe and secure with. Tell yourself it isn't a matter of *if* you will be able to enjoy a relationship but *when*.

- Look for evidence that you are beginning to attract or date others who have more of the qualities you are looking for. Believe this evidence to be a sign that you are growing and progressing because "birds of a feather flock together"—thus, your efforts must be making a difference.

TIPS that will help you progress in your relationship skills

- Solicit and listen to feedback from others about your behaviors and their effects on your relationships (especially those that relate to the skills of empathy, personal responsibility, and self-control). Then set goals to improve in these areas. The more you develop your emotional maturity, the more likely you will be able to attract emotionally mature men and maintain good relationship patterns.

- Choose to nurture the qualities that the kind of man you are looking for would appreciate, enjoy, and be attracted to. If you want a man who values education but you make no efforts to educate yourself, you may be setting yourself up for disappointment. If you want a man with strong religious devotions but you are inconsistent in your religious devotions, he may not see you as being equally invested in an area in which he needs compatibility. Be the kind of person you want him to be or that would be a good fit for him.

- Read books about communication, the differences between men and women, and how to have more effective relationships.

- If you are a single mom, read books that improve your parenting skills. Ask friends and family to give you additional support as you try a new discipline technique.

- Look for opportunities to practice new communication skills. Keep an open mind to constructive feedback about how your new approach felt for those around you. Refine the process until you feel confident in your delivery of your new skills.

- Invest in relationships with those who seem supportive when you express your feelings, wants, likes, and needs. Good relationships will give you more opportunities to receive constructive feedback with love, while also building your confidence in your ability to have good relationships.

- Be true to yourself about others' advice. Communicate to others that you will think about their ideas, but do what feels best for you.

- Practice asserting your feelings, needs, and desires with those men you know well or interact with every day. Even if you are far away from the hope of a romantic relationship right now, you can still practice the skills taught in chapter 7 with those you already know. Efforts you make now to improve your assertiveness skills with men will help you have a better and more effective relationship when you meet someone you like.

- When appropriate, take risks that will help you develop

love for those you know. Help and serve others (without doing for them what they alone should do for themselves). Express warmth and appreciation. Touch them. Sacrifice your time to be with them. Show them you are thinking about them through small acts of service, gifts, or phone calls just to say, "I was thinking about you." Give to them and let them give back to you. Express love, gratitude, sadness, pain, hurt, and anger. Be real with them and show vulnerability.

• Realize that no matter how close you become, relationships always evolve, change, and even come to an end. Love others anyway. Trust that when one relationship ends, another will soon begin.

Making progress in any one of these areas increases your ability to appear and feel more confident while preparing you for good men and better relationships. The more you act on these ideas, the more likely you will feel empowered, capable, self-assured, lovable, and confident.

CASE STUDY
REVIEW

THERAPEUTIC ASSESSMENT

Aubrey had several issues that were imposing on her ability to progress in meeting men and pursuing dating relationships, the most problematic of which was her sense of loyalty to her mother's, sister's, and friends' needs. As long as she continued to feel responsible for more than the immediate needs of her family (herself and her kids), she would not have time for herself or a relationship.

Aubrey decided she had to make some changes or she would never date (and remarry, which she really believed was in her and her boys' best interest). But where could you possibly begin? After talking with her counselor about the many issues in her way, she realized that she was giving too much of her time to her mother's, sister's, and friends' problems. She decided she would need to set some boundaries and only spend an hour or two a few times a week helping them if she was going to reduce the chaos in her life.

The next time her sister called to see if she could watch her kids, Aubrey stated, "I think I could make room to do that on Thursday but not tonight. I love being with your kids and can probably help out once a week if you give me enough notice." The next time her friend tried to stop by unannounced, she gave her a hug and said, "I love seeing you. Let's get together for lunch on Saturday. I am just so busy tonight that I won't be able to give you my full attention. I will call you tomorrow to set the time." And the next time her mom called in a crisis that Aubrey knew would take more time to deal with than what she felt comfortable giving, she said, "I don't know how you are going to work this out, Mom, but I trust you will find a way. Perhaps my therapist can help. I will be glad to give you her number. I have got to get the kids in the bath and do homework. Good luck. You will be in my prayers."

By prioritizing her time and energy and controlling how much she was giving to those whom she was not immediately responsible for, Aubrey was able to spend more time with her kids, feel less stressed, reduce the chaos in her life, and start making goals with her single girlfriends. She and her friends began going to lunch and whispering about which men at the restaurant appeared to be single. They even practiced smiling and making eye contact with a few of the men. Aubrey didn't feel ready to go to singles events or get on the Internet, but she felt freer to pursue her options and knew there was more room in her life for a man and a relationship than there used to be.

BE SUCCESSFUL

You have learned to be safe and confident. Now you must get onto the Field of the Dating Game, persevere in the face of challenges, and reach the Final Goal. It is time for you to be successful. Get out there. You can do it!

chapter twelve

You can't win
if you aren't in the game

As you enter the final section of this book, the Coach believes you need to hear, "You cannot succeed at the Dating Game if you are not on the Field. You have learned to be safe and confident. Now you must get onto the Field of the Dating Game, persevere in the face of challenges, and reach the Final Goal (marriage with a good man). It is time for you to be successful. Get out there. You *can* do it!"

However, you, like many women, may feel tempted to stall while replying, "But I don't like competitive sports or understand sports analogies. The idea of a Dating Game seems about as repulsive, confusing, and overwhelming as the idea of spending an evening watching any professional sport I don't understand. Thus, comparing dating to a competitive sport does not make it seem more attractive. I don't want dating to be a game. Can't it be something else?"

Like it or not, the Dating Game is a game because men like games.* Most men think competitively, act without realizing the feelings of the other players on the Field (thus unknowingly causing injuries), and only fall in love through the challenges and sacrifices of the game.

Thus, if you want to be more successful in dating men, you would be wise to think more metaphorically about the process and accept the fact that dating implies rules, strategies, and injuries just like any competitive sport. Thinking about dating as a game will actually make dating easier, not harder. Your efforts will be more successful when the process seems less personally rejecting (what happens in the game is just the way the game is—it's not personal). You will then be more likely to appreciate the Coach's game play strategies, hints for avoiding common mistakes, and tips for success. Chapters 12–17 will coach you on all the things you need to know to be successful, but first you must trust the Coach enough to confidently run onto the Field, believing her when she says, "There is a time to act and it is now. Nothing can fully prepare you for the actions you must take. Thinking and talking about relationships does not replace experiencing them. Get out there. You *can* do it!"

When you emerge from the Locker Room and take your first running step into the Dating Game, you will need to know where to begin, where you are going, and how to get there. So here is a quick primer of the rules of the game.

Rules

1. You can't win if you are not in the game. In order to succeed at the Dating Game, you must venture onto the Field. Being on the Field of the Dating Game means you are putting yourself where other singles are and you are flirting. Avoiding the places where single men are and refusing to flirt means you are anywhere but on the Field of the Dating Game; thus, your chances for success are unlikely.

2. Be safe. Avoid unnecessary risks. There are many serious dangers that need to be avoided in the Dating Game. Never forget your safety plan from the BE SAFE section (chapters 1–7).

....

* Don't be tempted into believing that the Dating Game only applies to guys who really like sports. Most, if not all, men (even the intellectuals) are driven by a desire to pursue and conquer challenges. Men who seem uninterested in sports are still often drawn to act competitively. Furthermore, do you want to be in a relationship with someone who acts passively interested in life (and you) because he has no competitive spirit or drive, causing you to be the one who has to do all the work in the relationship?

3. Tackles are against the rules. Tackles represent abuse and manipulation. Avoid tackles from others, and never tackle others. If you want to attract a good man, you need to portray the qualities that you want him to possess. Just as you expect the good men you are looking for to be emotionally mature in their ability to exercise self-control, feel empathy, and take personal responsibility, you need to have these qualities as well.

4. To play, you have to pass the ball. The ball represents active participation in this process (which can include anything from flirting and eye contact to dating, taking risks, and sharing your feelings). If the ball is to stay in motion, it will require the investment of both players. Passing the ball is something you must do through every stage of the dating process from flirting to marriage. If you want to be confident and successful at keeping the ball in motion, you will need to play your role and have faith that good men will play their roles. If the ball doesn't get returned, pick up another one and move on, trusting the good men you seek will find and play ball with you.

5. A date involves a man, a woman, and a ball. Only when the ball is kept in motion between two players is the game fun and rewarding. When the process works right, passing the ball will progress to a date, and you will begin to feel the rewards of being on the Field of the Dating Game.

6. Anyone can drop the ball at any time. Just when the ball gets going and progress can be seen, you or the other person can drop it without a word. Although this hurts the one left high and dry, it is both players' right and privilege to do so at any time. Every player is responsible for the quality of their life and knows best what they are looking for and need. When the ball drops, it is important to maintain your faith from the BE CONFIDENT section and remember that you will have the opportunity to marry the kind of person you said you wanted to marry, and the kind of person you are looking for is looking for someone like you; he will see you for what you have to offer, and he will pursue you. Having faith in yourself and others in the face of rejection can be a powerful confidence builder. Keep going. Don't give up. Don't lose faith. Play ball!

7. It takes a man, a woman, and a ball to get into the Final Stretch. The longer you keep the ball in motion with one particular player, the more likely you may partner up and venture into the Final Stretch of the game. As important as it is to get to the Final Goal, it is more important to be confident about the partner you bring with you. The longer you invest in a relationship you would *not* want to reach the Final Goal, the more likely you may discover that is exactly where you end up. Because it is much harder to drop the ball once you have invested so much of yourself (your time, energy, money, and commitment) to a relationship, it is always better to drop the ball sooner rather than later if a partner isn't right for you.

8. The game doesn't end until you reach the Final Goal. Marriage is the Final Goal of the Dating Game, but it is not the end of all trials. Nonetheless, when two emotionally mature people make the committed decision to choose their love and love their choice, knowing the challenges and trials they may face in marriage, the outcome is likely to synergistically make both individuals become more together than they could have been if they were apart. What men and women gain and learn from each other during a lifetime of service and sacrifice could never have been learned another way. Marriage not only refines individuals; it makes them more whole.

There is much the Coach is still going to tell you about how to be more effective once on the Field of the Dating Game, but you are the one who must break through the Locker Room door and race confidently onto the Field. So take a deep breath, go forward, and play ball!

CASE STUDY

As a divorced woman, Lorraine had taken up residence for many years in a place far, far, away from the Dating Game. She acted like a married woman in the singles world. She didn't look men in the eyes unless there was a purpose for doing so. She didn't wear makeup. She didn't dress up if she was going anywhere but to work. She didn't ask for blind dates. She rarely accepted blind dates. She felt content to stay were she was, believing it was better to remain safe than sorry.

Then one night she met a girlfriend for dinner. As they walked to their table, she saw two men sitting at a table near theirs and briefly made eye contact. She spontaneously smiled at one of them with a shock of coy enthusiasm she had not felt for years. Her body language immediately changed. She walked with a swing, and her shoulders straightened up. She sat down at the table and turned her body a quarter turn in the two men's direction and started talking in an animated way with her friend. Her hands were following suit, assuming as much animation as the rest of her body—and then she halted. She hadn't realized she was flirting until that moment.

She couldn't believe it. She hadn't felt these emotions or been this animated in years. It was an old habit that came back without invitation. It felt great and scary! She gave it up that instant. She rotated her body so her back was turned to the men and her eyes were unreachable. She flattened her hands and rested them on the table. She talked more quietly to her friend and with less enthusiasm. She just couldn't bring herself to act feminine and flirtatious. So she went back to being safe and perpetually single.

A few years later, a friend pressed Lorraine with the idea of going on an Internet dating site. She adamantly refused, stating she had heard about many women who had been raped by men they met on the Internet. Her friend continued to press her with the idea, stating Lorraine had only been on a few dates over the last few years—and those were all blind dates. How could she move on if she didn't invest more in the process? Her friend then argued that the Internet might also attract those like herself (busy with their careers, families, goals, and friends) who didn't have many opportunities to meet singles in other ways. Her friend wouldn't quit pressing the idea.

Lorraine thought about it and realized she needed to do her part. She read about how to be safe when dating and then joined a singles website that seemed to match her value system.

She had a great experience. She did detect those who were abusive and manipulative fairly quickly, which was a confidence builder. She also met some great men who were quick to respect her boundaries, fun to talk with, kind and considerate, consistent in their efforts to pursue her, and quick to make her feel comfortable. She enjoyed the experience, the men she met, and the feelings of progress and empowerment she felt.

Then she met Eric, and just like that time before, she spontaneously began flirting with him in ways she had long forgotten to do. She made jokes more frequently (in email and on the phone). She laughed more easily. She felt giddy and excited when she thought about him. And she looked forward to meeting him. For the first time in a long time, she felt like a woman again rather than just a professional businesswoman, mother, and friend.

At times, during the dating process, Lorraine wished the passionate and intense feelings Eric brought back had not returned. She saw herself as a controlled, analytical businesswoman, mother, and friend—not an enthusiastic, playful woman. These feelings were unwelcome but intoxicating. As much as she wished her emotions would go back to sleep (so she could be as controlled and analytical as always), she couldn't help but admit that she loved feeling passionate again and wanted these feelings to stay.

CASE STUDY
REVIEW

THERAPEUTIC ASSESSMENT

Lorraine's struggle between her analytical and controlled nature and her passionate and feminine nature was largely caused by her fears that her emotions could not be trusted. They had blindly rushed her into her first marriage, which had proven abusive. Might these emotions only prove to be foolish again, or were her emotions to be an important part of her future success? She wasn't sure, but she longed to feel whole again and wanted to give her emotions a try, as long as they didn't betray the logic and wisdom her rational mind had learned to trust would keep her safe.

Although Lorraine's passionate, intense, and romantic emotions became scary for her after her divorce, her emotions alone had not betrayed her. She blamed them for blindly rushing her into a bad situation that took her years to recover from, but in reality it was her logical and rational side that closed her eyes while her emotional side did the running. Shutting her emotions off in punishment for her lack of judgment was unwise and unfounded. She had ignored and minimized the many warning signs of her ex-husband's potentially abusive and manipulative behavior when dating him. She had then blamed her emotions for the realities she faced in marriage.

In the end, her eventual success in her relationship with Eric came from the merge of her emotional and logical parts of her personality. Her new theories about dating helped her find wisdom and balance while her emotions flattered and complemented Eric's male psychology (and her female psychology—she enjoyed being feminine again). Both were needed for him and her.

Integrating her passionate emotions back into her personality and relationship improved her life tremendously. She felt more beautiful. She acted more confident. She laughed more easily. She was excited and more animated with others. Together her emotional side and her analytical side made her whole again.

chapter thirteen

From flirting to the first date

So many singles say they hate all the games that come with dating. Perhaps they say this because they do not understand how to navigate dating effectively, so they keep getting manipulated and abused (tackled) or hurt (injured). There is so much to know about how to date effectively, and women spend a lot of their time trying to figure it out, yet their efforts remain ineffective, leaving many asking, "Why does it have to be so hard?"

But the Dating Game doesn't have to be as hard as women make it if they listen to the Coach's game play strategies, understand the male psychology, look for and avoid the common mistakes women make, and follow the hints and tips that will help them be successful.

In this chapter the Coach will call out two game play strategies for your success. Number 13: *Think like a man*, which will help you avoid the many mistakes, hazards, and injuries that can occur in the Dating Game when playing ball with good men; and number 14: *Be feminine, warm, flirtatious, and appreciative—while also being a challenge*, which will empower you with tips for your success so you can define your role and encourage him to play his role.

Be cautious and have fun!

GAME PLAY STRATEGY #13
Think like a man.

To be successful you must think like a man. In order to do this, you will need to better understand the male psychology. Chapters 10 and 12 introduced you to secrets #1–7. Now consider secrets #8–10.

♂ Have a male-friendly psychology

SECRET #8: Men like femininity.

Men like curves and things that are soft and round. They like things that are feminine, delicate, and beautiful on women (especially when that feminine woman can still jump in and enjoy the things men enjoy doing). They like women who are kind, gentle, loving, compassionate, friendly, helpful, and warm. They like it when a woman makes things beautiful, appealing, and clean. In some ways, their feelings toward women mirror the feelings they have for their mothers. In fact, many men are drawn to women like their mothers in that they long to feel nurtured, supported, and unconditionally loved. Yet, they want to have their cake and eat it too. They want nice girls who make them feel emotionally safe (like their mothers) when they are vulnerable and need love and approval, but they also want all the sensuality that surrounds femininity. They want all this without being mothered by women. They want femininity, warmth, and love but not the experience of being doubted, controlled, distrusted, and nagged, as if they aren't man enough to do what must be done.

SECRET #9: Men like women who have opinions and assert their needs.

Men try hard to surprise the women they love with gifts, service, and support (to then discover their power-tool gift, haphazard vacuuming, and quick advice giving were not appreciated). Men are often clueless about what it takes to make a woman happy (which secrets women often mistakenly withhold from men, believing men should intuitively know how to make them happy). They try hard and are eager to please but often miss the mark by a long shot. Good men are also surprised by how often they can unintentionally hurt a woman's feelings. This leaves men believing they must read a woman's mind to succeed, which they know will never work.

Thus, as much as men like loving, kind, and sweet women, men value and appreciate the woman they love telling them what she wants, feels, and needs. Men desire to be heroes but don't think long enough about their relationships to intuitively know how a woman needs her man to heroically rescue and support her. The more a woman tells him how to support her and then appreciates and loves him for his sacrifices, the more competent and capable he will feel in his ability to please her. The more he feels like a success (or hero) in their relationship and when with her, the more he will be drawn to the relationship and her.

SECRET #10: Good men pursue women who are approach-able and appear to be available.

Good men respect other people's choices and rights. As much as men enjoy being heroes and helping others, good men usually wait to be invited into someone's life, problems, or issues before getting involved (unless life and limb are on the line).

Good men trust that a woman knows what she does and does not want and sees no point soliciting unnecessary rejection. Thus, he will hesitate before approaching a single woman who doesn't look him in the eyes, smile at him, or encourage a conversation, because he doesn't know if she is unavailable, married, or just uninterested. Thus, he will respect her space and look for someone who seems to be approachable instead.

For this reason, women who confidently look men in the eyes, smile, show interest in others' conversations, and periodically touch others on the arm are more likely to have men approach and pursue them.

⚠ Exercise CAUTION—potential hazards exist and can cause injuries

Thinking like a man is essential to a woman's success because if she does not understand men, she is likely to repel them rather than attract them. In this way the secrets above, when hidden or ignored, create the stumbling blocks, potholes, curveballs, game-play collisions, and other mysterious and unseen hazards on the Field of the Dating Game (which chapter 8 alluded to) that keep tripping women and causing them to get injured and lose the ball. However, when these secrets are understood, hazards and mistakes can be avoided, and women can more confidently and successfully navigate the Dating Game.

The examples below outline some of the common mistakes women make compared to the secrets of the male psychology, from flirting (or the lack thereof) to first date. If you discover you are guilty of the mistakes below, do not despair. The suggested hints may help you and are complemented well by the tips that follow later in this chapter.

MISTAKE #1: Women often refuse to flirt.

Women often wait for men to pursue them while not recognizing their responsibility to appear available and approachable (or in other words, to flirt). They then make the fatal mistake of blaming men or believing something must be wrong with them rather than recognizing their error was in not acting in a way that was friendly to the male psychology.

The SECRETS that explain *why*: #5, #8, #10

(For a brief list of the secrets to the male psychology, refer to appendix e.)

Hint: If a woman is not getting attention, it's because she does not seek it or flirt. Women (of all ages, shapes, and sizes) who look men in the eyes and smile, dress in ways that make them look attractive and feel confident, and show interest in talking with men get attention. Those who don't, don't. Women decide their fate a lot more than men do. Thus, if you are not dating, it is likely that you do not know how to flirt or are choosing not to flirt. You cannot progress unless you change this behavior. Flirting is a must for success.

MISTAKE #2: Women often refuse to put themselves where other singles are.

Many single women don't go to places where other singles are (dances, singles events, the Internet) or act in ways that attract those singles (at the grocery store, library, park) who are in their everyday lives. Not only does their lack of effort hurt their progress, but many women also interpret this lack of progress to mean that they have been fated (by God or other unseen forces) to be alone and should just learn to accept it. This excuse gives them permission to stay in their comfort zone rather than taking those awkward steps that would put them where other singles are.

The SECRETS that explain *why*: #5, #8, #10

Hint: It is never too late to take responsibility for your own life. You decide your own future more than external forces do. If you are comfortable, you are really complacent. You cannot grow unless you stretch yourself and step out of your comfort zone. Thus, if you want to get married, start acting more approachable in your everyday life, start putting yourself where other singles are (dances, singles events, the Internet, speed dating), and start flirting.

MISTAKE #3: Women often waste their time analyzing men instead of thinking like men and realizing that if he isn't calling, he's not interested.

Women sit around talking and analyzing men too much. They diagnose why he hasn't called, what emotions he feels, what issues may be preventing him from pursuing them, and how they can cure him of these issues. They feel anxiety, depression, fear, and false hope for weeks, months, and even years while they patiently wait for him to come around. When they finally ask him if he is interested and he tells them no, they feel anger and resentment, as if he led them on. Whether he did or not, they are the ones in pain, not him.

The SECRETS that explain *why*: #3, #4, #10

Hint: If a man is interested, he will ask for your number and call. A man's behaviors define his commitments. He will not invest time or money unless he is interested. Men assume women know this and prefer not to spell it out for them. Thus, a man will not usually come right out and tell you he doesn't like you or want to date you. He hopes you will figure it out from his actions. Don't waste your time on false hopes—move on. He has.

MISTAKE #4: Women often sit by the phone, anxiously waiting for a man they just met to call.

Women often refuse opportunities to go out in case they might miss a phone call. They then feel depressed, worried, and self-doubting when the night was wasted and he still didn't call. A woman is then likely to analyze everything she could have done or said that turned him off. This usually just makes her feel rejected and more hopeless about her future.

The SECRETS that explain *why*: #3, #4, #5

Hint: Most of the time, a man thinks logically and practically about dating, which accounts for the twenty-plus reasons he didn't call. Most of these reasons have nothing to do with you and are not personal. Thus, you may want to think about the situation logically as well. Thirty to fifty percent of the time, a man you just met isn't going to call if you gave him your number, 50–70 percent if he asked for your number. Don't invest too much of your time, energy, or hope into a high-risk bet. And never take it personal. Get out there and have fun. The kind of guy you're looking for will pursue you. He will call and leave a message.

MISTAKE #5: Women often make themselves too available too quickly rather than risk turning a guy off—which turns guys off.

Often a woman may cancel plans with a friend to go out with a guy two hours after he calls, only to have him act like being with her is no big deal (because he shows up late, changes his plans at the last minute, or acts like he just wanted to make out—for a first date). Being taken for granted and treated casually is painful and embarrassing and adds to feelings of insecurity. Not only is being too available hurtful to the woman's sense of self-respect, but it also turns men off because things that are more challenging seem more rewarding to men.

The SECRETS that explain *why*: #2, #4, #7, #9

Hint: Being warm, grateful, and busy is very attractive to the male psychology. Men like challenges and competition. Thus, you would be wise not to rearrange your life or turn down other dates or opportunities in the hopes he will call or in the moment that he does call. Not only does this make him feel you are not a challenge, it also makes you look desperate, which is a turnoff—no matter how beautiful you are.

MISTAKE #6: Women often act like friends, eliminating their chance for being a potential girlfriend.

Women often believe nurturing easy *friendships* with a man will later cause him to develop romantic feelings for her. Thus, she acts like a friend instead of flirting. She gives her time easily and without much effort on his part. She stops flirting with other men and spends all her time with him in spite of the fact that there is no commitment from him. And she denies her feelings and needs so she can be accommodating, fun, easy, and the all-around-perfect girl (so he will fall in love with her like she is falling in love with him). When the friendship never changes or he falls in love with someone else, she is often devastated and wonders what went wrong.

The SECRETS that explain *why*: #1, #2, #3, #4, #5, #7, #8, #9

Hint: Men are physically attracted to a woman from the start or they are not—it rarely changes later. But men love having girls they are not attracted to as friends. They get lots of attention, quick and easy companionship, and trust and respect with no commitment. If you have a friend that you would like a relationship with, ask him if he is interested in doing that as well. Then let him know that if he is not interested, you will need to stop being as available so you can invest in other relationships. If he is okay with you doing that, he doesn't see you as a romantic option (and likely never will). Move on. Start dating. Don't return his calls as quickly or frequently. Invest in him like your other friendships. Put your dating relationships before his needs. If he doesn't like it and misses you (not just all the things you used to do for him), let him pursue you, ask you on dates, and spend money on you like any other date. You can help turn a friendship into a relationship, but only if you don't act like a *friend* anymore—expect to be treated like a girlfriend.

MISTAKE #7: Women often take the lead and pursue men, which sometimes only makes them look and act desperate.

Many women believe waiting for men to pursue them is old school and unnecessary in today's singles world, so they volunteer their phone number, call men, ask men out, and drop in unannounced to say hi. Once a woman's efforts to be with a man exceed his efforts, she may begin to feel insecure and, unfortunately, pursue him more. She is then likely to become a nuisance and not realize it. The longer she hangs on, the more embarrassed she will feel later, when she realizes her desperate acts only pushed him further away.

The SECRETS that explain *why*: #2, #9

Hints: Men love it when a woman pursues them—initially. However, for men, things (including women) that come easily are enjoyed and then discarded. If you like a man and want to encourage the process, flirt but let him experience the rewards and enjoyment that come from working hard for the things he wants. If you give him your number without him asking for it first or if you call him the first few times, let him know that you really want to get to know him but you don't feel comfortable calling guys more often than they call you so you will need to hear from him before you feel comfortable calling again. Then wait to see if he calls. Try to pace your interaction with his or preferably less (for every two times he calls, you call once). You will feel more appreciated and valued if you don't pursue a man more than he pursues you.

How you begin a relationship may define the course of how the relationship develops and maintains even after marriage, so it is important that you clearly define the role you feel comfortable playing early in the relationship or within the first few contacts. The more you stick to your role, the more likely the kind of man you are looking for will act in a way that supports that role because he also wants the relationship to progress. That is why avoiding the mistakes above can be so important to your success.

However, knowing what to avoid is not enough to help you be successful. Your next game play strategy will be needed for that.

Acting feminine, warm, flirtatious, and appreciative while also being a challenge not only complements the male psychology, but it is highly effective and potentially builds confidence. The challenge is to do your part of being warm and feminine, but not his part of being actively involved in pursuing you (remembering that if you play your role, he'll play his). The following tips may help you accomplish this as you learn the art of being flirtatious while also being a challenge, but first review the case study below. Consider how the tips that follow might help Angie and you.

If you play your role, he'll play his

> # GAME PLAY STRATEGY #14
> ### Be feminine, warm, flirtatious, and appreciative—while also being a challenge.

CASE STUDY

Angie had not dated much over the last few years. The demands of her career were great. She often worked fifty hours a week or more, and most of her friends were married, so she had few people to socialize with on the weekends. She felt limited in her options for meeting men. She had tried Internet dating, though somewhat reluctantly, and it just wasn't her thing. She refused to go to the bars, since she knew the kind of man she was looking for wouldn't be found there. And she very much hated the "meat market" feel of singles events. She wasn't sure if there were any other good options left.

TIPS for flirting

Flirting is an absolute must if you are going to be successful in getting attention. Here are some tips on how to support and encourage men in their efforts to pursue you:

- Look men in the eyes and smile warmly, sweetly, affectionately, tenderly, and playfully. This should be a feminine and soft smile that shows interest and warmth. Smiles that are businesslike, superficial, polite, or matter-of-fact are not encouraging. If you need to, practice your smile in the mirror to see what looks and feels best. Then start using it with friends and little children to see how their expressions and interactions with you change after you smile at them in this manner. Once you have the technique down, start using it with men. Do not mistakenly believe you can skip this tip and move on to the others. This one tip is a must for success and is core to flirting.
- Get a new hairdo, some new makeup, and more flattering new clothes. A woman doesn't flirt when *he* looks good; she flirts when *she* looks good. Start looking good at least three times a week, if not every day, when you go to the store, the library, your work, or a park. You never know when you might notice a single man you would like to flirt with, and you won't be as likely to flirt if you don't feel attractive.
- Start looking for single men in the everyday places you go. This will help you initiate eye contact. Trust and believe that there are lots of single men in the world because there are—it's a fact.
- If you notice a man from across the room:
  - Don't move in his direction or approach him, but turn your body at least a quarter turn in his direction.
  - Keep your peripheral vision turned toward him so you can catch his eye if you see him looking at you. Make brief eye contact with him, smile, and then turn away (if your smile turns up more on one side, appears shy, coy, playful, or excited, he'll get the hint that you like him).
  - Maintain good posture. Keep your back erect. Cross

your legs. Accentuate your femininity.

- o If you are talking with a girlfriend, start moving your hands a little more while you talk, lean slightly forward to show that you are interested in the person and their conversation, and periodically touch them on their upper arm, hands, or tips of their knees (which makes you seem more warm, friendly, and approachable).

- o Try to get a moment when you can be alone so he will be more likely to approach you. At the park, this may include walking over to a stranger's child who seems to need help but is also a little closer to the man you are flirting with. Provide this opportunity for only a few minutes. Only do this once or twice. If he is interested, he will take the risk and approach you as soon as the opportunity presents itself. He is more likely to approach you if you have made eye contact with him several times.

- o Leave when you feel sufficient time was given for him to take action. Lingering won't improve your confidence as much as leaving on a high note will. The point of flirting isn't to give out your number every time. The point is that you are playing your role and building your confidence along the way. You can be sure you will be asked for your number often enough.

- o Keep flirting, no matter how many dates you have been on lately. You will do better in the Dating Game if you are flirting with at least three to five men at a time (in separate locations from each other). Try diversifying where you are flirting, such as the store, the Internet, or your church group. Not only will you feel and appear more confident when you have multiple options, but also men tend to want women other men want. Don't limit your flirting options until you have been with a man who has consistently played his role for at least six weeks and has asked you to see just him.

The tips above for flirting are something you should be attempting to do at least once a week to once a month, especially if you are not currently dating.

Try making a commitment with a friend to practice the tips above while you are at a business lunch, the library, the park, a church social, or on a walk. Make a competition out of it, do it together, reward each other's behavior, or be accountable for cleaning the other person's car if you chicken out. The point is to use the support and encouragement of your friends to help force yourself out of your comfort zone so you can be successful in dating.

TIPS for managing the first contact

When a man approaches you with any kind of a startup comment or question, do the following:

- Assume he might have noticed something about you that made you look approachable. Reward him for noticing by immediately looking him in the eyes and giving him a warm smile (unless you feel the man is brazenly invading your space—good men don't do that. Feel no responsibility to reward bad behavior by responding warmly or encouragingly).

- Contribute to the conversation immediately. Ask him his name. Tell him yours. Comment on the weather, his tie, hat, shoes—whatever is immediately noticeable. Ask him where he is from. Encourage his questions by giving more than a "yes" or "no" response. Put detail into your responses, and ask questions that would solicit details from him. If you struggle with how to begin conversations, read more books about how to flirt, how to start a conversation, how to communicate through body language, or how to make others feel great about themselves.

- Learn and use his name several times in a conversation.

- Show interest in the conversation by leaning slightly forward. Keep your body turned toward him. Talk gently with your hands or bounce your foot gently in his direction.

- Be playful, make jokes, have fun, and tease. But do not act sarcastic. Sarcasm often makes others feel insecure about what you really think, feel, want, like, or dislike about them. Be fun, but don't cross the line. If in doubt about whether your teasing or joking behavior is going too far, take it back a notch or just eliminate it.

- Give sincere and warm compliments. Express appreciation. Observe the things he does, says, or talks about and comment on them. If he opens the door for you, give him warm appreciation. If he gives you a compliment, thank him.

- If the situation seems appropriate, take a risk and touch him briefly during the conversation or before you leave. Safe places to touch include the tips of the knees (if you are both sitting and talking, as long as the contact is brief and is intended to get his attention or to emphasize enthusiasm about a question you have) and the upper arm (a warm but gentle squeeze may be very encouraging, if not left to linger too long). When shaking his hand in greeting or farewell, clasping his hand in both of yours may add extra emphasis and warmth as you say, "It was such a pleasure to meet you. I would love to talk with you another time." For a first contact you may want to avoid holding hands or prolonged touching of his lower arm (if he were sitting closely to you) since it may be too forward. You don't want to look more excited about meeting him than he seems about meeting you. Touch can be a powerful tool that lowers defenses, creates warmth, and makes someone feel comfortable and accepted, but it can also make people feel uncomfortable and turn them off. Thus, measure your risks on the interaction you are having with the person. If in doubt, show warmth but hold off on touching the person until your next encounter.

- If your first contact with someone is on the Internet, you can still use much of the information in this section to start and maintain an email connection; however, it is usually best to move forward with talking on the phone sooner rather than later since you can't really get a good sense of how compatible you will truly be (or how much chemistry you will feel) until you talk with and meet the person. Moving on to the first phone call after three to five emails (if you feel comfortable with what you have learned about them so far) prevents you from wasting too much time.

TIPS for giving out your number

Never volunteer to do the role you want him to play. This includes volunteering your phone number. In most cases, it is not a good idea to offer your phone number before he asks for it. Instead:

- Tell him how much you enjoyed talking with him and that you would love to do it again (or, if on the Internet, tell him you would like to talk on the phone since it is easier to get to know someone that way). Then pause to give him a chance to ask for your number. Do not offer it. If he wants your number, he will ask.
- If he doesn't ask for it, tell him you hope he has a great day and that you would love to run into him or talk with him again. Then walk away.
- If he offers you his number instead of asking for yours, touch him on the arm and explain how difficult it would be for you to make the first phone call. State that you don't know how men get the courage to call women because it is so uncomfortable for you. And then say, "If you give me your number, I probably won't feel comfortable enough to call, but I would be glad to give you my number." Then wait a moment for him to ask for your number. If he doesn't ask for it, say a warm good-bye, and walk away. If he wants your number, he will stop you and say, "I didn't get your number." If he doesn't, walk confidently away, reminding yourself that you know you are worth the little bit of effort it takes to get a number and call and that your walking away is showing confidence. The kind of guy you are looking for wouldn't let the opportunity pass. It's better to wait for him than waste your time with someone who can't see your value.
- If he does ask for it, give him your number. Then state, "I can get busy sometimes, so if I am not home or available when you call, leave a message. I will call you back." This sends the message that your time is valuable and makes you appear to be more of a challenge.
- If he leaves a message, return his call. If he doesn't leave a message but you see his name on the caller ID, don't call

him. If he's interested, he will call back or leave a message.

- **There is one important exception to this TIP**. If your home address can be accessed from the telephone directory or Internet with just your telephone number, you may not want to give your number out (which everyone on the Internet should seriously consider). Accept his number rather than giving him yours. Then call him from a phone without caller ID. Most cellular phone numbers are not connected to a home address, which may protect you more than giving out your home number. So using a cell phone may be safer. Once you feel safe, give him your telephone numbers. Then explain to him how uncomfortable it is to call him first, and let him know how much you would appreciate it if he called you first from now on (or at least for a while). Tell him you will return his calls if he leaves a message.
- After you have given a man your number, don't waste your time rehearsing your experience with him or talking about him with more than two or three friends. The more you talk about him, the more disappointment you may experience when he doesn't call. Protect your emotional energy. Focus on your life and having fun rather than talking too much about a new man.

TIPS for the first phone call and setting up the first date

When he calls:

- Enjoy the conversation, but look for the warning signs of the potentially abusive and manipulative (explained in chapter 5). If you don't feel comfortable in meeting him or continuing to talk with him, tell him, "I've enjoyed getting to know you, but I don't feel enough of a connection to want to go any further. I don't want to waste your time. Thank you. Good luck."
- Try to keep your phone calls to him paced so as to not exceed his efforts. If he calls twice, call him once. Try to avoid calling him more often than he calls you. Calling him too often may take the challenge away and will likely

undermine your feelings of confidence and security that he is as interested in you as you are in him.

- If you feel safe in continuing future conversations or going on a first date, wait for him to ask you out, or tell him you would love to see him sometime. Either way, don't tell him what days you are available or make the arrangements until he starts to pursue the idea. If it all seems too vague and the conversation has come to an end, say, "Let me know *when* you want to go out. I'd love to see you. Good-bye."
- If he begins to make plans for the date, take the time then and there to plan it. Let him know going on this date is something you really want to do. Express sincere regret if you can't go out on the night he suggested, and then suggest two other nights that would work for you. Give him some ideas of activities or restaurants you enjoy that may work around his budget.
- Avoid accepting dates for *that night* during the first three to six weeks. If you do, you are setting yourself up to be easily taken for granted. Express your desire to go but your regret that you can't. Tell him what days you could see him. (For example: "I would have loved to go with you tonight, but I can't. Thursday or Saturday would work for me, though.") Be warm and sincere about your refusal. Remind yourself that men like and fall in love with women who are a challenge and assert their feelings and needs.
- Review the three-date rule from chapter 5. Set important boundaries that can ensure your safety (which chapter 6 described), such as meeting in a public place for the first few dates, asking to go on a double date first, asking to meet for a one-hour lunch, and so forth. Remember that you cannot discover who a man is if you quickly become everything he wants you to be. Assert your feelings and needs. Good men are defined by their actions in the face of challenges, not their actions when everything is easy. A good man will respect your feelings and needs and search for solutions or ideas that can be mutually agreeable. He won't act like a doormat, get mad, punish you after he gives you what you asked for, or belittle your opinions (which chapter 5 illustrates).

CASE STUDY
REVIEW

THERAPEUTIC ASSESSMENT

Angie didn't feel right about pursuing most of the good options available to singles (dances, singles events, the Internet). However, she had multiple opportunities to take advantage of her everyday situations. There were single men in many of the places she was going every day (the grocery story, the gas station, the movies, the park). All she needed to do was become more aware of when she was in their presence so she could notice them noticing her.

As she began having faith that she had opportunities all around her, she began looking for single men and looking them in the eyes and smiling warmly. The more she smiled at men, the more approachable, friendly, and warm she felt toward them. She also began spending extra attention on her appearance (adding to her confidence). It didn't take long for the dates to start coming in small spurts. Though she may have had more attention and success if she had put herself where a greater number of singles were, she was still able to maximize the opportunities around her. She, like a majority of women, was not without options for success even though her time and opportunities were limited.

chapter fourteen

From first date to the three-week drop off curve

All of the Coach's game play strategies you have learned so far have been intended to prepare you for this important stage of dating—the first date to the three-week drop off curve. Now, more than ever, you need the skills you have learned. Now is the time for you to practice the three-date rule to detect the abusive and manipulative. Now is the time to be sure you are breaking your pattern of attraction. Now is the time to recognize and appreciate good men. Now is the time to be true to yourself through defying your fears, asserting your rights, and thinking rationally (thus acting friendly to your female psychology). Now is the time to be confident you will have the opportunity to marry the kind of man you are looking for and he will appreciate and pursue you. Now is the time to think about dating like a man does and to act with men in a way that is friendly to the male psychology. Now is the time to be emotionally aware and expressive. Now is the time to be successful.

The initial six weeks of dating is pivotal to your future success because the patterns you create and maintain here (for good or bad) may follow you long into the relationship (if the relationship continues beyond the first six weeks). To help you to remember all the things you have learned, your next game play strategy is to stay connected to your mind and heart.

GAME PLAY STRATEGY #15
Stay connected to your mind and heart.

The trick to staying connected to your mind and heart is to remain grounded logically and practically to those things that seem right, stable, consistent, and true to yourself, while also being emotionally trusting and aware (as Lorraine learned from chapter 12). It is the combination of mind and heart—not just one or the other—that will make you successful. Acting with rigid logic, precise dedication to facts, or indifferent practicality is not good for the man you seek or yourself. You and he need your emotions intact, alive, and well. Warmth, love, passion, confidence, enthusiasm, playfulness, joy, fear, sadness, righteous anger, and all other emotions are part of the human experience and create a vitality that makes life and relationships seem real and exciting. However, these emotions alone, without reasoning and logic, can lead a person to make decisions that are emotional but not grounded in the truth and facts of the situation.

When a woman learns to merge her mind and heart, she is more likely to find wisdom and balance in her relationships. One is as important and essential to her success as the other, and the two together will make her and her relationships more complete. Finding the art of being both logical and rational while being emotionally responsive and expressive is no easy task and is one you will have to explore and test many times before you find how to do it in a way that is right for you—but you can do it.

Going on the first date can often be an exciting and nerve-racking time that makes many women wonder, *Will I like him? Will he like me? Will there be chemistry? Will he be the one?* However, many dates end up being duds, and many potentially good relationships end up going nowhere or ending by the third to sixth week.

CASE STUDY

Beth had been excited about her upcoming date with Chad for some time. They had experienced an immediate chemistry from the first time they met at a local singles event, and she believed tonight's date would be equally exciting. However, from the moment he picked her up, she could tell the evening would be a disappointment. He seemed cool and distant, preoccupied, and even a little depressed.

He was polite enough, but Beth could tell halfway through dinner that there wasn't enough happening on the date for her to be certain he would ask her out again. Truthfully, she wasn't sure if she would want to go out again. Her interest was fading fast. It seemed as if the night might be yet one more wasted experience. The thought was depressing and discouraging.

Then it occurred to Beth—the night didn't have to be a total waste. Yes, she would likely never go out with Chad again, but what if she treated the date as an opportunity for personal growth? If she could do a few things she normally would not do on a date that would make her more confident, develop her relationship skills, and give her a sense of personal empowerment, she could judge the date by just her own standards rather than its potential for building toward marriage. She could progress even though the relationship may not.

Beth's experience shows that a woman would be wise to set realistic and obtainable goals for every date. If she is able to practice new skills while on a date, whatever the outcome of the date, she will feel she personally progressed and is closer to her larger goal of having a good relationship. Doing this may help you endure the many highs and lows of dating relationships.

As you set specific goals, it is important that at least one is logical (thus connecting to your mind) and the other emotional (thus connecting to your heart). When appropriate, the goal can be both logical and emotional. For example: a logical goal may help you improve yourself, your relationship and dating skills, your confidence, your ability to be true to yourself, and your ability to recognize when you are breaking your relationship patterns. An emotional goal may help you listen to your gut feelings, express your faith and trust, or express your feelings of appreciation, warmth, affection, and even adoration, when appropriate.

As you attempt to set logical and emotional goals for every date, you may find it helpful to review previous chapters and the answers to previous questions or talk with friends and family members. However, you will also need to be mindful of the following secret to the male psychology, the mistakes that women make, and this chapter's tips for your success. The more you take action in your life, strive for personal progress, and improve your relationship skills, the more likely you will feel connected to your mind and heart. This can only help increase your self-esteem and confidence.

♂ Have a male-friendly psychology

Almost everything a woman needs to know about the male psychology to help her navigate the first date through the three-week drop off curve can be found among SECRETS #1–10 with one important exception—sex.

SECRET #11: Good men want sex with a woman who feels good about having sex with them and will wait until marriage.

Men want sex. There is no doubt about that. However, good men are not animals, unable to control their bodily functions; they exercise self-control and show empathy, care, and concern for the needs of others. They take responsibility for their own needs and problems in most (if not all) areas of their life—and sex is no different.

When a good man is with a woman, he would never abuse, threaten, or manipulate her into having sex with him. He may encourage, suggest, taunt, and even playfully tease her, but a firm and consistent "no" is enough for him to recognize and respect her desires. He may even admire her for them because he wants to do the right thing too.

Men seem to value, respect, and appreciate a woman who has firm sexual boundaries when dating. In the book *What Men Want,* the male authors state:

> Men don't tell women what they really think about the do's and don'ts of sexual behavior because we don't want to incite a riot. Political correctness has not yet entered the bedroom. A man still holds a woman to a stricter sexual standard. . . . If you have sex with him too soon, he will be less likely to consider you as a potential girlfriend or wife. The truth is that while men talk fast and seductively, deep down they are conservative and idealistic about the kind of girl they will marry. . . . Practicing caution at the beginning of a relationship allows a woman to weed out the guys who are ambivalent, the ones who want only sex.[1]

When a good man knows a woman's boundaries and sees that she is firm in her commitment to her morality, he feels an attraction to her for many reasons: (1) she is a challenge; (2) her boundaries show that she has self-respect, which engenders his respect; (3) her ability to exercise self-control causes him to feel confident in her ability to be faithful to him; (4) her boundaries give him an opportunity to avoid the shame and regret he feels when a woman is emotionally hurt after sex; and (5) he sees her as a woman who has the respectability needed for marriage, motherhood, and family life.

Television, movies, music, and magazines may portray sexual relationships as being an important and immediate development when dating, but good men have values and will respect others' values. In many cases, women who show they don't have strong values will turn off good men.

Thus, in spite of all the attention the media gives to sex in relationships, good men want a woman to do what is right and they will wait.

⚠ Exercise CAUTION—potential hazards exist and can cause injuries

Women will often give up what they want most (a loving, committed relationship) for what they want in the moment (immediate comfort and attention).

Many women do not plan to fail on a date—they fail to plan. Many hazards can be avoided on a first date (and over the three to six weeks that follow) if a woman plans in advance. When she doesn't, she may discover she feels unsafe and unnecessarily vulnerable on first dates, is unable to get second dates, gets used and taken for granted, or keeps cycling through the three-week drop off curve over and over again.

Thus, you would be wise to consider carefully the mistakes below before you go on your first date so as to create a logical plan for avoiding them.

MISTAKE #8: Women who trust without good reason are more likely to find themselves in bad situations they can't control.

Many women want to trust others, so they give their trust quickly and easily. If a woman gives out her address to someone she doesn't know (especially when she met him on the Internet), goes with him to places she is unfamiliar with or that are far away from the assistance of others, or invites him to her house or goes with him to his, she is at risk of losing control over her safety. Most of the time this poses little physical danger to a woman, but in those rare cases when she discovers she is with someone who is sexually forceful, the time to control the situation is past, and all she can do is hope to get away and recover from the experience.

The SECRETS that explain *why*: #2, #4, #5, #6, #9

Those who sexually abuse play by entirely different rules than good men. There are no secrets about good men that explain abusive behavior. However, there are many secrets that explain why a good man will support a woman's boundaries and need for safety—secrets #2, #4, #5, #6, and #9.

Hint: Every woman should take steps to ensure her safety when going out with someone she doesn't know well. Chapter 6 gives many safety tips, and chapter 5 helps women identify the potentially abusive and manipulative within the first three dates. If a woman follows the advice in these chapters, she will be more likely to navigate dating safely.

MISTAKE #9: Women who act cool, cautious, and reserved on dates often don't get asked out for second dates.

Oftentimes a woman may be quite interested in a man but fears acting foolish or desperate, so she acts cool, businesslike, or passive. This usually results in the man doubting her interest in him or feeling bored when with her. Thus, he is less likely to ask her out again (there is no point wasting his money or risking unnecessary rejection if she is not interested).

The SECRETS that explain *why*: #1, #5, #7, #6, #10

Hint: Men need some kind of emotional encouragement from women. Men love a reasonable challenge but will avoid challenges that are greater than their interest or appear likely to only result in rejection. Therefore, a woman would be wise to make her interest known. She can do this through warm and sincere expressions of gratitude, occasional and appropriate touch (handholding or sweet simple kisses), or through acting excited and animated when a man calls or takes her out.

MISTAKE #10: Women who become physically involved with men in the first three to six weeks are likely to get dumped sooner rather than later.

Many women falsely believe that getting physical is a must for solidifying dating relationships with men. They feel this in spite of the fact that sex often has a higher price tag for women than it does for men because women (1) usually become more emotionally attached and vulnerable following physical contact, (2) often feel regret and/or spiritual shame about having sex outside of marriage (3) are more susceptible to the life-altering effects of sexually transmitted diseases (such as infertility and cervical cancer), (4) are more negatively stigmatized by society and men as being loose, easy, or sluts, and (5) are more likely to bear the full emotional and financial burden of unplanned pregnancies and parenting than men are.*

Not only does pre-marital sex have emotional, physical, and spiritual consequences, it also increases the probability that a new relationship will end before the third to sixth week. Thus, when a woman engages in sexual conversations, sexual contact, and sexual intercourse before marriage, she increases her odds that she will be lonely and rejected rather than loved and adored like she had hoped.

The SECRETS that explain *why*: #2, #3, #4, #9, #11

Hint: The three male authors of *What Men Want* say it best:

> Sometimes, when a man is not interested in a woman, he will change the tone of his conversation and begin to talk in a sexually suggestive way. He will discuss sexual topics, hoping for a positive response so he can get some action. He knows he does not like her but will still try to get sex from her. If he does get sex, he will never call again. If he doesn't get sex, he may call again to get one more shot at getting laid. Once again, though, after they have sex, he will not call again. In general, if a guy is very open about sexual topics on the first date, he is not looking to build a relationship.[2]

If you want a loving, committed relationship, you cannot afford to waste your time and emotional energy on men who are sexual opportunists (who would gladly have sex with you even when they don't really like you), sexual predators (who would pursue and even manipulate you for the sole purpose of getting sex—and then dump you), or sexual abusers (who might exploit any vulnerability in you or your circumstances to manipulate, overpower, and rape you). You cannot always know if the man you are talking sexually with before your first date is one of the above or a good man who means no harm by what he is saying (either way, it is unlikely that a relationship with this person will last more than three weeks because it is already set up to become sexual). Can you emotionally, physically, or spiritually afford to take the risk? Good relationships rarely start out on a sexual note. Getting sexually involved is likely to cause the relationship to end or blind you to stay in a relationship with a man you have nothing in common with. How long can that last?

If you want a loving, committed relationship with a good man, you need to be committed to doing what is best for you in the long-term, not

---

* Please note: Marriage is the ultimate sign and assurance of a loving and committed relationship; thus, marriage is the only secure context for a sexual relationship.

the short-term. Consider again what you learned in chapter 7 about being true to the truth and true to yourself. Sex is one of those many issues that require self-control. Can you really hope to have a good, long-term and lasting relationship without both you and your partner exercising the skills of self-control? Are not your values truly expressed by what you do when it is hard to keep your values rather than when it is easy? Make a commitment to what you know is true and best for you and you will draw good men to you who will respect and protect your values. There are many women and men who choose to wait to have sex until after marriage. Don't be afraid to do the same (even if you have had sex before). After all, sex outside of marriage has a price and you have the right to know and do what is best for you.

MISTAKE #11: Women often falsely believe that if they meet a man's every need, he will love and appreciate them for it.

When a woman drops what she is doing to hang out at the last minute with a man, spends money on him, does his laundry, or runs his errands, though he has shown little to no commitment or involvement, she is likely to discover she is the good-for-now-until-something-better-comes-along girl rather than being the woman he loves and adores. Not only will she discover that he is not "into" her (and probably never will be) like she is "into" him, she will likely also feel used, exploited, and neglected as he continues to explore his other more attractive options or dumps her on a whim.

The SECRETS that explain *why*: #1, #5, #7, #8, #10

Hint: Men neither love nor respect women who do everything for them or make things too easy. Without sacrificing for the relationship, they feel no deep bond or connection to it. Good men don't mean to hurt those women they call when they are bored or lonely, but for some a quick fix is too easy to resist. If you become less available, only spend time with men who call days in advance, and start expressing your feelings and needs, men will value you more than if you are too accommodating, available, and easy.

MISTAKE #12: Women often try to make the good times last for as long as possible, which contributes to the three-week drop off curve.

When a woman is having a good time early in a relationship, she is likely to want to stay up late talking or being together for hours on end. Not only does this increase the likelihood that sexual interaction may occur, but it also wears the relationship out faster.

The SECRETS that explain *why*: #1, #5, #7, #8, #10

Hint: It is natural for a woman to not want to end a good date when things are going well, but for men too much of a good thing can be tiring and increase boredom (especially when dates last until one, two, or three in the morning). The more he learns about you early in the relationship and with little effort on his part, the more likely he may lose his curiosity and fascination with you. When there are no mysteries to be discovered early in the relationship, he will likely become bored and look for the next challenge in a different relationship.

MISTAKE #13: Women are often drawn to loving men who aren't in a position to love them back.

Women often fail to think about what a relationship has to offer them personally. Instead they give and give and give, only to discover that they are unhappy and unfulfilled in the relationship and even easily discarded by the man they gave so much attention and affection to. This can happen when a woman loves someone who is either emotionally immature or who is emotionally mature (a good man) but is unable to love her back because of his circumstances. Men who are recovering from a bad breakup, death, or divorce; are currently married; or are engaged in drug, alcohol, prescription, or pornography abuse and addiction have many needs that can be attractive to some women. However, men in these situations are so absorbed in their problems (and absorbed *by* their problems) that they are not able to give much love in return.

The SECRETS that explain *why*: #1, #2, #3, #4, #7

Hint: Men who are addicted to drugs, alcohol, prescriptions, pornography, or sex are often consumed by their addictions. These influences almost always affect their skills of empathy,* personal responsibility, and self-control, causing them to regress in their emotionally maturity to that of fourteen-year-olds.

The presence of an addiction can make it difficult for you to know if a man was once emotionally mature (thus likely to return to his previous level of functioning when in recovery) or if he has always been emotion-

....

* The effects of pornography on empathy can be great. When a person begins to see others as sexual objects, their perceptions of others' rights, feelings, and needs can become distorted, causing problems in many areas of the relationship. This is particularly the case when the pornography addiction developed early in the person's childhood.

ally immature (thus likely to remain so even after recovery). Therefore, dating someone who is addicted to substances, pornography, or sex (or appears to be abusing these influences enough that addiction in the future is probable) is not a wise choice. The likelihood that the addict's loyalty to his substances will override his loyalty to you is great. The resulting emotional, financial, physical, and personal suffering you may experience from these relationships is likely to only end in tragedy, not your loved one's recovery. Thus, it is best to avoid romantic relationships with those suffering from addiction until they have had at least two to five years of recovery (which increases their odds that they will not return to the substances). An emotionally mature person who has been in long-term recovery for at least two years can be a great marital choice, if he has regained his empathy, self-control, and personal responsibility.

A rebound romance is just that—a rebound. Once the crisis is over, he is likely going to want to explore his other options. He will be grateful to you for the companionship during the crisis, but his logical nature will tell him he shouldn't make quick commitments. This may happen either before or after he has already married you on the rebound (which partially explains why second marriages that occur quickly after a death or divorce are more likely to fail than first marriages).

A married man may be eager to give you some of his attention (because you are more exciting to be with right now than his wife), but he is probably not going to give you all of his time, energy, and other resources because the consequences of doing so are too complex and potentially life-altering. If you are ready to love deeply, you deserve to be loved deeply and fully. Married men cannot offer that unless they divorce their wife. If a married man does divorce his wife for you, she and their children will probably blame and hate you for it. Furthermore, when his clouded thinking clears and his logical nature returns, he may see you and the relationship differently, preferring his old life to the new or desiring the excitement of another relationship (an affair).*

You are responsible for your own happiness. Start your next relationship off with the best possibility for a good outcome by detecting men who can't love you back as soon as possible. Then end your contact with them until they are in a better position. You are ready to love and be loved. Don't waste

....
* Remember, good men don't do drugs, get drunk, or have affairs. Don't waste your time with men who do. You can't afford to lose your self-respect or the respect of good men by having an affair with a married man. The personal consequences of affairs are terrible. Avoid infidelity like the plague.

your time. Love yourself enough to only love good men who are good for you—right now!

MISTAKE #14: Women tend to put all their hopes into one relationship too early in the dating process.

Women often stop flirting or dating other men as soon as they meet someone they really like, especially if the relationship progresses quickly. However, the emotional excitement and neediness they feel for just the one man can create heavy burdens for the relationship and him before he has sufficiently invested. When the relationship ends, she may feel devastated while he feels relieved.

The SECRETS that explain *why*: #2, #3, #4, #5, #7, #8, #9

Hint: Women often scare men away when they become too invested or needy early in the relationship. Not only do men get bored when there is no challenge, but they also resist complications and commitments early in a relationship, even if they are having a good time. A woman who becomes overly emotional, takes his behavior too personally, or demands more emotional investment or commitment than a man feels ready to give (especially during the first three to six weeks) is likely to get rejected. Keeping your options open to dating others will not only make you more of a challenge, but it will also keep you from getting too emotionally needy too soon. Do not stop flirting with or dating other men (because men like women other men like—*it's the challenge*), until the guy you like has played his role for at least three to six weeks but preferably longer, like three to six months, and has asked you to stop seeing others.

After reviewing the above secret to the male psychology and the mistakes women make, set some logical and emotional goals for when you are on a date so you can manage and avoid these issues. Write these goals down. Then use the tips throughout the rest of this chapter as options for additional goals and dating ideas.

If you play your role, he'll play his

TIPS for recognizing, encouraging, and appreciating good men when on a date

Good men so often go unnoticed and unappreciated for the seemingly small, everyday, and consistent things they do. When you take notice of a good man's everyday choices and sacrifices and recognize him as important and valuable to you, you may find the men you date are drawn to you.

- When setting up the first date, if a man is supportive and respectful of your needs to meet somewhere public, be sure to thank him warmly for being so understanding.
- When walking to the car, don't leave him guessing about whether you would like him to open the car door for you (good men would want to treat you well). Smile warmly, lean next to him, or touch him on the arm while you are walking and say, "I know guys aren't sure if they should open the car door on a date or not. I love it when guys do that. So, if you want to, please do. I'll always appreciate you for it." If he doesn't, don't comment on it. If he does, give him a warm smile and say, "Thank you."
- When deciding where to go on the date, if he thought about it enough to have already planned several possibilities for the night, especially if they were creative options, comment on the effort he showed. Say, "Wow! You've put a lot of thought into this date. That makes me feel special. Thank you."
- When expressing your personal preference, need, or desire to go to a certain restaurant or movie or to be home at a certain time, if he responds immediately or respectfully, smile warmly and touch him on his upper arm to show gratitude for his response.
- While with him, notice the things he talks about. If he shows signs of empathy *(as indicated by how respectfully he talks about his mother, sisters, ex-girlfriends, the way he treats you and the waitress, the way he respects your boundaries, property, feelings, and needs)*, self-control *(as indicated by how he talks about his experiences with managing money, debt, anger, prescription use, alcohol, pornography, the law, and authority figures)*, and personal responsibility *(as indicated by how he acknowledges his mistakes and issues, works to correct them, shows concern for resolving how his behaviors affect others)*, acknowledge those things with a sincere comment.
- Show respect for and take interest in the things that demonstrate his long-term commitments and investments.

This could include anything he values enough to sacrifice for, such as his career, home, family, friends, children, religion, education, and athletic interests. If he continues to make these things a priority over the next few weeks, while also slowly fitting you in among these priorities, acknowledge his efforts to fit you in. When he calls each week for a date, in spite of his busy schedule, show warm appreciation. *A good man will likely only see you once or twice a week at first because he cares about keeping balance among the many important things in his life. Do not expect a relationship with a good man to be fast. It will be steady and constant, not fast and chaotic. Also take comfort in knowing that a man who doesn't abandon the things he loves on a whim, even to be with you, is likely to not abandon you on a whim. One of the many signs of a good man is that you can trust and respect how he handles the things he commits to and loves.*

- Look for and acknowledge those things that make a man good and stable, such as his long-term employment, commitment to financial responsibilities, and dedication to family, friends, or religious/community services. *Good men do not expect recognition for doing what is "right" or their "duty" and "responsibility." They will keep sacrificing without appreciation or recognition, since "it's just the right thing to do," but nothing feels quite as good as being noticed for one's voluntary choices to do what is right.*

- Recognize and show him appreciation for anything he does for you that shows interest in you, your thoughts, opinions, feelings, or needs, from opening the door to showing interest in your opinion.

- When eating dinner and you are not sure if he intends to pay for both of you, assume that he is a gentleman and planned on paying. Do not look awkwardly at him to find out his intent. Instead, smile at him and say, "That was a great meal. Thank you." *(If you feel bad that he is paying for the meal and want to pay your half, resist this urge. Men spend money on things they value and grow to love things they work hard for and sacrifice for—don't deny him the privilege of sacrificing for you. He valued you enough to ask you out. Show your appreciation. Do not diminish his perception of your value by offering to pay your half of the meal. If he asks you out again, you will know he really is interested and values spending time with you.)*

- When he shows interest and concern for how dating may affect your family (and especially your dependent children) and tries to accommodate their needs, take time to give him special appreciation for his interest and concern. *Any man who sets boundaries to protect your family and kids from unnecessary pain, confusion, or problems deserves recognition for his empathy and respect.*

- If he has paid for several things on the date and you would like to show your appreciation to him, express how much you enjoyed the evening. Be specific about what you thought was special or was particularly thoughtful. Tell him how much fun you had. Let him know his sacrifices were valued and appreciated.

TIPS for encouraging further dates

Men often feel uncertain about a woman's interest in them. If you want more dates, you will need to give a good man some indication of how you feel about him or the date.

- At the end of every date, make sure you have tried to touch him warmly at some point during the date, or do so at the end. This could include giving him a warm touch on the upper arm, a kiss on the cheek, or a hug; putting your arm in his as you walk to the door; grabbing his hand and holding it briefly; and even giving him a sweet kiss good night. Do what feels most comfortable for you among those options, but be sure to touch him, unless you do not want to encourage another date. If you felt he was potentially abusive or manipulative, avoid touch, warm statements, and even eye contact at the end of the night. If he indicates he wants to go out again, say, "Thank you for your time. I just don't feel enough of a connection to continue with another date, but I appreciate the opportunity to get to know you." He can't successfully argue about whether or not you felt a connection, so keep repeating that statement if he tries to talk you into another date, unless you are afraid. Then mumble a half response of "ohhhhh, sure" and quickly end the date and go inside. Later when you feel comfortable, you can tell him you're not interested over the phone.

- If you want to go on another date, make your interest known, but don't set up the date. For example: touch him on the arm, look him in the eyes, and smile. Then say, "I really enjoy being with you. I'd love to see you again. Thanks for a wonderful time." Wait for him to ask for the next date. You did your part; if he's interested, he will do his.

- If he asks you out for a night that won't work for you, express disappointment, and suggest another night instead (never rearrange a date with someone else to accommodate him). Let him pursue planning that date, but at least he'll know you want to see him.

TIPS for preventing him from becoming bored by the third week and therefore triggering the three-week drop off curve

- If you want to keep his fascination and interest in you going, try to end the date on a high note, not three hours after it hit its peak. Say good night instead of spending hours making out. Making out won't accomplish much (especially this early in the relationship). A simple affectionate kiss can end the night better than a makeout session can. Warmly tell him, "I could enjoy talking with you for hours, but I must call it a night. I'd love to see you again sometime next week, though." Then trust that if he is interested, he will call (or someone else will).

- Keep flirting with and dating others, but do not rub your dating options in his face, which would be a turnoff. He'll know you're dating others because you're not always available when he asks you out. If he asks you directly if you are dating others, tell him. If you are dating more than one man at a time, it's not emotionally fair or honest to be physically involved. Keep your affection simple and clean. Care about others' feelings by controlling your passion.

- Don't accept a date for the same night, especially during the first three to six weeks, unless there is a rare circumstance (like he won tickets to a concert that night, which he seems to really want your company for). Just don't make a habit of being available at the last minute. He may stop pursuing you as much if he feels getting your attention is something he can have as a quick fix whenever he wants it.
- Take many of his calls, and return his messages fairly quickly (but at least every third or fourth call, wait a few hours before you call him back so you don't seem excessively available). When you do talk with him, be happy and excited to hear from him, but don't seem too available—thus, not much of a challenge.
- Call him periodically so he sees that you are interested enough to take a few risks, but don't call too often. He will appreciate the reassurance of knowing you like him too, and he won't be as likely to feel annoyed because you aren't calling him excessively (even if a guy says he likes you calling him a lot, many men get annoyed by it and won't tell you). By not calling him too frequently, you will give him a chance to miss you, which will help keep him interested in you.
- Pace your dating. Try to only see him once or twice a week for the first three weeks and not more than three times a week for the next three weeks, which is about as much time as most good men may be interested in spending with you early in the relationship. They have responsibilities, family, and friends they will want to keep in balance. You should try to do the same. If you keep your life in balance and then experience the three-week drop off curve, it will hurt less than if you had wrapped your life around his for three weeks. Furthermore, pacing your dating will make you more of a challenge for him to pursue. If he seems to want to go out more than twice a week, resist the urge to do it; he will be more likely to get bored faster if you do. Tell him how much you would love to see him that often but that right now you can't. If he asks why you can't, tell him you are too busy, it is just something you don't do this early in a relationship, or you need to keep your friendships and life in balance. An emotionally mature

man who is really interested will pursue you and will not dump you just because you won't see him every day.

TIPS for when you go on additional dates

- If you have been on several dates and he has paid for the dates, you could show him how much you appreciate his sacrifices by offering to pay for an occasional meal, a dessert at the end of the date, or the movie. Let him sacrifice for you and be generous to you, and you start to do the same. (His ability to love you will come from his sacrifices, so don't completely match or exceed his efforts or tell him he no longer needs to sacrifice for you. Just start being generous with him in small ways.) Do things that show your appreciation. Take a risk and buy him something you think he would like. However, never go halves on a date. Paying half of the meal is like paying for yourself; thus, neither of you are sacrificing for the other.
- As the relationship progresses, let him kiss you, and you kiss him. Be sweet, adoring, and simple in your kisses. This will show your interest and keep the relationship clean, fresh, uncomplicated, and encouraging. Passionate and prolonged kisses are not necessary and can actually begin to turn a potentially good relationship into a sexual relationship, accelerating and complicating the relationship too quickly. Furthermore, too much of a good thing can create boredom and bring the relationship to a quick end for a man. One of the easiest ways to keep the relationship from becoming sexual is to limit kissing to just a few minutes. Don't lie down and kiss, which makes prolonged kissing and potential sexual contact easier to do. And be sure to explain your desire "to go slow and just kiss" so he understands how to support you.
- Warmly and affectionately resist commitment for now, even if things are going great. If he really likes you, he will continue to pursue you over a period of weeks. Be realistic. This new relationship could end by the third week, like so many others. Why get attached too quickly? Additionally, becoming committed early in the relationship can

blind you to important warning signs and increase your likelihood of becoming more sexually involved than would be wise. Ask him to go slow and give you time.

- Start telling him what you like or what makes you feel special. For example: tell him how much you like it when men pick you up at your home or surprise you at work. Tell him what activities you enjoy doing, what foods you like, and so forth. Then ask him if he would be willing to do some of them for you.

- If you have dated a few weeks and have not shown affection to each other because you feel uncomfortable trying to hold his hand first or kissing him first, warmly tell him that you would love to hold his hand, cuddle with him, or kiss him, but you are too uncomfortable with making the first move so you hold back. See what he says or does. Whatever he does to please you or fulfill your requests, give him tons of recognition and appreciation (he'll love being appreciated and feeling like a hero).

- If he agrees to participate in activities that involve your friends or family and then tries hard when interacting with them, give him warm and affectionate appreciation. Many men in new relationships avoid such activities. His willingness to go and then act so friendly is a sign of his sacrifice and goodness. You would be wise to recognize and appreciate his efforts, especially if you hope this relationship will progress. How hard he works to develop relationships with your friends and family will improve the quality of your life and the likelihood that your relationship will be successful. Reward these efforts; they will mean a lot to you in the long-term.

Once on a date, always remember to alter any of your goals or the tips above that don't seem wise or logical in your current situation.

CASE STUDY
REVIEW

THERAPEUTIC ASSESSMENT

Beth realized that Chad's quietness was making her feel distant and uncomfortable. She had hoped he would maintain most of the conversation on the date, since it wasn't a strength of hers, but she quickly realized that wouldn't happen and the date could be a failed experience. Instead of letting that happen, she began telling Chad about some of the vacations she had been on during her life, including details she normally feared others would think were unimportant or boring. This time she decided to share her stories at the risk of boring Chad, because she might never see him again anyway. She might as well build her confidence and skills of talking about herself with others. She kept telling herself, "These skills will likely be needed in later relationships. Why not take a risk? If I don't see him again, I will recover. The kind of man I am looking for will ask me out over and over again in spite of my imperfections. This isn't my last chance for happiness or love. I can be brave and talk a little about myself."

By the end of the evening, she had even experienced enough courage to reach across the table to touch him on the arm a few times, which is another problem she often struggled with (showing affection).

She went home that evening, walked in the door, and smiled confidently to her roommate, who said, "Wow! That must have been a great date."

Beth replied, "No. It was actually quite awful but I feel great. Let me tell you what I did."

Beth's decision to maximize her growth through dating made her more confident, relaxed, and even playful on a date. Through worrying less about whether there would be a second, third, or fourth date or relationship and thinking more about her own skills and progress, she not only managed the highs and lows of dating better, but she also became more attractive and challenging to the men she dated and began attracting the kind of relationships she wanted.

Notes
1. Gerstman, Bradley, ESQ; Christopher Pizzo, CPA; and Rich Seldes, MD. *What Men Want: Three professional single men reveal to women what it takes to make a man yours.* New York: HarperPaperbacks, 1998, 17–18.
2. Ibid, 115.

chapter fifteen

Building the relationship

In the Final Stretch of the Dating Game, a couple needs to do two important things: keep their eyes open and keep the ball going.

Many women hesitate to trust their judgment, but time is a great teller of the truth. If a woman keeps her heart and mind connected, she won't miss the truth she needs to see. Most people who are abusive or manipulative cannot maintain a deception for more than four to six months unless those closest to him or her don't want to see the truth. A woman who talks openly (with at least two good friends) about everything she sees and experiences with the man she is dating will discover the truth, both good and bad.

When a woman is dating a good man, most of the time the truth is good and can build confidence in her judgment and in him while also revealing the issues or problems she will need to decide what to do with (since everyone has a few problems). Many issues and problems are ones a woman merely needs information about and ideas for managing. Other issues may cause her to end the relationship because of incompatibility. Whatever the issue, a woman needs to know she can handle the truth (about herself, the man she is dating, the relationship, and the problems that both of them bring to the relationship). If she keeps her mind and heart connected, it is not a matter of trusting her judgment (there is nothing wrong with her judgment); it's a matter of deciding what to do with the knowledge she has.

This stage of a relationship can be difficult and complicated at best. In order for a woman to effectively support this process, she will need to be effective in building the relationship (keeping the ball in motion) while also learning and dealing with the problems in the relationship (keeping her eyes open), which is your next game play strategy.

GAME PLAY STRATEGY #16
Be effective in how you build your relationships while confronting and dealing with problems in your relationship.

CASE STUDY

Marissa had been dating Hunter for about three months. He had been persistent in pursuing her, respectful of her needs, and emotionally mature in his responses and behaviors. Yet, she feared moving forward with the relationship and becoming exclusive with him. There were just so many things she didn't know about him, and she feared limiting her options until she had more information.

Marissa had been married before, though only for a few months. Shortly after the wedding, she had discovered her husband had been dishonest about his exorbitant debt, past relationships with other women, and his involvement with pornography. Though the details and facts he had withheld were disturbing, it was his dishonesty and excuses that had damaged her trust and brought their relationship to a quick end.

Marissa just couldn't bear moving forward with a relationship again to only discover the issues were too great

for her to choose or the person had been dishonest. She
needed more information and needed to see that any man
she became serious with would be completely honest and
willing to answer any questions she had. Nonetheless, she
wasn't sure how to approach the situation without appear-
ing accusing or causing him to take offense.

There is a difference between being *right* in why a woman does what
she does and being *effective* while doing it. When it comes to men, a woman
can change many things in her approach that will help her be more effective
and friendly to the male psychology as she warmly solicits a man's support,
so he can respond in a way that is friendly to her female psychology as well.
The following secrets, mistakes, hints, and tips may help you learn the art of
being effective.

♂ Have a male-friendly psychology

SECRET #12: Men need to be needed.

Most men need to feel important, needed, and valued. When a man
feels needed and feels that his sacrifices make a difference for others or
fulfill a greater purpose or good, he often feels a deeper sense of love,
commitment, and loyalty for those he serves while also feeling a greater
sense of self-respect. This is not to say that sacrificing a selfish desire is an
easy task, but emotionally mature men know that their contribution is
necessary to the overall success of those they love, so they sacrifice without
resentment or demands of fanfare. When the need is great and they see
what they must do for others, good men feel it is their duty to provide.

SECRET #13: Men are repelled by criticism, nagging, and whining.

A man's desire to be trusted and respected by the women he loves as well
as his desire to be a hero can cause him to do many things to please a woman.
Her trust, respect, love, appreciation, and recognition are all he needs in
return. Most women do not understand this important dynamic of the male
psychology and mistakenly believe that pointing out a man's failures, mis-

takes, and inconsiderate actions is an effective way to motivate him to change and meet her needs.

Men internalize criticism, nagging, and whining as a sign that they have failed somehow. Taking it personally and feeling attacked, their bodies respond with powerful chemical reactions used for fight or flight. In new relationships, these emotions often drive a man to try harder, hoping to please the woman he loves. However, when criticism, nagging, or whining become chronic, he believes that removing himself from the situation (through tuning her out, leaving the room, breaking up) or fighting back (through defensive arguments that point out her weaknesses) is his only recourse. As much as a man wants to please a woman, when he feels all his efforts only result in failure, he will stop trying and begin avoiding her rather than trying to please her.

SECRET #14: A man experiences anxiety in every conversation a woman initiates until she tells him what she wants him to do

Because a good man wants to be a hero and likes to be needed, he will often listen to a woman's feelings and try to support her when she is upset; however, this is no easy task. Heroes don't rush in and then sit down and contemplate the situation at large. They take action, and that is what he wants to do. Yet a good man will put this need aside and spend up to about twenty minutes listening, hoping for some clue to how he can help. Doing this is a tremendous emotional sacrifice for him, but he will listen, somewhat patiently, if he thinks it will help.

However, as a woman goes on and on about a problem, a man is likely to become increasingly more anxious. After fifteen to twenty minutes, he may begin to panic under the looming and growing anxiety that the conversation may never end. Good men then begin to give advice, get upset that their advice isn't helping, and even become frustrated, stating they don't want to hear about it anymore. They mean no offense to a woman when they do this. After all, they started out wanting to help. They just don't understand what she needs or if they are making a difference, and they feel chemically overwhelmed by the negativity that seems to have no end.

SECRET #15: Men bond through doing activities and talking about things more than they do through talking about people, problems, feelings, or ideas.

There are three ways people tend to build relationships:

- **Doing activities and talking about things:** Men tend
  to need an abundance of leisurely, peaceful, everyday
  activities and conversations. Enjoying leisure activities with
  others such as watching television together, doing sporting
  activities, doing physical things, going on vacations,
  talking about politics, or talking about the kids' activities
  are all things that make good men feel bonded and close to
  those they love. Having too much conflict in a relationship
  and not enough peaceful interaction can sometimes make
  a man distance himself (because the relationship just feels
  too stressful). However, if stressful conversation is kept in
  balance with an abundance of leisure enjoyment (about 60
  percent or more of the time), good men will feel bonded
  enough to endure moderately stressful conversations in a
  relationship.
- **Talking about people and problems:** Women tend to
  need a lot of time to process and discuss their relationships
  and problems. For a woman, this is a healing and helpful
  activity that reduces her stress and helps her feel hope and
  confidence in what she is experiencing and what she needs
  to do. It also creates a bond between her and the person
  with whom she is sharing. For men, it can create stress and
  feel more like gossip, negativism, and pointless complaining.
  A man and woman's differences, in their desires to talk
  about people and problems, can tax the relationship
  and cause one or the other to emotionally distance
  themselves from the other person. For example: too little
  communication for a woman can cause her to feel lonely
  and emotionally distant from the relationship, whereas, too
  much communication about problems can make a man feel
  more stressed and dissatisfied with the relationship.
- **Talking about feelings and ideas:** Talking about feelings
  and ideas is often mutually rewarding to both men and
  women. Good men often enjoy hearing about a woman's
  ideas and feelings (unless those feelings are accusing him),
  and he usually likes sharing his own (when his opinions,
  feelings, and beliefs are heard and valued). Women

often enjoy feeling a deeper connection through open discussions and sharing. When discussions about people and problems transition into respectful sharing of feelings and ideas, both the man and the woman may feel their needs are better met (especially if after the conversation they share some relaxing time together).

Thus, if a woman wants a man to feel as bonded and connected to her as she feels to him, she would be wise to spend less time talking about people and problems (although definitely some time must be spent), more time talking about feelings and ideas, and the majority of their time enjoying activities or talking about things.

SECRET #16: Good men adore women who give them love, attention, and affection.

Nothing quite motivates a person like love does, for both the giver and the receiver. However, helping someone to feel loved isn't always as easy as it appears. Most people give love to others the way they like to receive love, not the way the other person needs love; thus, communicating love and affection in a way that is meaningful to the other person is something all couples should learn early in the relationship.

The sooner a woman understands how to communicate her affection effectively (the way the other person likes to receive love), the more likely she will be adored and appreciated for her efforts. Likewise the sooner a woman learns how she likes to be loved and effectively encourages and supports others in meeting her needs for love, the happier and more fulfilled she will be.

The secrets to communicating love can be broken down into five basic love languages:

- **Touch**: which can include physical touch, holding hands, kissing, cuddling, etc.
- **Words**: which can include sincere statements of appreciation, praise, recognition, being heard and validated, or lengthy conversations about one's feelings.
- **Acts of service**: which can include back rubs, getting someone a glass of water, putting the kids to bed, doing dishes, ironing clothes, running errands, or making dinner.

- **Time together**: which often includes doing activities together, shopping together, or going for walks together. Those who feel loved through time together need more than just the minimum amount of time that is necessary to keep a relationship going. They need an abundance of time.
- **Gifts**: which can include buying something the person likes, giving love notes, taking them out for a date night—anything that makes them feel special.[1]

Everyone has a preferred way to receive love with the other ways falling in second, third, fourth, and fifth place behind the primary love language. For instance, one person may need touch above all else, making it the number one love language, with words coming in second and acts of service third. Their fourth and fifth love languages (of gifts and time together), although important, may make little difference in the person's ability to feel loved if the top three have not been met.

One way to determine a person's primary love languages is to look at those forms of love that have the greatest healing or calming effect upon the person when he is upset. Another way is to look at the things he most commonly does to show others love. He might be showing how he wants to be loved in the ways he gives love.

Whatever a man's love language is, when he feels loved, there is little he won't do for the person who is giving him that love. If you want to be adored, your best bet is to show an abundance of love and assert your love needs as well.

Once you discover a man's love languages, never use them against him when you are angry. Punishing others by withholding their love language is like starving a child when he does something wrong. Denying the other person your acts of love will threaten the survival of the relationship and impair your relationship's ability to weather trials. There are better ways to express your feelings and needs than through punishing a person with the one thing that endears them to the relationship—your expressions of love.

SECRET #17: Good men are often willing to talk openly and honestly when they feel it will help them or another person to do so.

Most good men do not feel the necessity to share their thoughts, feelings, and problems with others. They feel confident they can work through most of their issues on their own, so a man is likely to only involve others when he knows he or the other person could benefit from his sharing (this could include a family member, a neighbor, a coworker, or a perfect stranger).

Without seeing any potential benefit for others or himself, a good man may keep important issues from a girlfriend or wife, believing he is sparing her the burden of his problems. It is not that a good man feels he must hide his issues from her; he just feels no need to burden her with his issues. Many women feel this is just an excuse to "cover his sins" (which in some cases may be true), but men do not see it this way. Oftentimes, a man is willing to share and divulge; he just needs to see how it would help others or the situation.

If a woman asks a specific question and explains her need to know while being respectful in her approach to asking him, he will often tell her what she needs to hear even if it paints him in a bad light. All he asks in return is that she respect his information and not gossip about it to others. Men are often private and feel betrayed when their problems or dark secrets are shared without permission. Although a woman may need a few confidants and a man may allow her to share with them, he will expect her to make sure they are trustworthy and will protect the information as well.

⚠ Exercise CAUTION—potential hazards exist and can cause injuries

Women want so badly to have loving, committed relationships, and yet getting one seems to evade many women. Here are some common mistakes women make that interfere in the progress of their relationships or the fulfillment of their needs.

MISTAKE #15: Women often forget that men have feelings and needs too.

Many women will complain about how self-centered and neglectful their men are, but when pressed to explain his emotional needs, they simply cannot express them. Some women spend a lot of time thinking about their relationships but often do not think to see it from his perspective (or ask questions to get his insight)—which seems pretty self-centered and neglectful.[2]

The SECRETS that explain *why*: #1, #5, #6, #7, #10, #12, #13, #15, #16

Hint: Whether women believe it or not, they have more power to affect a love relationship than they may think. A man is easily motivated to meet a woman's needs when she meets his (or when he hopes she will meet his). Thus, if you want to keep him engaged and active in the relationship, you simply cannot afford to forget his needs for appreciation, trust, and love. A man's feelings and needs are not something many good men will assert until they feel backed into a corner or criticized. You would be wise to learn as much as possible about the needs of the man you love through watching his reactions to your efforts to meet his needs and asking him questions about his needs, feelings, and preferences. (Even if you think you already know his needs, you are likely wrong, so ask him.)[3]

MISTAKE #16: Women often fail to assert their needs long enough for a man to respond.

Women often fail to express their needs in a way that registers with men. When a woman gives hints, beats around the bush, or feebly expresses her needs, she can be assured of disappointment. To add insult to injury, she often responds to his failure to meet her poorly expressed needs by stating that his lack of action means (1) he must not think she deserves to have her needs met, (2) he must not really care about her or the relationship, or (3) he is just selfish and self-absorbed. If she mentions her hurt, anger, or resentment about her unmet needs and he becomes defensive (often stating, "Well, I didn't know! I can't read your mind"), she usually backs off (feeling further offended or unworthy), stating, "My needs don't really matter. Forget I said anything," or tells him bitterly, "Never mind. I'll do it myself," or criticizes him at length for his selfishness. Her reactions then make him feel more anxiety and confusion about how to please her. The greater a man's anxiety or confusion about how best to proceed, the more likely he will avoid or stall taking action.

The SECRETS that explain *why*: #1, #4, #6, #7, #9, #13, #14, #16

Hint: If you lovingly assert your needs five or even seven times without getting angry, you will likely hear a man who loves you express regret for not taking action sooner, stating he will work on the issue. The more you continue to lovingly assert your needs (while not taking the challenge away from him and trusting he cares enough to meet your needs), the more confident he will feel about his ability to please you, and the stronger his desire to please you will become. (This technique is referred to as the 7–11 rule and will be discussed in more detail in chapter 16.)

MISTAKE #17: Women often prefer to see their relationships idealistically rather than realistically. When a woman is forced to face the realities she has been avoiding, she is then likely to feel like a victim who has been betrayed or deceived.

Single women often contribute to the dilemmas they experience later in marriage through their refusal to see things as they really are when dating. When a single woman avoids, covers, makes excuses for, or denies the facts and problems she doesn't want to see in herself and the man she is dating or their relationship, she is setting herself up to eventually face the issues and live with the consequences they impose on the relationship. Unfortunately, she may then feel like a victim who is now being burdened with a secret problem she did not feel she chose. Her anger would be founded if her boyfriend or husband was truly manipulative or outright deceptive, but when she consciously or unconsciously avoided the truth all along, her sole anger at him is unjustified. She owns some responsibility for how she enabled, supported, and contributed to the problem. Feeling like a victim and mischanneling her anger will not help the situation. Assuming a victim position usually results in the woman delaying her ability to effectively resolve her part in the problem or in her making emotional decisions that later prove to be rash or unwise.

The SECRETS that explain *why*: #7, #9, #13, #16, #17

Hint: If you want to know the truth, you can get it. If you state why you need to know the information and how it can help you, while showing respect, you will likely solicit a good man's support and understanding of your need for the truth. Many good men will reveal more details than you may think they will. Tips for effectively approaching a man with your need for information will follow later in this chapter.

If you play your role, he'll play his

The secrets to the male psychology, along with the above mistakes women make and the hints for avoiding those mistakes, can do much to build the relationship (or keep the ball going); however, they are not enough to make a relationship compatible. You will need to ask some difficult questions, deal with some real problems and issues, and work out these issues now, while dating. Without doing this now, how can you realistically feel good about marrying him? Your problems and incompatibilities will still be there after marriage. You need to know what those problems are before you are married. The following tips may help you play your role in this process as you learn to recognize and address the problems in your relationship.

Note: People who are emotionally immature (thus lacking skills of empathy, self-control, and personal responsibility) will probably not respond well to the tips below. If a man looks good for a few months but later shows his true colors as being abusive or manipulative, a woman should not ignore these behaviors based on the first few months. Anyone can maintain a façade or deception up to four to six months. Thus, you would be wise to immediately end a relationship that has become abusive or manipulative.

TIPS for communicating in a way that is friendly to the male and female psychology

- Support the health and happiness of your relationship. Always remember to:
  - Spend a lot of time having fun, enjoying leisure activities, or participating in sporting events with the man you love. He needs this as much as, if not more than, you do. Make this a regular (daily, weekly, and monthly) priority.
  - Spend a lot of time expressing your love in his preferred ways for receiving love (touch, words, time together, gifts, acts of service). Make this a daily practice.
  - Address small problems or complaints (especially those that might prove to be only critical or nagging in nature) with a brief but effective request. Refrain from complaining or commenting on what he did wrong; just ask him for a new behavior. For instance, don't say, "Why do you come to my house to sit on the couch? Can't you see I'm bored?" Instead say, "I know you are tired right after work and could use a little rest, so it will be a big sacrifice to jump up and go do something with me right now, but would you be willing to do it anyway? I sure would appreciate it." *Ignore any grumbling or hesitation on his part.* You expressed your need. Give him a minute to change gears and get going. Within a few minutes, he will likely be ready to meet your request if you didn't get upset, critical, nagging, defensive, or more demanding in those few short

minutes. Avoid bringing up his past mistakes to defend your request. Just make the request and give him space to meet it. A quick request can save hours of negativity. Remember, the goal is to be effective, not to prove to him how right you are (and have been in the past) and how wrong he is (and has been since the first day you met him).

- Share your difficult feelings, needs, and problems with the goal of being effective and loving:
  - Before you begin the conversation, accept the fact that 80 percent of the time you will be the one bringing up issues in the relationship. Don't complain about this fact. Just be confident in yourself, your rights, your feelings, and your needs.
  - Begin with a soft start-up such as, "I know you would never intentionally ignore my needs if you knew what they were. I also know you can't read minds, so I need to tell you my needs. I thought you would want to know that." This works best if you touch him as you talk.
  - Tell him what you need or want from the conversation and how long it might take right from the start. Don't leave him guessing. If you want advice, let him know you would love to hear some options. If you don't want advice, tell him his understanding and support would do you the most good right now. The point is, tell him how to support you best. If you haven't figured out what you need, share your struggle with a girlfriend first so you can take all the time you want to figure out what you need to express before you talk with him.
  - Ask him if now is a good time for him to give you his complete attention or if later would be better (and when). If he chooses to do it later and he doesn't bring it right up at the appointed time, gently touch him and say, "I appreciate you being willing to talk with me about this problem. Is now a good time like you thought it might be?" Don't get angry if he postpones the talk for another time later that day. Trust that he means to get to it. Thank him for his willingness to help (refer to the 7-11 rule from chapter 16 for further ideas).

o Touch him periodically, and let him know his efforts are making a difference.

o Use "I" statements to express your comments, complaints, feelings, needs, or wants. (For example: "I felt disappointed when you . . ." or "I would prefer . . .")

o Try to keep your complaints specific, and avoid bringing up more than two or three complaints during the conversation.

o Avoid saying, "You always . . ." "You never . . ." or "You are so. . . ." Statements like these often just increase defensiveness and sidetrack the conversation from being constructive and effective.

o While you are talking about the problem, if he tries to cheer you up; lighten the mood with humor; or bring the conversation to an end, laugh with him, smile at him, and then tell him he's getting you off the subject and you still need five more minutes. Go along with him in lightening the mood or breaking the tension so as to prevent the conversation from becoming excessively heavy or conflictual, but keep the conversation from being dropped altogether or ending without a resolution.

o If a solution to a problem is needed, use words that are not too firm or appear to suggest that you have already decided how the problem should be handled (since that would invalidate his potential contribution to the problem), but make your thoughts and ideas an important part of the discussion. Support his thoughts, ideas, and suggestions for resolving the problem. Show your trust in his good intentions, and seriously consider his suggestions for having a potential benefit to the problem.

o Keep negotiating the options until you can reach a mutually rewarding outcome.

o Tell him what you feel comfortable doing (never do something you feel you will resent later) rather than telling him what he should do. If you stay firm in only committing to and doing what feels right or appropriate for you, he will likely consider taking more responsibility for the needs that remain. For example: say, "I feel comfortable cooking the meals. How do we want to negotiate getting the dishes done?"

o Never seek to win a battle at any cost and right now; you will lose the war. If the issue goes on beyond thirty minutes to an hour or becomes too heated or negative, be willing to take a break and talk about it later (set a date and time to come back to the issue). Part ways with some form of a loving act or statement like, "I know you love me and don't want us to feel this tension," "I know we can work this out," or "We have worked through bigger issues than this. We'll figure it out."

o Acknowledge the problems that are likely perpetual problems, and work to only solve what is immediately relevant or necessary for now. Then bench the conversation until further need arises. If a solution is unlikely and unnecessary, agree to just disagree, and drop it. Not every issue needs to be fixed; some issues are best ignored with greater attention being placed on what is going right in your relationship. Remember the point is to be effective and maintain the relationship.

o When the conversation is over, give him a lot of appreciation. Tell him what he did that made a difference for you. Express how close you feel to him when he helps you in these ways. Touch him. Kiss him. And then go back to putting more time and attention into leisure activities or casual conversation and into expressing his love languages. *Try to keep the ratio of positive to negative interactions five to one overall.*[4]

o If the experience seemed like it was not effective or mutually rewarding, ask him how you could have been more sensitive to his needs during the process. Consider how you could have better coached him on how to give you what you needed during the conversation. Ask yourself if you really needed a girlfriend for the discussion rather than him (because only a girl could have given you the understanding and support you were ultimately looking for).

The above tips will help you support the relationship and communicate effectively, but you will also need to bring up some difficult questions that would not come up naturally if you are to get all of the information (both good and bad) that you need.

It may never be easy to bring up difficult questions about someone's past or present mistakes, problems, issues, or weaknesses; however, you need the information if you are going to remain true to yourself and if you are going to be confident about your decision to remain in a relationship that could eventually progress toward engagement and marriage.

How and when you bring up the many difficult questions that need to be asked is up to you. The sooner the better so you don't get too attached before you discover an issue that is a deal breaker (but probably wait at least three to six weeks into the dating relationship or you might overburden the relationship too soon).

Provided below is a general list of important issues you should discuss and some tips for how to initiate and maintain a conversation about them. Please note, *you would be wise to have answers in all of the areas below before you commit yourself to marriage. This is an important time for you to be true to the truth and yourself through being fully informed.*

- Addiction problems (from drugs to alcohol, prescription abuse, spending, gambling, sex, and pornography)
- Work related problems (from periods of unemployment to being fired, anger management problems, work discipline issues, sexual harassment, issues with authority, or dishonesty)
- Family problems (from violence to addiction, abuse, or mental illness)
- Financial problems (from bad spending habits to debt history, credit card misuse, and bankruptcies)
- Sexual problems (from pornography use to sexually transmitted diseases, sexual infidelities, sexual hang-ups, or sexual disinterest)
- Legal problems (from shoplifting to felonies, child-support delinquency, or protective orders)
- Abusive behaviors (from verbally, physically, or sexually abusive behaviors to destruction of others or their own property and financial or physical neglect of dependent children)
- Mental health problems (from depression to anger management, suicide attempts, and mood swings to past

counseling experiences or other efforts to get help)
- Physical health problems (from injuries and diseases to family predispositions for specific illnesses)

TIPS for lovingly and respectfully bringing up difficult questions that may effectively help him disclose the truth

You may be surprised how effective the following tips are. If you approach the conversation with the respect and warmth suggested below, you will likely see that when you play your role, he will play his and tell you what you need to know.

To begin a conversation about any of the above issues:

- Start with a brief description of why the conversation is important to you or potentially helpful for you. Then respectfully ask if he's okay talking about his personal information with you. (For example: you might say, "I know this is your personal information, but it would really help me if we could talk about your involvement with pornography [drugs, alcohol, gambling, or any other addiction] at some point in the future. I fear surprises more than I do facts, and if I know what I might be dealing with, I feel better. Would you be willing to answer some personal questions about it?")
- Express your willingness to discuss your issues as well.
- Encourage him to express a desire to "pass" on any question he does not feel ready to answer yet. Assert your right to do the same. Express your need to eventually know the answers to all of the questions you have before the relationship can progress to engagement, but let him decide when he is ready to answer all of the questions.
- Ask questions that will potentially help you get more, not less, information. Here is a list of questions that might help:
  o When was the last time you . . . (used any drugs; drank alcohol; took a prescription medication for the fun of it or to feel emotionally better; lost your temper; viewed pornography; acted violently; attempted suicide; were verbally, physically, or sexually abused by a parent,

girlfriend, or ex-spouse; had a depressive episode)? Be sure to ask your questions in this open-ended manner. Do not ask, "Do you have a problem with . . . (the above)?" Most men who view pornography, drink to excess, or have employment issues do not believe they have a problem. Thus, they will say, "No. I don't have a problem with . . ." because they, like most people, are in various stages of denial about their issues and problems. But if you ask, "When was the last time . . . ," they will be specific, and you will get a more complete picture.

- o How often did it (or does it) occur?
- o How old were you when it first happened?
- o How did it develop from there?
- o How far did the problem go?
- o What was its worst moment or consequence?
- o How did it affect you and those you love?
- o What feelings did it create?
- o How did others react when they found out?
- o How did you keep it hidden for so long?
- o What excuses for your behavior did you make to others or yourself?
- o How did you avoid dealing with the problem for so long?
- o What happened when you tried to change or stop the problem?
- o When did you first start reaching out for help?
- o What is your commitment to changing the problem now?
- o What have you tried so far?
- o What has worked? What has not?

- As you listen to his responses, be aware of your reactions so as to not act disgusted, shaming, or belittling.
- Give just as much attention to how he deals with the problem as you give to the details of the problem. Focus on his willingness to divulge, not your judgments. You will have time later to decide if his issues are compatible with your needs, but for now respect his sacrifice of honesty and treat him with respect.
- Touch him periodically. Tell him how much you appreciate his honesty and willingness to share with you

and his willingness to meet your needs.

- Act curious and interested in the problem, seeking to better understand it all.
- Show him you care, but don't let his frustration, anger, or attempts to change the subject throw you off the subject of the information you need (in other words, don't be manipulated). Give him options about when to talk about it, but expect to get the information at some point. Your request for the information is important and appropriate. Don't feel guilty or uncomfortable. Don't give up.
- Recognize and vocally express your appreciation for the things he has done in the past or said in the moment that cause you to respect how he has or is addressing the problem.
- Empathize with how difficult the problem is. Try to see it from his perspective. Try to understand the hidden shame that may have been as painful as the problem itself. Don't leave him hanging with fear about what you think of him. Express some of your thoughts. Recognize his sacrifice in sharing. Touch him. Communicate what you respect about him. Don't feel pressure to say his problem is okay if it is not okay, but show respect for him.
- Be disclosing as well. Share your issues and trials. Be honest with him. Answer his questions. Pass on those you don't feel ready to share yet.
- If some of these issues directly affect you, in that he was dishonest with you or unfaithful to you, be genuine about your emotional reactions. If you feel betrayed, hurt, angered, or even unsure about where you are in your commitment, express your feelings appropriately. (These feelings are consequences of his choices in interacting with you. He needs to experience these consequences if they are affecting you. You need to see if he will justify, blame, or excuse his behavior or if he will express concern about your hurt [show empathy and take personal responsibility].)

Like many other women, you may doubt whether a man has been truthful or whether you can really see his issues clearly. The tips below may help you feel the confidence you need.

TIPS for feeling confident in your ability to recognize the truth

Both during and after the conversation:

- Look for inconsistencies that may reveal deceptions, partial truths, or manipulations. Respectfully and warmly ask for clarification. If the confusion you felt is easily clarified and the pieces easily come together in a way that feels right, makes sense, and rings true, then he was likely honest. Look for and trust your internal feelings, thoughts, and experiences. Truth seems to carry its own conviction and often speaks to the mind and heart or resonates from within one's gut feelings. You may also benefit from using spiritual or religious practices of prayer or meditation to help you sense what feels right or true. If the confusion or inconsistencies remain, you are probably picking up on a deception.

- Talk to others who can corroborate, verify, or correct the information you are hearing (this may include ex-wives, ex-girlfriends, family members, friends, or former coworkers). Do not let guilt or feelings of loyalty prevent you from taking this step. It is your responsibility to be true to yourself more than to feel loyal to him while you are still dating. You do not want to later regret that you did not corroborate his stories. If he is emotionally mature and has been honest with you, he will feel he has nothing to hide. If you fear that a vindictive ex-wife might lie and attempt to deceive you, trust your own judgment and ability to sense the truth. You are not gullible or stupid. Just talk to her, and then you can discern what feels real. At least you will know you did everything possible to get the truth before you married him and exposed your children, present or future, to this man and marriage.

- Talk about everything you learned with at least two friends or family members who seem wise in their ability to see and speak the truth. Be very careful about sharing his personal information with people who will not keep your confidences or who will hold it against him later. You may want to ask for permission to discuss it with someone. (However, at this stage, you are not married to him. Your first loyalty is to yourself and your future.) But definitely discuss the information with someone—a counselor, if necessary, to protect his privacy—so you can be sure it makes sense and rings true as you talk out loud about it with others. If the other person has the same impressions as you about how wisely he has worked to resolve the problem, you will likely feel more trust and confidence in him and your decision to remain in the relationship.

You may greatly respect and appreciate him for being so honest; yet you must still decide if the issues you now see are:

- Ones you can choose because they are acceptable.
- Ones you can choose because you respect how he is handling (or has handled) his problem (he showed emotional maturity).
- Ones you are open to learning more about so you can increase your coping skills for being effective with the issues and increase your options for supporting him as he resolves the issues.
- Ones you can choose willingly, without resentment, and without fear of becoming someone you would not want to become (a nag, someone who is depressed all the time, or someone who has no life or hobbies because of the problem).
- Ones you just can't live with.

The quality of your life is up to you. It is your responsibility to choose what is best for you and your children. (If you don't currently have any children, you may likely have some in the future. How might these issues affect them?) No one else can decide what is best for you like you can (and no one else will worry like you do when you see the effects of these issues on your children). Trust your judgment. Think of what is best for you now and in the future, because later you may find love is *not* enough.

If the issues seem acceptable or are ones you would be willing to learn more about, do the following:

1. Ask him if he would be open to you learning more about the problem together. Suggest getting counseling, reading books about it, or talking openly about it as needed until

you feel more confident about the issue and your options for managing the problem effectively.

2. Ask him to describe how he intends to manage his problem. Ask him how you can support him, but resist owning his problem or acting in a way that makes you more responsible for fixing the problem than he is.

3. Accept the problem as one you choose (at least for now). Avoid assuming a victim position, resenting him for it, or feeling deceived. Going through appropriate stages of grief, surprise, and sadness about the issue may be needed, but accepting responsibility for your choice to remain in the relationship is necessary if you are to begin managing the issue more effectively.

4. Accept responsibility for the problems and issues you bring to the relationship, and be willing to make similar commitments to improvement and progress.

For the next four to six months:

• Observe how he talks about the problem, responds to your needs relative to the problem, and takes actions to correct the problem (especially in those areas where it affects you).

• Be careful to not care more about his problems or take more action to fix his problems than he does.

• Resist any temptation on your part to worry about, criticize, or try to control portions of the problem that do not affect you and likely will not affect you. (For example: if he is managing his work responsibly, there is no real threat of him losing his job, so do not preoccupy yourself with the things you think he could be doing better at work).

• Define what you would need resolved relative to the problem before you could consider becoming engaged or getting married.

If you see him handle the problem with increasing self-control, concern for others, and an abundance of statements and actions that show he is taking personal responsibility, you will likely feel more confidence in him and the future of your relationship. These kinds of responsible and self-controlled actions may encourage you to move forward with the relationship with more confidence in his skills of emotional maturity and in your future.

CASE STUDY
REVIEW

THERAPEUTIC ASSESSMENT

Hunter felt immediately uncomfortable with some of the questions Marissa asked. It wasn't difficult to talk about his past drug and alcohol use, since he hadn't had any problems with either of them, but talking about his masturbation and pornography history was difficult for him. He had a few issues in the past with them. He preferred to stay away from pornography and masturbation and strived to do so, but even recently he had viewed a few pictures and masturbated.

Hunter knew his viewing of pornography would be hurtful to Marissa, though he honestly wasn't sure why so many women take it so personally. Nonetheless, he didn't want to see Marissa in pain over it, and he feared being shamed or criticized. He had worked at avoiding pornography and masturbation in the past and would be willing to work on it again to help Marissa feel the confidence and loyalty she needed, but would Marissa trust him and his statements? He feared he was going to be in a lose/lose position if he told her what she wanted to know, but he told her anyway.

Marissa's reactions and follow-up questions remained respectful and warm, so it became easier and easier for Hunter to tell her what she needed to know. At the end of the conversation, Hunter felt a bit relieved to know he had held nothing back.

Marissa was deeply concerned about living with pornography or mastur-bation in a marriage. It was offensive to her and fed on her self-doubts. She shared this with Hunter and asked him to come up with a plan for how he was going to prevent viewing pornography in the future and how he would tell her if he did view it. He felt willing to help her feel better and hoped his efforts might strengthen their relationship, so he committed to do what Marissa needed. She decided to just trust his efforts, watch, wait, and see what he did with the issue.

The more they talked about his issues (and hers) over the next few months, the more she felt confident in his honesty. He even let her check his computer and Internet browsing history anytime she wanted because he knew honesty was the bigger issue, and he wanted her to feel confident that he wasn't hiding anything. This meant a lot to Marissa and added to her faith that he was handling the problem with self-control, personal responsibility, and empathy for her feelings. After learning more about pornography and seeing his reactions to her needs, she began to feel they could manage the issue in a way that she could feel good about, especially because he seemed committed to staying away from pornography.

Nonetheless, a few months later, Marissa was still anxious that Hunter might be hiding something. In many ways, she knew this fear was not based on fact. Hunter had demonstrated his honesty. He openly answered her questions, and she never found any fact inconsistent with what he told her, but she still felt on guard.

One night, Hunter stated, "I know why you have the issues you do. I know most of them come from your first marriage, and I am okay with it for now, but I am looking forward to the day I am innocent until proven guilty and not the other way around." Marissa realized in that moment the depth of his sacrifices. She didn't feel ashamed or bad about the fact that she had needed to ask so much from him (that was just life and the demands of a mature relationship), but she did realize that if they were to progress, she would have to start trusting her judgment of him as a good and honest man and move on with faith and trust in him.

Over the next few weeks and months, she made a conscious effort to resolve her issues and to show him the trust and faith he had earned and deserved. They got married six months later, and trust has never been an issue since.

Notes
1. Chapman, Gary D. *The Five Love Languages: How to express heartfelt commitment to your mate.* Chicago: Northfield Publishing, 2004.
2. Schlessinger, Laura. *The Proper Care and Feeding of Husbands.* New York: HaperCollins Publishers Inc., 2004.
3. Schlessinger, Laura. *Woman Power: The Companion to the Proper Care and Feeding of Husbands.* New York: HaperCollins Publishers Inc., 2004.
4. Gottman, John M. and Nan Silver. *The Seven Principles for Making Marriage Work: A practical guide from the country's foremost relationship expert.* New York: Crown Publishers Inc., 1999.
   Gottman, John, PhD. *Why Marriages Succeed or Fail: And how you can make yours last.* New York: Simon and Schuster, 1994.

chapter sixteen

From engagement to marriage

Once in the Final Stretch of the Dating Game, you will have to make many decisions and face many challenges before you reach the Final Goal (marriage). You will have to decide if the relationship you have developed and encouraged over the last year is one you want to continue with more permanence and commitment; you will have to recognize, address, and accept the challenges that both of you bring to the relationship; and you will have to act in a way that encourages the process so it will progress toward marriage.* With these challenges in mind, the Coach will provide two new game play strategies for you during this important stage of engagement to marriage.

Game play strategy number 17 will help you clarify the challenges you might face in choosing the man you love so you can love your choice, and number 18 will help move and encourage the man you love to ask you to marry him through always keeping him in pursuit of you.

When you marry a man, you marry his problems, his children from

....
* Whether you are considering marriage or are just beginning to date, you may still find this chapter and chapter 17 helpful since they will coach you through the mistakes you will want to avoid. Once you are in a relationship, you may want to review these chapters again, since it will have a renewed relevance to your situation.

GAME PLAY STRATEGY #17
Choose your Love. Love your choice.

GAME PLAY STRATEGY #18
Always keep him in pursuit of you.

CASE STUDY

Taylor felt anxious, frustrated, and powerless about the slow progress of her relationship. She had been dating Ben for over a year. She loved him, trusted him, and knew she wanted to marry him, but he seemed content to keep the relationship as it was. She couldn't understand his fears about moving forward with the relationship. What more could she possibly do to convince him that they should get married? Did he not love her as much as she loved him? Was he just content and comfortable with her but didn't see her as the type of woman he would really like to be with? Was she wasting her time because he would never really marry her?

Taylor believed Ben was a good catch, but it wasn't like he didn't have issues. He had a child from a previous marriage (which would limit the amount of time they would have alone together as well as their financial freedom since he was responsible for a considerable amount of child support each month). He had an ex-wife who seemed unstable and manipulative (and as such, more likely to create stress for Ben and her from time to time). And his work placed a lot of demands on his time (sending him out of town and even calling him at all hours of the night). Their relationship would inevitably be stressed on occasion by these circumstances. So Taylor often felt a bit unappreciated and even resentful that Ben didn't realize how much she was willing to work with and accept his issues. Was he not committed to doing the same with her? Several of Taylor's friends had given her advice that she feared would only make her seem unloving, critical, or nagging if she followed it. She also feared giving him an ultimatum of getting married or breaking up, because she wasn't sure she was ready to end the relationship just because he wasn't ready for marriage. She felt powerless and simply didn't know what to do to help the relationship progress.

previous relationships, his family, his financial limitations, and his needs. Likewise, he does the same with you. But you don't just bring your issues and problems to a marriage. You also bring your strengths and love.

On a separate piece of paper, define what you would be choosing if you choose your love. *Much of the information you need about the problems you will probably experience in marriage are evident in your relationship even now (especially if you followed the tips in chapter 15)—but you may feel more confident in your ability to make this choice if you complete the following questions, take some premarital tests together, and seek premarital counseling.*

Define what you would be choosing if you chose your love.

On a separate piece of paper, answer the following questions about your current relationship.

1. What are the problems you believe you will likely face in this marriage (financial stresses, communication problems, religious differences, cultural differences, sexual struggles, family problems, emotional problems like depression or anxiety, parenting differences, step-parenting, and blended family issues)?

2. What is your plan for dealing with these problems?

3. In what ways might you be incompatible with each other?

4. Do you experience problems communicating effectively in these areas?

5. What problems might you or he have with:

exercising **self-control** (over emotions, eating, anger, spending, substance use, pornography)?

expressing **empathy** (through showing concern for a spouse's feelings or perspective, respecting a spouse's belongings, encouraging a spouse's interests, putting the children's needs above one's own selfish desires)?

or taking **personal responsibility** (through taking actions to change problems, personally accepting when he is or either of you are in the wrong rather than blaming, excusing, or avoiding responsibility)?

How might these issues affect your relationship?

6. If either of you have children, what problems might these children face personally (ADD, learning issues, anger management problems)? How can you help the children work through those problems and adjust to the new marriage (since they didn't choose any of your or their parents' problems or decisions)?

7. How might issues with your extended families or ex-spouses cause problems in the marriage?

8. What strengths do you both bring to this marriage that will help you manage your problems more effectively?

9. How might you cope better with these problems if you recognize that you chose them instead of reacting as if these problems were forced upon you?

10. What reactions from either of you might make your problems worse, not better? How could either of you help prevent these reactions?

11. Does the man you are considering marrying match the kind of man you said you wanted to marry from chapter 9? If so, how? If not, why or why not?

12. Define what his and your role should be in addressing the problems you have described above.

13. If you choose this man, his problems, and this relationship, could you see yourself being happy with him? Why or why not?

When two people are compatible, have good communication, and possess the skills of emotional maturity, they are more likely to effectively manage their problems and succeed in marriage. Making sure you have these qualities in your relationship before you get married may help you stay committed when marriage gets unexpectedly complicated and hard. Making the decision to marry the man you love when you are fully aware of your potential trials and challenges is no easy task, but when you move forward with your eyes open and your mind and heart fully committed to the man you love and the life you are choosing, you will likely approach the situation with greater wisdom, faith, hope, and effectiveness. In essence, you will both be *choosing your love and choosing to love your choice.*

Can you in good faith and conscience choose this man and willingly endure with patience the trials that come with him? YES/NO_____

If you answered no, it might be best for him and you if you do not choose to marry him. If yes, never forget that you chose the problems you have foreseen. You are no victim to them. You had a choice and you made it. It is now your responsibility to embrace, love, and maximize your choice to the best of your ability.

If you decide to continue your relationship, you may find the following ideas about the male psychology, the mistakes women make, and the tips that follow helpful as you try to progress the relationship toward marriage.

♂ Have a male-friendly psychology

Secrets #1 through #17 of the male psychology gave you the basic information you needed to more successfully navigate dating to this point. The additional information you need to succeed from here should now come from the good man you love. Many, if not all, of the seventeen secrets will continue to apply to him and your relationship, but receiving clarification from him about his needs, thoughts, and feelings will be necessary if your marriage is to be successful and if you are to have the trust and confidence in him that both of you need. The good man you love needs to become your guide to the secrets of his male psychology. Thus, to have a male-friendly psychology, ask him how!

Warning! A man's descriptions of how he and other men think can sometimes be aggravating and elicit strong feelings that their ways are simply flawed; however, if you listen carefully, ask more questions, and take the time to see it from your man's perspective, it will make so many things you have observed about men more clear. You may not initially like what you discover, but you will be amazed at how much sense it will begin to make. In time, you may even come to appreciate the simplicity behind how men think about their relationships. Once you learn to understand the man you love, you may find negotiating your needs, pleasing him, and enjoying the relationship is easier than you previously thought.

⚠ Exercise CAUTION—potential hazards exist and can cause injuries

If you want to move toward marriage, you would be wise to avoid some of the following mistakes.

MISTAKE #18: Women often waste their time in a dead-end relationship that has little chance for progressing toward marriage.

A woman who has made the mistake of being the convenient friend (mistake #6), the good-for-now-girl (mistake #11), or the rebound/recovery girl (mistake #13) may hope her love will eventually win the commitment and loyalty she desires from the man she so eagerly serves, but if she looked at the situation realistically, she would likely see that it will not (especially if he was only in the relationship because it was too easy and convenient to end). A man usually knows if he would eventually want to marry a woman. Good-for-now girls rarely become more than that. If a man feels pretty confident he could get something better anytime he wants it, he will likely feel there is no point in limiting his options through marriage.

The SECRETS that explain *why*: #2, #3, #4

Hint: If you have been hanging on to the hope that your status as a friend, your willingness to please, and your love and support will eventually win the heart of the man you love, your best bet is to find out what he is logically looking for in a relationship. If you do not fit that description, you need to know so you can end the relationship and move on. He may be just enjoying the convenience of the relationship (all the while knowing he would never marry you). However, if you fit that description, he may be content to avoid commitment for as long as you seem willing to not demand it.

If you pressure him to commit and he feels restless about making that commitment because he is not sure if he could still do better, he may prefer to break up with you to test his other options. Therefore, if you have maintained a relationship for over a year and he seems unwilling to progress toward marriage, you might be wise to push the issue rather than waste more time in a potentially dead-end relationship. He is either "into" you or he is not.[1] You need to find out before you waste more time. Pursuing commitment is one way to define if he has any intentions of marrying you. If you end the relationship, be prepared for him to not know what he had with you until he has lost you. He may be likely to not really believe he has lost you until you are long gone, so don't keep looking back, wondering if he has gotten a clue yet. Move on as if he is not there. If he ends up figuring out that he wants you before you are with someone else, great. If not, good news—you are with someone else.

MISTAKE #19: Once in committed relationships, women often train their men to not pursue them or sacrifice for them.

After a man and woman become comfortable in their relationship, a woman often makes it easy for her man to stop pursuing her and sacrificing for her. This makes the relationship easy, comfortable, and secure (which for a man can sometimes be boring or easy to take for granted). A woman may do this in several ways, from calling him all the time to always being available, dropping in frequently, telling him he doesn't need to pay for date nights anymore, and even taking care of all the problems in their lives (the cars, the yard, the bills, the dry cleaning, the needs of friends and family members). These behaviors hamper the relationship and make it less likely to progress toward marriage.[2]

When a woman (or wife) calls a man (or husband) frequently, never goes out with friends, or waits on him hand and foot, she denies him the opportunity to miss her. When she quickly does everything herself, she makes it easy for him to let her. He doesn't feel a need to pursue or sacrifice for her because she is always there and everything is always done. He then begins to think about her and the relationship only 5 percent of the time instead of the 20 percent of the time he used to spend. There is no challenge or need to spend more time focusing his thoughts or energies on her. He knows she will always be there. He can take the relationship for granted.

Even if you do what you think is the opposite of doing things for him (impatiently nagging, criticizing, and demanding things of him), you will in so many words be telling him you don't trust his commitment to you or his competence to do the task (which will not solicit his support as much as it will create his defensiveness and avoidance of you).

Remember, men fall in love through serving and sacrificing; they are driven to succeed and face challenges, and they need to be needed and trusted. Thus, a man's sense of belonging and importance in the relationship (as well as his sense of self-respect) depends upon him being indispensable and his sacrifices being valued and needed in the lives of those he loves. When a man's sense of challenge, success, and importance cannot be found in his primary relationships, he is more likely to become increasingly self-centered and self-indulging. His relationship does not make him feel masculine, important, and needed, so he looks for emotional fulfillment elsewhere (through flirting, buying toys, working, hanging out with friends, drinking, gambling, viewing pornography, or having affairs).

When this happens, men will also resist making their life and relationships more difficult, demanding, or complicated without good reason. Marriage isn't normally a challenge men look forward to (with all of its demands and losses of freedom); thus, why would a man feel driven to add more work and complications to a relationship that he can take for granted just the way it is?

The SECRETS that explain *why*: #1, #2, #4, #6, #9, #12

Hint: Start practicing patience, tolerance, and faith in him while lovingly communicating your needs, and trust in him to meet these needs (albeit in his own unique way). He will become more invested, involved, and loyal to you through his sacrifice for you. Use the 7–11 rule, which is in the tips that follow. Get him back in the habit of pursuing you, and then show a lot of appreciation and love in return. Once he is in the habit of sacrificing for you and feels like a hero who makes you happy, he will not want to lose you. The inconveniences and complications of marriage will not be too high of a price to keep you (if he logically believes he is somewhat ready for marriage). He will ask you to marry him and will be anxious to make you his permanently. You just need to avoid the trap (now and forever more) of training him out of pursuing you and sacrificing for you.

MISTAKE #20: Women are often too eager to discuss marriage when in a relationship, which can cause men to back off or get frightened away.

Women who seem eager in the first few months to talk about marriage and serious commitments may burden the relationship before a man is sufficiently invested in it. A man who has not convinced himself that he wants a relationship with her enough to sacrifice more and more for it will become repelled by pressure to increase his sacrifices.

A woman who tries to pace her commitments at or below the level the man seems interested in pursuing will remain a challenge and prevent frightening him away. This can sometimes be a difficult and confusing process for a woman because a man may bring up the idea of marriage, meeting his family soon, or going on an expensive vacation together six months down the road, but as soon as she jumps all over the idea, he might become anxious and stressed by the pressure these developments contribute to the relationship and back off. She may then look (to him) like the pursuer while he feels like the prey that must make a quick escape.

The SECRETS that explain *why*: #2, #3, #4, #15

Hint: You would be wise to hold back on believing a man is ready to progress the relationship until his behaviors and words remain consistent and persistent over time. By doing so, you will be less likely to pressure him. However, you would also be wise to let him know that somewhere around nine months to a year into a relationship, you will be deciding whether or not the relationship has the potential to progress toward marriage. If it doesn't appear to have that potential, you will begin exploring dating others again. Then drop the subject. Don't bring it up again—he heard you.

As the common mistakes above illustrate, you do not have to ask a man to marry you if he is totally "into" you. He will play his role. You just need to know how to encourage and support him in his pursuit of you.

If you play your role, he'll play his

The role you have played from the first flirt to now will be in many ways the same role you will play throughout the years to come. The secret to success with a man is found in your ability to encourage him to keep pursuing you. The best way to do this is through responding to any of his efforts and sacrifices with your warmth, femininity, and love. A man will sacrifice much to keep getting love and affection. The ticket to keeping a man anxious to come home, willing to complete honey-do lists, and motivated to buy you flowers is the love and appreciation you give him in return.

The following tips will give you specific ideas on how to keep him in pursuit of you. They should work at any stage in your relationship, from early dating through fifty years of marriage. These tips, when followed, will work as long as you are with a good man and being loving, appreciative, warm, and affectionate with him.

TIPS for always keeping him in the habit of pursuing you

- Avoid the temptation to call him more often than he calls you overall. On those days when you don't need to talk to him right away, limit your calls so he will have the opportunity to miss you.
- When he calls or attempts to pursue you in any way, be warm, excited to hear from him, and glad he wanted to talk with you. Be happy and cheerful.
- Seem busy and happy when he calls you. He will likely feel that you seem somehow more attractive or challenging.

He may even feel a slight degree of anxiety and a stronger need to keep connected with you. Thus, he will be less likely to take you for granted. *If you discover that getting busier, though you remained warm and inviting, proved to only make him drop you out of his life, he was probably not as "into" you as you were "into" him. You are better off discovering his apathy toward the relationship now—rather than two years from now—so get busy.*

- When he walks across a room and wraps his arms around you, melt a little into them and snuggle up for a minute (your reaction will help reinforce and reward his behavior, making it more likely he will do it again).
- When you hear him brag about you to his friends, wink at him.
- When he goes out of his way to always kiss you before he leaves, enthusiastically give him two extra kisses.
- When he invites you to do something recreational (that you really don't enjoy much), recognize the fact that he wanted to spend the time bonding with you, and go make it fun. Remember how much he doesn't want to change your tire or listen to you talk for thirty minutes about your problems with the neighbors, but he does it anyway.
- When he leaves you love notes or does anything you find romantic, loving, or exciting, tell him how much you appreciated it, make him a great meal, or give him a hug (whatever his primary love language is).
- Try not to be around him all the time so he can develop the habit of stopping, looking around, and wondering where you are sometimes. If you are always there, he'll be more likely to take you for granted. Let him know that he is your first priority and you will always fit him in if you can or have enough notice, but do not drop plans with friends or family on short notice (unless there are special circumstances).[3]
- Encourage and support his desires to do things with the guys. He'll be likely to enjoy his time away but be even more likely to pursue you and your time when he comes back. *Let him know what activities would interfere with your feelings of safety and security in the relationships (such*

as going to singles clubs, flirting, or spending so much time with the guys that you are in second place or neglected). As long as he is willing to respect those needs that make you feel safe and secure, do not try to tell him how to be a man when with other men. Give him the space to pursue his guy time in his own way. Don't put down, criticize, or tease him for the things he and his friends enjoy doing.

- Be flirtatious with him often. Dress up. Wear makeup. You are more likely to act flirtatious when you look good.
- Don't bring up marriage, talk about how things would be if you and he got married, or how much you would like to be his wife. You will know you are playing your role and using these tips effectively because he will want to spend time with you, tell you that you would be a great wife, or suggest that you go ring shopping with him. When he does this, give him a great smile and be warm, responsive, and sweet, but don't get too excited about it, and definitely seem resistant to taking him too seriously. Most men toy with the idea in theory but aren't ready to put it into action. Don't assume he is really serious, or he will feel cornered. Don't get too excited; he might back off or run. Instead, tell him you are not interested in talking about such things until you know he is truly serious about it. No matter how serious he seems that night, resist believing him. Be warm and loving but state you are not sure if he is certain until you have a ring and a wedding date. If he truly is serious, he will make a point of letting you know his intentions (that night and the next and when he gives you the ring).

The more a man feels like a success in the relationship (because he knows he makes you happy), the more he will desire to pursue you, call you, and spend time with you. The more a man thinks about you during the day and spends time serving you, the more he could never imagine being without you. The more investment he makes in your relationship, the deeper his sense of loyalty and commitment to the relationship will become. But how do you, or any other woman, encourage a man to give that much of his mental energy, time, and investment to the relationship when you feel you have to passively wait for him to pursue you (since you can't risk becoming the pursuer yourself)? Does a guy just naturally become that intensely involved in meeting your needs, or do you have to encourage the process?

If you are to be successful in progressing your relationship to marriage, you will need to do more than passively wait to respond to his attention and efforts. You can inspire and invite him to do quite a bit more for the relationship than he might do naturally through using the 7–11 rule.

To use the 7–11 rule

- Consider your top three love languages (as discussed in chapter 16: words, gifts, touch, acts of service, and spending time together).[4] Clarify the ways you like to receive love the most (flowers, help around the house, kisses before you leave, reassuring words, long walks together).
- Touch him on the arm, back, neck, or shoulders, and express to him how much you enjoy getting love in these ways. Put words of emotion into your descriptions (for example: say, "I love it when I get flowers," "I feel so appreciative when you help me around the house," "I feel so loved and important when you call me before you go to bed").
- Then ask him if he would be willing to do those behaviors again sometime because you appreciate them so much. Say "would you," not "could you." Men *can* do many things, which often makes them feel like they *should* do it because they *can*. However, when someone asks if a man "would be willing" to do something, then his actions are a gift and an option. He gets to be a hero, not just someone who is doing his duty.
- If he says he would be glad to but fails to follow through, trust that he meant to please you but just forgot. Many people need to hear things in repetition (five to seven times) before they will remember something (even when it is important). Be patient with him until he gets in the habit of remembering your desires.
- Commit yourself to waiting a little while (at least a week or month) and then expressing your desire or need again

without commenting on how you have already mentioned it. If he forgets and doesn't fulfill your request again, don't focus on it. Be happy, warm, and appreciative about the things he is doing. Give it more time and make the request again.

- Commit yourself to continue expressing and asserting your need or desire seven to eleven times. Be sure to do this in loving ways, especially the first five to seven times. If you express your need with anger, criticism, complaining, or a scolding tone (because he keeps forgetting), don't count it. Around the fifth time, it may be appropriate to briefly express sadness or confusion about why he hasn't followed through with your request when he said he would, but try to not be critical or negative, just confused or hurt. Once you add some personal but brief expressions of sadness, it will often increase his motivation to please you, especially since you have been so patient.

- Any time from that point on, if he takes action to please you, get excited. Show him you appreciated it by doing something for him that is his love language (give him a big hug, tell him how much you enjoyed it in an animated way, buy him a gift, spend a lot of time with him).

- A few weeks or months later, make the same or another request. Tell him how special and secure it does (or would) make you feel and how much you do (or will) appreciate his sacrifices for you and your needs.

- If he follows through with your request, immediately reward his efforts with love and appreciation. As you continue to repeat this process, he will get in the habit of remembering and doing things he knows please you. The more he feels like a success in pleasing you, the more he will want to please you, and the more he will feel he can handle the task of pleasing you in marriage.

- *Warning: If by the eleventh time you have lovingly expressed your need and he still has not met your request, stop asking. If he hasn't met your need by then, it is not because he didn't understand or remember your request. It is because he is intentionally withholding your needs from you (which is something those who use a passive aggressive response are likely to do—the more you want something, the more they will withhold it or give it to you grudgingly and with strings attached). If this is the case, seriously reconsider the relationship but don't keep asking for what you want—it just gives him power to hurt you. The reason this process is called the 7–11 rule is that by the seventh time, a good man will usually give you what you need, whereas by the eleventh time the emotionally immature will still not freely and lovingly give you what you need. This is one simple tool for defining those who are potentially abusive and manipulative from those who are good men who just need your faith and loving, consistent, and repetitive communication and patience.*

The tips for keeping him in pursuit of you along with the 7–11 rule should help keep your man thinking about you and sacrificing for you. However, you should also frequently review chapter 15. The skills you learn there (such as the five love languages, the importance of doing things and activities, the need to avoid criticism and contempt, the necessity of keeping the positive to negative ratio five to one) will be important to your relationship's ongoing health, progress, and success.

When building and solidifying a man's commitment to the relationship, there is one thing you should rarely (or never) do—threaten to end the relationship, especially when angry or on a whim. Throwing around threats of abandonment greatly damages the relationship. Think through any threat to leave or significantly change the relationship until you are ready to take action (even if you are in a bad relationship*). Those who manipulatively threaten relationships or give ultimatums to make the relationship progress toward marriage will likely find they damage the relationship more than they cause it to progress. Be emotionally honest about any threats you make to the relationship. Make sure you are only threatening to leave it because it is necessary for your continued progress because of

....
* If you are giving an abundance of love and getting abuse, demands, criticism, or neglect in return, you are likely not with an emotionally mature man and may be wise to end the relationship sooner rather than later. However, most people are rarely ready to follow through with threats they make on a whim, even when there is abuse. Take more time and get support before you try to leave or you may find you just end up going back. Additionally, never use threats of breaking up as a tool for making a man change who he is (it won't last). Be with someone who is a compatible fit with your needs, and let him find someone who will appreciate him as he is.

the relationship's lack of progress, unhealthiness, or incompatibility with your needs or desires. Think it through well.

Think of threats to the relationship as an unstable bridge that can only handle one or two crossings before it might collapse. Don't use it unless absolutely necessary, or you may find that once you are on the other side of the bridge, there is no coming back.

If you strongly believe you need to (and are ready to) change the relationship, unless there is a commitment of marriage, then clearly express your positive emotions about him and the relationship before you make the change. Acting cool, cold, angry, or mysterious as a way of clueing a man in to your needs will not usually work. A man won't typically figure out what you are feeling or needing unless you explain it. Your coldness, distance, or anger will only make him feel rejected and cause him to believe you need your space. Instead, express your positive emotions for him and then explain what you would need him to do if he would like the relationship to continue. Then give him his space and time to figure out what he wants to do about the situation.

Warning: If you use the 7–11 rule with a man and it doesn't get a positive response from him until after you threaten to end the relationship, know that he is passive aggressive. He may now be ready to marry you, but he will only continue to act passive aggressive or aggressive once married. Don't go back. He is probably not going to change. After marriage, he will only do the minimum necessary to keep you (and oftentimes, only after you threaten to end the relationship again).

CASE STUDY
REVIEW

THERAPEUTIC ASSESSMENT

In the beginning, Ben had always been passionate about pursuing Taylor, but lately it seemed she was the pursuer and he was the prey, which was making Taylor feel insecure, sad, moody, and irritable. She knew there were two possibilities for making herself feel better: (1) Ben could resume the role of pursuing her, which would make her feel more confident and safe in the relationship or (2) she could start doing more things to make herself feel happy and fulfilled. She only had control over the second option, which scared her because she didn't want to distance herself from him, but she also knew that to be true to herself she couldn't stay in this relationship for more than three to six more months without a hope of marriage. She would need to move on at some point if the relationship didn't progress, so if she started to spend more time with friends and family or pursuing her hobbies, she would be in a better position either way.

Pursuing her happiness separate from Ben seemed like a practical solution, though it was a bit depressing. But there was also the possibility that if she started focusing more on her life and less on Ben, he might feel less pursued and more like pursuing again—but she could not be sure of that. She just had to have faith that the kind of man she was looking for would pursue and marry her if Ben did not.

So she stopped any behaviors that seemed like she was pursuing Ben (such as calling him more often than he called her, talking to him about marriage, or nagging him about the things he wasn't doing for her). She increased her love, warmth, and appreciation of his behaviors when he did pursue her (such as calling to say hi, asking to spend time with her, going out of his way to snuggle up with her, or doing something for her). She started calling him only when absolutely necessary and started making her time with him something he would have to ask for in advance (by expressing her sad regret that she couldn't see him the night he called but would love to make plans with him for the next day or weekend). And she started calling her friends and family more to go do things together.

She hated having to be so formal and rule-oriented like in the early days of when they had first begun dating, but she had fallen into the mistake of making the relationship comfortable and unchallenging. Now she had to step back so he could step forward.

About a week after she changed her behavior, she felt it best to let Ben know that she had been feeling depressed about their relationship and Ben's indecisiveness and knew she just needed to get busier and happier in her life. She told him he was still a great priority and she loved him; she just didn't feel good about living her life around his when he wasn't sure of his commitment to her. She stated, "I just need to pull back and match your efforts and commitment level—rather than exceed it. So, that is why I am changing my behavior."

At first Ben didn't notice much of a change at all or even worry much about it (though he sent her flowers the day after their talk). It took a week or more before he realized that she wasn't calling as much, but that was somewhat of a relief. He started calling her a little more (just because he wanted her to know he loved her), but for the most part he didn't feel worried about the changes. Life seemed good, their relationship had less pressure, and he felt comfortable.

However, Ben's feelings of comfort shifted one Friday night (about five weeks after their talk) when he called and Taylor stated she was heading out the door to go to a movie. He asked her whom she was going with. She said she was going by herself. He then said, "I'll take you. Just give me about an hour and I'll come get you." She replied, "I'm sorry but when you woke up this morning, did you have the impression that we were going on a date tonight?" He said, "No." She gave a long pause and then said, "That was my impression as well. I need to go to the movie without you. I love you, and I can do this on my own. Good night."

He then started to realize how many things she had been doing on her own lately. With that, he began to feel anxious about Taylor's ability and determination to live without him. He started to fear they were becoming too distant and he could lose her. She was so warm and loving; he didn't want to drive her away or live without her.

He started calling her every day and complaining that they were drifting apart. She continued to maintain some resistance to spending more time with him but stated that if he made plans with her in advance, she would usually be able to make time for him and do occasional spur-of-the-moment activities with him. She still didn't call him more often than he called her, and she rarely rescheduled plans once she scheduled them with friends. She also seemed to be avoiding the topic of marriage (though he wasn't bringing it up either). By the third month, he began hinting that they should go ring shopping. He had to mention it three times before she finally went with him. They were engaged by the fourth month.

Notes
1. Behrendt, Greg and Liz Tuccillo. *He's Just Not That into You: The no excuses truth to understanding guys.* New York: Simon Spotlight Entertainment, 2004.
2. Gray, John, PhD. *Men Are from Mars, Women Are from Venus: The classic guide to understanding the opposite sex.* New York: Quill, 1992.
3. Fein, Ellen and Sherrie Schneider. *The Rules: Time-tested secrets for capturing the heart of Mr. Right.* New York: Warner Books, 1995.
4. Chapman, *The Five Love Languages.*

chapter seventeen

The art of making
two hearts become one

Leaving the Dating Game and moving into married life has many ups and downs. The excitement and thrill of a new, passionate relationship can quickly settle into boredom and disillusionment. Yet, when an emotionally mature woman is with a good man, she keeps a greater perspective on his goodness than she does on his slow and often uninterested efforts to fix things around the house, his occasional disheveled appearance, his tendency to grope or playfully pinch her when the kids are just in the other room, and his filthy, cluttered, or disorganized garage, bedroom, or office.

An emotionally mature woman keeps the bigger picture in mind because she understands and appreciates everything else he brings to the relationship. She knows her recognition of his contribution and sacrifices make him feel more content, loyal, fulfilled, happy, and giving in family life. And she knows that her gratitude goes a long way in helping him to overlook her many annoying, somewhat controlling, critical, demanding, and emotionally inconsistent behaviors as well.

It is a husband's and wife's willingness to overlook each other's personal, mostly benign, bad habits and annoying ways, while emphasizing each other's strengths, intentions, and good natures that keeps them focused on what matters most—their commitment to their marriage and family. In this way they become one, with a singular goal that means more to them than anything else.

When a lifetime of decisions has led to good and bad consequences, no amount of success or failure in the world seems to matter as much as having succeeded in marriage and family relationships. When two lives have been driven by care and concern for the other, a desire to improve and change, and a willingness to control selfish behaviors for the greater good of the marriage and family, a man and woman can truly feel self-respect, contentment, and gratitude for seeing past individual moments of criticism and into the heart of the person they love. It takes both individuals' sacrifices to create the opportunities and lasting blessings that make individuals and marriages complete; thus, the sacrificing of two makes them become one.

As the Coach helps you past the Final Goal, she knows your marital success depends upon a new goal or purpose, to become one with your spouse (which is your final game play strategy).

GAME PLAY STRATEGY #19
Become united.

CASE STUDY

Marissa had always looked forward to marriage with a good man, which she had great confidence Hunter was. However, she was surprised, confused, and somewhat frustrated by how different she and Hunter were.

Marissa's first husband had always been complacent, easy-going, and private about his feelings, needs, and opinions during their short marriage, while Hunter was communicative, opinionated, and assertive about his (which was one of the reasons she trusted and respected Hunter enough to marry him). She knew her ex-husband's people-pleasing behavior was probably linked to his secretive double life and emotional immaturity, so she had been very specific in looking for someone who would be completely honest, up front, and loyal to her; however, she had not expected marriage with Hunter to be so entirely different and in some ways more difficult than her first marriage.

She almost felt as if she had never been married before. Every time she and Hunter talked about something, it was as if he was coming from such a completely different perspective that she wasn't sure how they would negotiate their differences (her ex-husband had never expressed such feelings, problems, or opinions). She often felt Hunter's perspectives were outright wrong and shortsighted, especially as he shared his thoughts about how men think or what they need. She wasn't sure how to express her faith and trust in him when he seemed so slow to complete projects, which he insisted she let him do in his own way. And she often felt confused by her frustration and lack of interest in sex, which he seemed to want more often than she did. None of these problems had been an issue in her first marriage because her ex-husband had always told her what she wanted to hear, waited for her to bring up issues, dodged their problems, and seemed silent and apathetic, though brooding, about their sexual relationship. Thus, her second marriage seemed strange and uncomfortable in some ways.

She couldn't deny that Hunter's approach to their relationship seemed honest, assertive, and committed (which made her feel ten times more secure in his loyalty to her than she had felt in her first marriage), but she was surprised by how different they were in how they perceived life, their problems, and their marriage. How could they become more comfortable and united when they seemed so different? Or was there just something wrong with their relationship?

Becoming united will require both of you to develop greater feelings of respect and empathy for each other. Developing and refining your ability to empathize with your spouse will only happen as you seek to understand and respect his perspective without a desire to control or change his views (which empathy and respect he should offer you as well).

This is not to say that those who empathize with others do not on occasion contribute to the person's ability to change. Those who are loving and accepting often have great influence on others. It just means that truly accepting and understanding someone as they are right now involves respecting their right to change or not change. When you observe someone's past and present experiences and how those experiences have shaped the person's thoughts, feelings, and behaviors, while lovingly respecting where they are now (without imposing where you think they should be), you will likely find the person is endeared to your love and respect. What husband or wife does not desire this kind acceptance from their spouse?

Having a male-friendly psychology (and female-friendly psychology) means accepting and respecting men (and women) for all that makes them different. Women often look at how men think and act differently than they do and conclude that men are flawed and wrong for doing so (and vice versa). Just because someone is male (or female) does not mean he (or she) is wrong. How is it that one-half of the world can be wrong just because they are different from the other half? Men and women think, feel, act, and need in many similar and different ways, and they are both right for doing so.

When a bridge is developed between the male and female minds, more understanding and peace can be found between the sexes. To help provide that bridge, you may benefit from the following tips.

TIPS for becoming united in marriage

The following tips build on everything you have learned so far with special attention to some common issues in marriage. When followed, these tips will not only help you show respect for his male psychology, but they will also help you address the issues that are common to your female psychology.

- **When feeling insecure about whether your husband is attracted to you, whether he believes you are sexy, or whether he secretly wishes you would lose twenty pounds,** realize that sharing these thoughts or fears with him will only put him and you in a lose/lose position. No matter what he says that is positive, he knows you will likely not believe him, you will only think he is trying to be nice, or you will find something wrong with what he says. So instead, go look in the mirror, find five loving things to say to yourself about yourself, review in your mind all the loving things your husband says about you, and then repeat in your mind, "My husband is no fool. He would not have sought a relationship with me, pursued me, and then married me if he wasn't attracted to me. He thinks highly of me or he wouldn't value me enough to work hard for me and our family so we can have a good life." Then go give him a big hug and tell him, "I am grateful you love me and find me attractive. Please know, sometimes I have self-doubts about my appearance, like most women, so when you tell me I am beautiful or try to romance me, I feel reassured that you are attracted to me. I just thought you would want to know how much that helps me to feel beautiful."

- **When frustrated with how busy your husband is,** realize that a man thinks you know that everything he is doing is really for you and the kids. From his perspective, going to work every day, taking care of the lawn or cars, running to the grocery store to buy you eggs, rearranging his schedule so he can make it to a soccer game, and stopping in to see his mother or help a friend is somehow connected to meeting your needs and being a good man for you. Women usually do not see it this way. They just believe he is avoiding them and resent the neglect. If you are to be happy and fulfilled in your relationship, you cannot afford to expect your husband to read your mind. If you share your feelings and needs in a respectful way, a good man will listen and try to meet your needs, especially if you use the 7–11 rule (from chapter 16).

- **When tempted to feel resentful about the things you are doing for the relationship and family**, choose instead to realize that from your husband's perspective, he believes he is giving a lot to the relationship too (albeit in his own and different way). Women often keep score about all the things they are doing for the family in a direct way (such as changing diapers, cleaning the house, making meals, driving the kids to activities). Having a shortsighted perspective with careful attention to score-keeping isn't good for either spouse. Someone always ends up feeling misunderstood, taken for granted, overburdened, and resentful. So, when tempted with victimizing beliefs that you are overburdened and neglected, rather than choosing resentment, tell your husband how much you love and appreciate him, give examples of things you know he does every day to sacrifice for you and the family, and then say, "I could really use your help, and I know that you would want to help me if you knew what I needed. Would you be willing to vacuum or make dinner tonight (put the kids to bed or do the dishes, go grocery shopping for me, or watch the kids for the next few hours)?" *The point is to communicate that you believe he is working hard for the family too but also to share with him the many things that need to be done for the family. If he believes that doing more work around the house (after a hard day at work himself) helps you, makes you happy, or wins your appreciation and gratitude, he will do it (not because it is the right thing to do but because he is willing to sacrifice for your happiness).*

Just remember to (1) share your positive feelings and make statements that show your faith and trust in his goodness and his willingness to sacrifice for you; (2) use "would you," not "could you" requests;[1] (3) give him examples and options for what he could do to help you; (4) give him room to do the things you requested in his own way unless it is absolutely necessary that it be done in a specific way (which you must be willing to clearly explain). Do not micromanage him in the things he does for you or he will not want to continue to help you; (5) let him choose when he will help you (now or in an hour, today or by the end of the week) as often as possible rather than expecting every request to be done now; and (6) express your appreciation for his sacrifices in ways that match his top three love languages.

If you choose to follow these six steps, you will have to give up lecturing him on how right you are and how much he has been missing the boat. Such lectures are unnecessary when soliciting the support of a man. Just warmly telling him what you need will work best. In this way you will be choosing what is effective in preference to that long-standing tradition, which so many women have followed, of being an over-responsible, self-righteous martyr who holds vehemently to her resentments rather than telling others what she really needs and then letting them fulfill those needs.

- **When tempted to believe that a man's needs for recreation or guy time is frivolous or immature**, stop and consider that a man would never appreciate a two-hour conversation with a friend. Men and women have different needs. Don't judge his. You would not want him to judge yours. Instead ask questions. Try to understand what a hobby, computer game, sports activity, or night out with the guys means to him or how it helps him to relax. Try not to interfere with these activities, especially when he seems willing to quickly meet your needs. If he likes to play computer games but will quickly turn them off to help you with the kids, dinner, or some other need, recognize that he is treating you as the greater priority.

  Help him to understand what specific activities would interfere with your sense of safety and security (such as going to singles events, flirting with other women when out with the guys, and so forth), and ask him to refrain from those activities. If his activities would cause you concern only if they were done to excess (such as spending ten hours a week golfing on top of his fifty-hour-a-week job or watching sports with the guys three times a week), ask him to limit the time he spends in the activities because too much time would cause you to feel neglected and would threaten your sense of safety and security in the relationship. However, do not use your sense of safety and security as a manipulation to control him. Be sure you are supporting his guy time a couple of times a month.

  If you respect a man's need for recreational activities and guy time, he will likely come home with more enthusiasm and appreciation for you and the relationship. Additionally, if you participate in his recreational activities with him (which would include doing things and activities as discussed in chapter 15), he will feel more positive about the relationship. A man who feels his needs are respected will usually not question your individual and different educational, recreational, or social needs.

- **When tempted to talk about a problem just because**

you need a friend to listen, understand that a man wants to help you, but he needs to know how. Do not just vent about your day to a man without first telling him, "I could really use a listening ear for fifteen minutes. I don't think I need advice as much as I need to vent. Would you be willing to do that for me? Is now good or in a half hour?" Then recognize how painful this is for a man. He is holding back his advice-giving, telling himself it will be over in fifteen minutes, looking at the clock as he counts the minutes down, and consciously trying to say "I see" all because he loves you and wants to help, but it is an anxiety-producing activity. Don't go on and on about it; his good intentions have a limit. Men do not chemically respond the same as women in the presence of a problem. Their anxiety builds, which is why they tend to want to give advice or take action to fix the problem (since these activities reduce his anxiety). If you need to vent for more than twenty minutes, consider calling a friend. Your husband cannot be all things for you all the time. Let your girlfriends give you what you need sometimes. He will appreciate you and your girlfriends for easing this burden for him.

- **When tempted to bring up the past**, realize that your resentments will make you less attractive to your husband. A good man rarely lingers in the past for very long. He doesn't like to dwell on past injuries because it stirs negative feelings that often can't be resolved and make him feel powerless. Men don't like to feel powerless, so they often try to focus on what is happening right now, since that is what they can control. That does not mean they are indifferent to how your past has hurt you. They want to listen to and support your feelings about your past when it is about someone other than them. In this way they can be your hero and helper. However, the more you seem to go on and on about your past with no resolution, the more discouraged they become. Their efforts haven't helped and they feel powerless. They will then begin to tell you, "You need to just get over it and move on." *Some past injuries or losses don't just go away, but be careful not to let the past* *throw off the positive to negative ratio in your relationship now.* Learn to live in the present, because the good man you are with now is willing to help you have a good life and future. Go see a counselor or talk with a friend until you can resolve your past. Update your husband on your progress and the things you are learning; he will want to hear about it. *Even if you can't resolve your past issues, living more fully in the present will help you feel empowered and give you the control you need (and didn't have then—which can be very healing).*

When your husband is the source of your past injuries or resentments, realize that bringing up the past reminds him of his failures. A man immediately feels defensive and overwhelmed when he can't fix something, and he believes he cannot fix the past and what he did to you. This does not mean you shouldn't bring up the past. He may not understand how talking about what happened will help you. As a woman, you know it will. In many ways, if you don't talk about the past, you may never regain your trust in and respect for him. So if needed, do discuss the past, but explain how and why talking about it will help you. Go to counseling to help him know how to restore your trust and respect. He needs to have hope that talking about the past can make a difference so the issue can eventually be put into the past. *Additionally, it would do much to help him patiently hold on if you occasionally express your regrets to him that the process isn't going faster and that you also wished you could just make your feelings all better— if for no other reason than just to help him.*

Once the issue is resolved, over the period of time that you needed, you will have to practice forgiving and forgetting the issue. The issue cannot be held over his head indefinitely, or he will feel hopeless and begin to wonder if you would be happier without him.

- **When frustrated with your husband's mother, grandmother, or sisters**, realize that he views his loyalty to them in the same way he views his loyalty to you. He first learned to connect to, love, and nurture women from his connection with these women. He offers you

the loyalty and commitment he initially gave them. He
wants to continue his dedication to them. He will give
you his greater loyalty if he must, but it will pain him to
do so. He just wishes you and they could love each other
as he loves you and them, and he doesn't understand why
you don't or can't. It may take him time to see that his
mother or sister are treating you badly, and if he sees it he
will give you his support, but he really wishes you could
just not take it personally so everything can be peaceful
and happy. If you feel your relationship with his mother,
sister, or grandmother has a toxic and painful effect on
you and you must limit your contact with them (and in
some ways the contact he and the kids have with them),
be sure you communicate with him that you know what a
big sacrifice he is making. Show him your empathy for the
difficult position this puts him in. Express your gratitude
for his loyalty. This is not easy for him. Then tell him
specifically what you need so he can succeed in giving you
his loyalty. Share your ongoing struggles about his family,
your resentments, or your hurt with your friends rather
than him. *He can give you his loyalty, but don't burden him
excessively with the negative feelings you have toward the
women in his family that he loves. And try not to limit his
time with his family if it is not absolutely necessary to your
sense of safety and security.*

- **When tempted to overburden or overstress yourself
  with others' problems or the petty details in life**, realize
  that your husband does not share your enthusiasm for
  stress, difficult relationships, or perfection. He will support
  you in the things that are important to you, but he won't
  appreciate being neglected. He may not tell you until he
  feels the neglect has gone too far for too long because he
  doesn't want to be the bad guy who tells you no. He wants
  you to set your own reasonable limits so he can be a priority
  in your life. Once married, most men put a majority of their
  time, energy, and loyalty into their families. You and your
  attention mean more to him than you may realize. He has
  emotional, social, and sexual needs that he doesn't try to
  meet outside of the relationship. He needs you to realize

his vulnerability and desires in the relationship without having to be the one who holds you back or tells you no. So, carefully consider where you are placing your priorities. Learn to say no to projects so you can say yes to him. If you don't have the skills of saying no, you will find your family and husband will suffer and be neglected on some level. Ask yourself, "When I am eighty, what relationships will be most important to me, and what relationships will I have wanted to endure the longest?"

- **When tempted to put your relationships with your children before your marriage**, realize the message this sends your husband. Most men focus their parenting on the goal of teaching their children to be independent and responsible. If they succeed at this goal, they know their children will grow up and move on with their lives away from home. Therefore, a man usually worries more about maintaining his relationship with his wife, because she is the one he wants to grow old with. He may enjoy his kids, but he wants a lifetime companion. When a wife focuses more on the kids or outright tells her husband that the kids come first, he feels dismissed, dispensable, and unnecessary—a servant to the family rather than the head of the household. Remember, a man who is not needed (and valued) dies a slow death.[2] Do not deceive yourself into believing your husband can endure your neglect and be taken for granted. A good man will eventually realize that if you don't love and value him, someone else could and would. Though his commitment to his values and integrity may keep him from doing immoral things, you will be leaving a tremendous vulnerability in the marriage that another woman could exploit. *If you loved your man enough to marry him, don't force him to live in a loveless marriage. Keep him a priority. It will be better for your children in the long run.* Using your children to fulfill your emotional needs is a form of emotional incest and will burden their emerging individual and social needs when they become teenagers and young adults. Instead, give them an example of a loving, committed marriage so they know how to create and invest in one of their own someday.

- **When tempted to become angry at the problems in your marriage**, remember to take some personal responsibility for the fact that the evidence of these potential problems probably existed before the marriage. If you know, or should have known, that your husband had some of these issues, tendencies, or problems before you married him but you married him anyway, don't waste your time nagging, criticizing, or trying to change him now. Instead, focus on how you can make the situation better, what you can do to manage the problem more effectively, or how you can lovingly respect and enjoy him as he is. You may make a request that he change how he acts in the relationship. You may ask him to consider changing parts of his life because it would mean a lot to you, but you do not have the right to expect him to be someone he was not before the marriage. Show him respect, and don't try to force him to change, or you will threaten the marriage. You chose your love; choose to love your choice. Don't waste your time on resentment or regret that you married him.

  If the relationship proves to be abusive, then certainly you may need to get help or end the marriage. But hopefully that won't be the case, because you stayed true to the truth and yourself through keeping your eyes wide open before you married him. If he is a good man with some annoying, tacky, or difficult traits but overall ensures your sense of safety and security, learn to ignore these traits, and count your blessing or find things to appreciate relative to what he is doing right. *Refocus your attention on the positive while focusing on improving yourself.*

- **When tempted to ignore your sexual relationship in marriage,** realize that your husband, in part, bases his feelings of acceptance and validation on whether or not you want to have sex with him. If you reject him repeatedly, don't have sex with him weekly, or never initiate sex, he will feel in some ways you do not believe he is acceptable, attractive, or good enough. This will not make him work harder for the marriage. Instead he will likely withdraw, feel sorry for himself, or refocus his attention on the things in his life that make him feel good (like his work, friendships, or hobbies).

Many women get caught in the trap of feeling that sex can be used as a tool for rewarding or punishing men and their behavior. When sex is seen as power, it will hurt one or both of the spouses. Sex is best when seen as a gift that is given to oneself and one's partner. Learn to look at sex as part of your nature. All people are created with a sexual nature. Learn to recognize your sexual feelings as being a part of you, a tool for pleasure and enjoyment, and a means for sharing oneself and creating closeness with a spouse. *Learn to view sex as something that brings you relief from stress, takes you away from the cares of the day, and helps you to feel more connected and close to your spouse.*

If you feel tempted to use sex as power or to see sex as dirty or something that must be given or taken from you but is not something you can choose to give, read some good books or get some professional help. *You can embrace your sexual nature and feel it is a beautiful part of who you are and how you express your love in marriage. Your husband needs this connection, and so do you. Don't ignore this important connection in marriage.*

Women who feel tempted to use criticism, nagging, neglect, or sex as a reward or punishment to change or control their relationships would be wise to consider the real power they discovered early on—the power of their loving emotions.

From flirting to marriage, you have been encouraged to basically do the same thing:

- Touch him.
- Look him in the eyes and smile warmly.
- Give him sincere compliments.
- When he does something you like, recognize it and express your appreciation.
- Be affectionate.
- Make time for him.
- Do things that show him you care.
- Help him when he asks for your help.
- Provide acts of service, just because you love him.
- Encourage his phone calls by calling him (but still call him less than he calls you so he can realize he misses you and then pursue you).
- Accept his forgiveness and give your own.
- Listen to him.
- Ask for his thoughts and feedback.
- Treat him like you trust and respect him.

From the beginning of this BE SUCCESSFUL section, you have been encouraged to be emotionally expressive with the men you like as a way of supporting and encouraging them while they play their role. Now, as always, your loving emotions have more positive effects and influence in your relationships than you may realize. Your faith in his goodness, your trust in his desire to please you, your expressions of confidence that he will meet your needs if you express them, and your occasional feelings of sadness, disappointment, or concern will be enough to motivate a man to meet your needs without use of any compulsory means or manipulations.

All he needs you to do is play your role and he will play his. Your role is simple: love, accept, appreciate, and encourage him. He will give you all that he has to give in return.

You do not need to do anything you would resent later. You do not need to be over-responsible. You do not need to fix everything or worry about everyone else's problems. You do not need to be perfect. And you do not need to walk on eggshells when you want to ask for something or discuss a problem.

As complicated as this book may seem and the process of analyzing your role may appear, it is really quite simple. Your loving and real emotions are the best source of power you possess in the life of a man who loves you.

A woman's loving emotions are the connection a man wants the most. He is not an animal or alien to the human race. He was a child once who loved to be praised and adored by his mother. He learned to be emotionally connected to her and value her acceptance, warmth, love, and approval. In the world of men, he has become trained in doing what must be done, but he wants the same emotional connections he enjoyed in childhood as a lifetime experience. He looks for the relief from the harshness of the adult world when he comes home to you, wanting the love and peace he enjoyed as a child (not every man or woman had the joy of a loving, safe, or peaceful family life, but it seems all souls long for it nonetheless). He loves you, and when he knows you love him, he feels complete.

When you embrace all that makes you who you are, from your analytical nature to your tender feminine emotions to even your own sexuality, you are enough to make him love and cherish you. Be the woman you want to be—whole, complete, and self-loving. Embrace all that makes you a woman. Do not fear the fact that your need to communicate, analyze things, and even bring up problems 80 percent of the time in the relationship. Just change your approach so it is effective and friendly to the male and female psychology while you do it. You already have the ability within you (you have been practicing it). The approach you and he need for success is your touch, tenderness, and love.

It may seem too simple to be real, but that is the joy of being married to a good man. Good men are simple in their needs. As you learn to trust yourself and him, you will find the ability to unite with him in a way that makes you both whole—or one.

CASE STUDY
REVIEW

THERAPEUTIC ASSESSMENT

The fact that Hunter was so different from Marissa made her feel, in some ways, confused, powerless, and insecure in her relationship. However, that was just a temporary condition. His consistency, commitment to communicating his needs and feelings, his dedication to hearing her needs, and his observable desire to please and support her gave her a sense of safety and security that was ongoing and endearing. In time, she began to recognize, value, and appreciate their differences.

Some of their differences were resolved through obtaining a better understanding of the other person (such as expressing and asserting their preferences and opinions until one or the other agreed to do it the other person's way), others through compromise (such as having sex two to three times a week versus every day like he wanted and once a week like she preferred), and a few through a commitment to agree to disagree and then drop the issue (such as when discussing the other person's problems with extended family members).

Within a year, and after reading many books about the differences between men and women, Marissa had not only found humor in their differences, but she had also felt freer from doubt and insecurity. And she trusted Hunter's loyalty and honesty more than ever.

Notes
1. Gray, *Men Are from Mars, Women Are from Venus*.
2. Ibid.

conclusion

On a personal note

I have had two dating experiences, the one before my first marriage and the one after my divorce.

During my first dating experience, I made nearly every common mistake women make. I was desperate for love, needy, and often ready and willing to be the good-for-now girl if that's what it required to get and keep a man's attention. I never thought like a man about relationships, though I thought about men all the time. I called too often and quickly asked too many questions about the relationship. I was often critical in my approach when my needs weren't being met and not often praising and adoring when a good man showed me the respect and kindness I craved. This regularly equated to me experiencing frequent and repeated short-term relationships. But I didn't know that was the problem.

Thus, when I met my first husband, I didn't look at the situation and his history with the careful logical and emotional connectedness I needed to make a wise choice. This was my chance to get the love and commitment I had desired for so long. So, I rushed into marriage with all the dreams and aspirations of any woman. And I had great confidence everything would just work out.

As one might anticipate, life follows the law and order of natural and logical consequences. In spite of my hopes, efforts, and expectations, in time my dreams were forced to give way to the truths and realities that were always there but I didn't want to see or accept, in him or myself.

In the wake of my divorce, I was left with many questions, most of which required that I take personal responsibility for my unhealthy beliefs, actions, and relationship patterns. But it wasn't enough for me to change myself. I also needed to change the types of men I was attracted to and the types of relationships I would involve myself in or I would just keep repeating the past.

Because of my naturally analytical nature, I drew upon the theories of my profession as well as the insight of friends and family, who knew me best, and took a year and a half to work through my issues. This protected me from repeating the past by jumping into relationships too soon, but it also gave me the ability to clear my mind of the effects of my marriage, restore my self-confidence, and confront my fears so I could be more assertive and true to myself. The results of my efforts created the substance of the BE SAFE section of this book.

Unlike my fist experience with dating, I felt confident the second time around because (1) I knew clearly what I wanted and didn't want in relationships; (2) I had a fierce understanding that being happily single was much better than being miserably married; (3) I was in no rush this time to get married; (4) I was deeply committed to being logical rather than just emotional about the process; (5) I had a firm conviction that I was lovable and had a lot to offer, and that others would value and appreciate me; and (6) I had a spiritual faith and hope that helped me to combat the many fears singles have.

A single woman has two options—fear or faith—although most single women don't know that there is another option besides fear. My second experience with being single was successful because I didn't choose fear. I had a spiritual conviction that I would have the opportunity to marry the kind of person I said I wanted to marry and the kind of person I was looking for would be looking for someone like me. I believed that if I did my part, God would help me meet the kind of men I was looking for. My faith wasn't easy. I was choosing to believe in something I couldn't see, touch, or know for sure would happen. But that is what faith is, and it certainly led me to a happier, more confident, and higher path than fear would have taken me down.

Had it not been for my faith in these two ideas, it would have been so easy to go back to my old patterns, to give in to destructive thoughts, and to feel despair and anxiety about my life and future. But instead, faith helped me harness my mental and emotional energy so I could believe in men, my future, and myself. Thus, I wrote the BE CONFIDENT section with faith as a core principle, because I personally know faith works, and I know that any woman who wants to feel confident must base her faith on something, even if it is just the principle that she can "fake it until she makes it."

Whereas the BE SAFE and BE CONFIDENT sections of this book were in many ways drawn from my personal experiences when I was single, I must admit, the BE SUCCESSFUL section was a work in progress even years after I married my husband, Eric. Because I acted more confident and logical when dating the second time around (I set a lot of logical dating boundaries and rules to help me control my emotions so I wouldn't rush into another bad relationship), I experienced great success, but I really didn't know why until later when I started to learn and understand the male psychology.

Once married, Eric's thoughts and behaviors were so different from my own that I was drawn to asking a lot of questions and reading a lot of books to better understand the male mind. It was then that I made the connections of why my first dating experiences had created so many short-term relationships while my second dating experiences had resulted in my husband's consistent pursuit of me.

From a male perspective, my first approach to dating had taken away the challenge and pursuit because I was always ready and available. Furthermore, I had poor dating boundaries, I didn't flirt enough, and I acted insecure. If only I had known then what I know now about the male mind, I wouldn't have taken the rejection so personally. After all, my poor success with dating wasn't really about me at all. It was about my dating techniques (which can be easily changed).

With an understanding of the male mind, the process of helping my clients be more successful in their dating relationships became easy. The answers were really quite simple when seen through a man's perspective, but this required that a woman change her view of the dating process. The idea of a Dating Game was the simplest way for me to help shift a woman's thinking. Women don't tend to think in terms of games, strategies, and rules when it comes to dating. They just want to be loved for who they are. But men are motivated by challenges, pursuit, and conquest, and if a woman wants to get a man to be interested long enough to get to know and love her personality, she needs to think and act in a way that motivates men. So in the Dating Game, a woman learns that she must think like a man, act warm and feminine, maintain the challenge, keep to the rules (because they work), act confident (or at least fake it until she makes it), and always keep him in pursuit of her. It seems complicated, but it really makes finding success quite simple.

So, on a personal note, this book in many ways chronicles my story when I was single: my struggle to be safe, my struggle to be confident, and my struggle to be successful. I wrote this book because I love single women. Having lived through the challenges of single life twice, while still so young, I wanted to help others navigate the dating process more quickly and easily than I had been able to. I wanted to coach others along the way so they could avoid the dangers and hazards I had experienced and so they could find the confidence and success that few singles intuitively discover. But I also wanted to be the kind of coach who the other players could relate to, who they could trust to understand their pain and frustration with being single, who they could sense truly grasped their fears of being abused and manipulated, and who they knew could still remember the anxiety that risking and trying when flirting, dating, and building relationships created.

I hope in all this I have been successful and you are now better prepared to recognize, meet, date, and marry a good man.

Good luck, and God bless your efforts.

—Alisa Goodwin Snell
Licensed Marriage and Family Therapist

appendix a

Identify the emotionally immature /
Assess your own emotional immaturity

Chapters 2 through 5 in the BE SAFE section focused on helping you identify the potentially abusive and manipulative through recognizing their emotional immaturity. If you do not practice the skills of identifying those who are emotionally immature now (even among your acquaintances, colleagues, friends, and family members), you will be more likely to tolerate and support unhealthy relationships and relationship patterns. You will then be more likely to dismiss or ignore important warning signs when dating. Thus, you simply cannot afford to wait until you are on a date to practice your discernment of others' (or your own) emotional immaturity.

When trying to determine if someone is emotionally immature, it is best to just focus on the person's struggles with feeling empathy for others, controlling self-serving behaviors, and accepting personal responsibility for their choices and consequences rather than trying to look for extreme examples of their behaviors (such as drug addiction, abuse, infidelity, self-harming behaviors, or excessive spending), which can take months or years to see.

Consider self-control, empathy, and personal responsibility to be like a three-legged stool. If one leg is missing, the stool will be unstable, likely to tip, and unable to support much pressure or weight. Though a person with two or even one of these skills (but not all three) may have many strengths, the skills they are lacking will greatly tax and disable the relationship and its potential growth, making the relationship difficult to maintain (especially if the skill he lacks is empathy).

As you complete the checklist below, consider anyone you believe may be emotionally immature. Do this assignment three, four, and even five times and with anyone (including yourself) or any relationship you find difficult to emotionally cope with. The more you learn to recognize these problems, the better you will become at seeing them in the moment. **Put a checkmark next to the descriptions below that fit the person you are thinking of.**

Problems with self-control

___acts dishonestly

___uses drugs

___drinks irresponsibly or excessively

___misuses prescriptions

___tries to get involved sexually very quickly

___is a drug, alcohol, or sex addict

___has been unfaithful

___has had affairs

___acts fourteen, seems to have never grown up

___acts irresponsibly

___spends money the family needs for food or basics on wants or selfish desires

___spends recklessly, doesn't pay bills, filed bankruptcy

___is noncommittal, a player

___has secretive behaviors like pornography, drugs, alcohol, Internet flings, flirting, gambling

___preaches but doesn't live his values—hypocritical

___breaks the law

___steals, shoplifts, etc.

___racks up credit cards he can't pay off

___violates others' space even when the person tells him to stop

___hits, slaps, grabs, pushes

___forces or manipulates others to do things they don't want to do

___threatens, intimidates

___won't allow others to leave

___has criminal charges

___has a history of violence, assault, sexual assault, etc.

___has history of emotional breakdowns

___has a history of multiple suicidal threats or attempts

___has lost jobs due to poor anger management, theft, drug use, laziness, sexual harassment, etc.

___has a history of jumping from one relationship to another or only leaves relationships if there is another one to go to

___treats others as objects, possessions for their use or pleasure

Problems with empathy

___calls names, belittles

___yells, screams, says hurtful things when angry

___is easily offended by others' feelings, requests, needs, complaints, etc.

___says he is smarter, more capable, better than others

___acts selfishly: buys clothes, plays golf when there is no money left for it

___shows no remorse

___gets angry when others express sadness, hurt, fear—sees it as a weakness or manipulation, doesn't try to understand why

___helps neighbors, friends, coworkers but not family, spouse, or children

___assumes others are talking about him, paranoid, accusing, won't believe others if they disagree

___believes his feelings, ideas, and emotional control make him superior to others—spouse, supervisors, doctors, etc.

___holds grudges for years

___refuses to forgive or forget even after the person has tried to resolve the issue

___expects immediate forgiveness after saying he is sorry

___expects trust after very little effort to fix things

___gives with expectations of receiving

___gives with resentment

___disregards others' space, property, feelings, body

___does what he wants without consideration for how it may affect others

___touches others or their things without asking

___refuses to accept that others have been hurt by his behavior

___refuses to accept that others did not consent to the things he did to them

___has rigid and inflexible rules or expectations

___apologizes but does the same hurtful things

Problems with accepting responsibility

___lies, deceives, denies

___blames others

___excuses his behavior

___gets angry, intimidating, or threatening when confronted about their behavior or deceptions

___feels justified in his behaviors and reactions

___feels his situation is the exception to the rule, he is above the rules, or he should be given special treatment

___uses guilt trips, sympathy

___plays the victim

___actions don't match words, excuses change but behaviors do not

___makes promises with no plan or follow-up

___minimizes the problem, downplays it, etc.

___tells only partial truths so he can hide other behaviors

___states he is worthless, unlovable, incompetent, etc., when others become upset or confront him

___cuts on his body, threatens or attempts suicide when things don't go the way he wants or expects

___justifies indulging in an addiction, affair, or other self-destructive behavior because he feels rejected, hurt, or ignored by others

___uses gift-giving, pleading, kindness, playfulness, etc., to convince others to give him what he wants

___gets angry or resentful if the consequences he receives do not match his expectations

___acts sick, needy, helpless, vulnerable, or fragile to get the support, help, enabling, or forgiveness of others or to avoid responsibility for his choices or needs

___admits his behaviors or deceptions were wrong but doesn't appear to feel remorse; doesn't seem to "really get it" and doesn't change

Remember, birds of a feather tend to flock together. If you are unaware of your areas of emotional immaturity, you may be attracting those who are equally or more impaired. This can be a valuable time for making important changes. If you hope to attract a good man, **you need to be the kind of person you are expecting him to be**. Thus, if you see weakness in your emotional immaturity, now is the time to work on those issues.

appendix b

Recognize good men by their skills of empathy, self-control, and personal responsibility

I f you are to be successful at identifying those who are emotionally mature when dating, you may want to practice recognizing the skills (both within others and yourself) of the emotionally mature now. Provided below is a list of many of the qualities, characteristics, and behaviors that are common for those who are emotionally mature.

*Caution: the list below should not be used to replace the three-date rule from chapter 5. Many people who are emotionally immature will demonstrate the behaviors below during the first few months of dating; however, they will also act consistent with many of the warning signs mentioned in chapter 5; thus, the emotionally mature can only be identified when the warning signs of the abusive and manipulative are not present and the skills below are evident over four to six months. Everyone is going to have a few issues, but if the person fits many of the qualities in all three categories below **and** they do not have significant warning signs of emotional immaturity from appendix a or chapter 5,* **then they are likely emotionally mature.**

Practice your ability to identify those who are emotionally mature by analyzing someone you suspect may have skills of empathy, self-control, and personal responsibility. *Consider someone you know well and have over six months of experience interacting with. Put a checkmark next to the descriptions below that fit this person.*

Skills of self-control

___keeps balance in their recreational, sporting, and athletic activities

___enjoys having fun, being playful, and telling jokes

___is able to laugh at himself, his life, and his mistakes

___thinks through his choices and possible consequences before acting

___pays bills, fulfills financial obligations

___spends money responsibly

___saves up for luxuries or considers carefully any debt-related purchases

___looks to the future (saves, gets additional education, plans for retirement, makes investments)

___tells the truth even when the truth may paint him in a bad light

___has clearly defined beliefs, values, personal standards

___lives what he preaches

___obeys the laws, even the small ones, or pays fines for breaking small laws without anger or blame

___asks for permission before touching others' things

___makes work a priority

___acts honestly

___acts responsibly at work

___respects others' boundaries, stops when someone says no or seems uncomfortable

___lets others leave when they want to go

___expresses anger through words and real expressions of emotion

___has a history of exercising emotional control

___has a history of long-term employment (three years or more) or consistent academic achievement

___has a history of long-term relationships

___has a history of being okay when they are alone—may take a break after a death or breakup

___says no to others

___completes his goals

___exercises caution to prevent injuries

___takes time out when too angry to control emotions

___follows through with rules or boundaries with his kids, even when it is inconvenient to do so

Skills of empathy

___controls himself when angry and to prevent hurting others' feelings

___is not easily offended by others' feelings, requests, needs, or complaints

___gives others credit for their work, praises and recognizes others' achievements

___donates to charities, helps others, volunteers time

___shows loyalty and commitment to family, treats family as a priority

___shows weakness, vulnerability, imperfection

___asks for help

___gives without expectation

___allows others to give to them to keep the relationship balanced

___works hard to forgive others, doesn't hold onto resentments

___gives others the benefit of the doubt

___exercises patience when others show weakness, vulnerability, or have difficult emotional needs

___often gives or helps others without wanting recognition or praise in return

___gives others their space

___shows appreciation

___accepts others' rights and feelings

___doesn't expect others to trust or forgive them but appreciates if they do

___apologizes

___expresses his feelings, needs, and wants with "I" statements that are free of demands on others

___encourages others to express individual feelings, needs, or rights

___validates others' feelings, even if he doesn't understand or agree

___protects children, animals, and those who are weak from abuse or neglect

___supports human rights

___participates in counseling to support the needs of those he loves

___has flexible and negotiable rules or expectations

___often acts kind and playful

___takes time to resolve problems and listen to others

___says what he means and feels even when things are good—not just because he is mad

___expresses sadness, hurt, fear, anger

Skills of accepting responsibility

___tells the truth

___admits blame

___accepts responsibility

___acknowledges times when his actions have hurt, manipulated, abused, neglected, betrayed, or deceived others

___appropriately describes situations and events that factored into his choices while using caution to not excuse his behavior

___accepts consequences for his choices

___acknowledges the harm he may have caused others, shows remorse

___works hard to change any behaviors that don't match his values

___creates plans for change, reads books, gets help

___follows through with commitments

___keeps his promises

___accepts expectations, boundaries, rules, and laws

___gets along with authority—police, bosses, etc.

___treats his body with respect, takes care of his body, uses caution

___seeks and accepts medical care, advice, etc.

___takes action to improve his problems, change his behavior, or address emotional issues

___trusts the advice of experts

___acknowledges his problems when helping others

___sets boundaries when interacting with others, helps others on his terms so he won't do things he'll resent later

___asks for help without expectation

___shows gratitude

___has strong beliefs that support good mental health which often include religious, spiritual, moral beliefs about forgiveness, faith, service, etc.

___has a positive belief about his value, goodness, etc.

___stands up for himself

___speaks about his good traits, shows self-love

___listens to feedback and constructive criticism

___talks and listens

___sacrifices personal wants for the greater good of the family or to be an effective parent

appendix c

GAME PLAY STRATEGIES

1. Recognize your vulnerability to abuse.
2. Shun any and all forms of abuse and manipulation in your relationships.
3. Accept that not all men can love, that loving them will hurt you, and that you cannot make someone emotionally mature.
4. Keep to the three-date rule.
5. Don't take unnecessary risks. Stay in safe places and around others until you know you are safe.
6. Recognize and change your pattern in relationships.
7. Be true to the truth.
8. Recognize, appreciate, respect, and enjoy good men.
9. Be true to yourself.
10. Exercise faith that you will have the opportunity to marry the kind of person you are looking for.
11. Believe that the kind of man you are looking for is looking for someone like you—and he will pursue you.
12. Fake it until you make it (to feel confidence).
13. Think like a man.
14. Be feminine, warm, flirtatious, and appreciative—while also being a challenge.
15. Stay connected to your mind and heart.
16. Be effective in how you build your relationships while confronting and dealing with problems in your relationship.
17. Choose your love. Love your choice.
18. Always keep him in pursuit of you.
19. Become united.

appendix d

17 secrets to the male psychology

1. Men seek out relationships that make them feel trusted and respected.
2. Men love through sacrifice.
3. Good men are largely logical about their relationships and commitment. Thus they do not commit easily to things they have not invested in over a period of time.
4. Men are driven to succeed, face challenges, compete, and conquer.
5. Men like women who like themselves.
6. Men love to be heroes.
7. Men like being appreciated.
8. Men like femininity.
9. Men like women who have opinions and assert their needs.
10. Good men pursue women who are approachable and appear to be available.
11. Good men want sex with a woman who feels good about having sex with them and will wait until marriage.
12. Men need to be needed.
13. Men are repelled by criticism, nagging, and whining.
14. A man experiences anxiety in every conversation a woman initiates until she tells him what she wants him to do.
15. Men bond through doing activities and talking about things more than they do through talking about people, problems, feelings, or ideas.
16. Good men adore women who give them love, attention, and affection.
17. Good men are often willing to talk openly and honestly when they feel it will help them or another person to do so.

appendix e

20 common mistakes women make

1. Women often refuse to flirt.
2. Women often refuse to put themselves where other singles are.
3. Women often waste their time analyzing men instead of thinking like men and realizing that if he isn't calling, he's not interested.
4. Women often sit by the phone, anxiously waiting for a man they just met to call.
5. Women often make themselves too available too quickly rather than risk turning a guy off—which turns guys off.
6. Women often act like friends, eliminating their chance for being a potential girlfriend.
7. Women often take the lead and pursue men, which sometimes only makes them look and act desperate.
8. Women who trust without good reason are more likely to find themselves in bad situations they can't control.
9. Women who act cool, cautious, and reserved on dates often don't get asked out for second dates.
10. Women who become physically involved with men in the first three to six weeks are likely to get dumped sooner rather than later.
11. Women often falsely believe that if they meet a man's every need, he will love and appreciate them for it.
12. Women often try to make the good times last for as long as possible, which contributes to the three-week drop off curve.
13. Women are often drawn to loving men who aren't in a position to love them back.

14. Women tend to put all their hopes into one relationship too early in the dating process.
15. Women often forget that men have feelings and needs too.
16. Women often fail to assert their needs long enough for a man to respond.
17. Women often prefer to see their relationships idealistically rather than realistically. When a woman is forced to face the realities she has been avoiding, she is then likely to feel like a victim who has been betrayed or deceived.
18. Women often waste their time in a dead-end relationship that has little chance for progressing toward marriage.
19. Once in committed relationships, women often train their men to not pursue them or sacrifice for them.
20. Women are often too eager to discuss marriage when in a relationship, which can cause men to back off or get frightened away.

about the author

Alisa Goodwin Snell is a licensed marriage and family therapist with over thirteen years of experience in treating a wide variety of mental health issues. Over the last six years, she has primarily worked with single women's issues: from coming out of abusive and manipulative relationships to navigating dating and getting married (or in many cases, remarried). She has been a favorite speaker at many singles events, seminars, and conferences, and is the guest on many radio shows nationwide. She is currently a weekly guest of the KSL Nightside Project. To learn more about when you can hear Alisa on the radio, go to askalisa.org. This website may also answer many of your other dating questions.

Alisa is married and has one son. She owns a private practice counseling center, Davis Counseling Center, Inc., in Farmington, Utah.